Make It Tonight

Make It Tonight

Canadian Living

Delicious, no-fuss dinner
solutions for every cook

BY THE CANADIAN LIVING TEST KITCHEN

Transcontinental Books

Contents

CHAPTER 1

Make It Tonight... in 15 to 20 Minutes

Rainbow Trout with Dijon Mayonnaise

Trout is a fast choice for dinner. This method of coating fish with seasoned mayonnaise is so versatile. Try it with salmon, tilapia or catfish for equally easy prep and tasty results.

4 **rainbow trout fillets** (about 6 oz/ 175 g each)
2 tbsp (30 mL) **light mayonnaise**
2 tsp (10 mL) **Dijon mustard**
¼ tsp (1 mL) each **salt** and **pepper**
1 tbsp (15 mL) chopped **fresh parsley**
Lemon wedges

Pat fish dry; place on greased rimmed baking sheet. In small bowl, combine mayonnaise, mustard, salt and pepper; spread on each fillet. Broil 6 inches (15 cm) from heat until fish flakes easily when tested, about 6 minutes.

Sprinkle with parsley. Serve with lemon to squeeze over top.

Makes 4 servings. PER SERVING: about 226 cal, 29 g pro, 11 g total fat (3 g sat. fat), 1 g carb, 0 g fibre, 82 mg chol, 282 mg sodium. % RDI: 10% calcium, 4% iron, 11% vit A, 13% vit C, 14% folate.

VARIATIONS
Rainbow Trout with Curry Mayonnaise
•Replace mustard with mild curry paste.

Rainbow Trout with Thai Mayonnaise
•Replace mustard with 1 tsp (5 mL) Thai red curry paste.

Green Beans with Sun-Dried Tomatoes

1 lb (500 g) **green beans,** trimmed
2 tbsp (30 mL) slivered **oil-packed sun-dried tomatoes**
1 tsp (5 mL) **extra-virgin olive oil**
¼ tsp (1 mL) **dried oregano**

In saucepan of boiling salted water, cover and cook beans until tender-crisp, about 7 minutes.

Drain and toss with tomatoes, oil and oregano.

Makes 4 servings. PER SERVING: about 49 cal, 2 g pro, 2 g total fat (trace sat. fat), 8 g carb, 3 g fibre, 0 mg chol, 10 mg sodium. % RDI: 4% calcium, 5% iron, 7% vit A, 20% vit C, 14% folate.

Corned Beef and Avocado Rolls

An avocado needs three to five days to ripen. Set it on the counter and out of the sun, or seal it in a paper bag with an apple to speed up the process. Once ripe, it will keep in the fridge for several days.

4 large **flour tortillas**
2 cups (500 mL) torn **mixed salad greens**
8 oz (250 g) sliced **corned beef**
1 **avocado,** halved, pitted and sliced
½ cup (125 mL) thinly sliced **red onion**
LIME MAYONNAISE:
⅓ cup (75 mL) **light mayonnaise**
1 tbsp (15 mL) **water**
1 tbsp (15 mL) **lime juice** or lemon juice
2 tsp (10 mL) chopped **fresh cilantro**
Dash **hot pepper sauce**

LIME MAYONNAISE: In bowl, combine mayonnaise, water, lime juice, cilantro and hot pepper sauce; set aside.

On work surface, spread tortillas with Lime Mayonnaise. Layer one quarter each of the greens, corned beef, avocado and onion on bottom third of each. Fold bottom up; fold in sides and roll up.

Cut each roll in half on the diagonal.

Makes 4 servings. PER SERVING: about 439 cal, 17 g pro, 24 g total fat (5 g sat. fat), 40 g carb, 5 g fibre, 62 mg chol, 1,090 mg sodium. % RDI: 5% calcium, 26% iron, 9% vit A, 15% vit C, 59% folate.

Carrot and Celery Slaw

2 **carrots,** coarsely grated
2 **radishes,** grated
1 rib **celery,** grated
2 tsp (10 mL) **white wine vinegar**
2 tsp (10 mL) **vegetable oil**
2 tsp (10 mL) **prepared horseradish**
Pinch each **salt** and **pepper**

In bowl, combine carrots, radishes and celery. Add vinegar, oil, horseradish, salt and pepper. Toss to combine.

Makes 4 servings. PER SERVING: about 41 cal, 1 g pro, 2 g total fat (trace sat. fat), 5 g carb, 1 g fibre, 0 mg chol, 26 mg sodium. % RDI: 2% calcium, 2% iron, 113% vit A, 10% vit C, 5% folate.

Bok Choy and Pork Stir-Fry

A stir-fry is even faster when the ingredient list is short – like this one. For our easy No-Fail Rice recipe, turn to page 22.

1 **pork tenderloin** (about 12 oz/375 g)
1 tbsp (15 mL) **cornstarch**
1 tbsp (15 mL) each **soy sauce** and
   hoisin sauce
2 tbsp (30 mL) **vegetable oil**
6 **baby bok choy,** halved lengthwise
3 **green onions,** sliced
2 tsp (10 mL) grated **fresh ginger**
½ tsp (2 mL) **five-spice powder** or
   grated fresh ginger
1 clove **garlic,** minced
Pinch **hot pepper flakes**
4 cups (1 L) **cooked rice**

Thinly slice pork crosswise; set aside.

In measuring cup, whisk together ¾ cup (175 mL) water, cornstarch, soy sauce and hoisin sauce; set aside.

In wok or large skillet, heat half of the oil over high heat; stir-fry pork, in 2 batches, until browned, about 3 minutes. Transfer to bowl.

Add remaining oil to wok. Stir-fry bok choy, green onions, ginger, five-spice powder, garlic and hot pepper flakes until greens are wilted, about 3 minutes.

Return pork and accumulated juices to pan. Add soy sauce mixture; stir-fry until sauce is thickened, about 1 minute. Serve over rice.

Makes 4 servings. PER SERVING: about 473 cal, 28 g pro, 10 g total fat (1 g sat. fat), 66 g carb, 3 g fibre, 50 mg chol, 410 mg sodium. % RDI: 14% calcium, 22% iron, 31% vit A, 55% vit C, 30% folate.

Monte Cristo Sandwiches

Make sure the bread soaks up plenty of the egg mixture so that it makes a satisfying French toast–style crust.

4 **eggs**
⅔ cup (150 mL) **milk**
¼ tsp (1 mL) **pepper**
Pinch **salt**
8 thick slices **white bread**
1 tbsp (15 mL) **Dijon mustard**
4 slices **Swiss cheese**
4 oz (125 g) each sliced **smoked turkey**
   and **Black Forest ham** (or 8 oz/250 g
   turkey or ham)
1 tbsp (15 mL) each **vegetable oil**
   and **butter**

In large shallow dish, whisk together eggs, milk, pepper and salt.

Spread 4 of the bread slices with mustard; sandwich cheese, turkey and ham with remaining bread. Dip each sandwich into egg mixture, turning to soak well.

In large nonstick skillet, heat oil and butter over medium heat; fry sandwiches, turning once, until crusty and browned and cheese is melted, about 5 minutes.

Makes 4 servings. PER SERVING: about 507 cal, 30 g pro, 22 g total fat (8 g sat. fat), 46 g carb, 2 g fibre, 238 mg chol, 1,277 mg sodium, 393 mg potassium. % RDI: 36% calcium, 28% iron, 15% vit A, 49% folate.

Poached Salmon with Salsa Verde

Tangy and a little salty, salsa verde adds a burst of fresh flavour to this moist salmon.

1 each **onion** and rib **celery,** thinly sliced
3 thin slices **lemon**
4 sprigs **fresh parsley**
½ tsp (2 mL) each **salt** and **peppercorns**
4 **skin-on salmon fillets** (each 6 oz/175 g)
Lemon wedges
SALSA VERDE:
⅓ cup (75 mL) **fresh bread crumbs**
3 tbsp (45 mL) **red wine vinegar**
1 **hard-cooked egg,** coarsely chopped
1 bunch **fresh parsley,** stemmed
2 tbsp (30 mL) drained **capers**
2 **anchovy fillets**
1 clove **garlic**
¼ cup (60 mL) **extra-virgin olive oil**

In wide low pan large enough to hold fish in single layer, bring 3 cups (750 mL) water, onion, celery, lemon, parsley, salt and peppercorns to boil. Cover, reduce heat and simmer for 5 minutes.

Add fish; poach just below simmer, covered, just until salmon flakes easily when tested, 5 to 7 minutes. With slotted spatula, transfer fish to plates; remove skin.

SALSA VERDE: Meanwhile, soak bread crumbs in vinegar for 5 minutes; transfer to food processor. Add egg, parsley, capers, anchovies and garlic; chop finely. With motor running, drizzle in oil and 3 tbsp (45 mL) of the cooking liquid. Serve with salmon. Garnish with lemon wedges.

Makes 4 servings. PER SERVING: about 476 cal, 37 g pro, 34 g total fat (6 g sat. fat), 4 g carb, 1 g fibre, 149 mg chol, 562 mg sodium, 702 mg potassium. % RDI: 7% calcium, 19% iron, 25% vit A, 65% vit C, 38% folate.

HOW TO GET HELP IN THE KITCHEN

•Expect everyone to pitch in. When kids are little, take the time to teach them to set the table, peel carrots and potatoes, shake salad dressing and tear lettuce. As they grow, let them try new dishes, especially the ones they like.

•Keep a binder of favourite recipes, chosen by you and your family. Or keep them in a virtual recipe box on your computer. Enlist everyone's aid in planning weekly menus, building them around dishes they like (with your guidance, of course). Make the shopping list based on their choices.

•Shop from a list and bring along family members so you can pass on your wisdom about choosing the best fruits and vegetables. This encourages children to make wise choices with the amount of money the family has budgeted for food. And it means you can pass the shopping chores on to them later.

•Post the week's menu on the fridge or a kitchen whiteboard or blackboard. If kids are old enough, encourage them to start supper when they get home.

•Draw up a schedule and assign everyone a job. Rotate duties so no one is stuck making the salad – or taking out the garbage – every night.

•Cook together as a family. It provides lots of opportunities to hear about the day's events. This time can be just as valuable as the time you spend together at the table. Consider it a warmup!

•Make regular dinner together a priority in your family. Studies show that this pays off for kids, both in school and in relations with their peers.

Open-Faced Shrimp and Egg Sandwiches

With these Danish-inspired sandwiches, a weeknight meal is just 10 minutes away.

2 tbsp (30 mL) **butter**
8 slices **white bread**
8 leaves **red leaf lettuce**
32 thin slices **English cucumber**
8 **hard-cooked eggs,** sliced
¼ tsp (1 mL) each **salt** and **pepper**
16 thin slices **sweet white onion**
SHRIMP SALAD:
12 oz (375 g) thawed cooked peeled
   cold-water shrimp
2 tbsp (30 mL) **mayonnaise**
1 tbsp (15 mL) minced **fresh dill**
1 tbsp (15 mL) **lemon juice**
Pinch **pepper**

SHRIMP SALAD: In bowl, combine shrimp, mayonnaise, dill, lemon juice and pepper.

Butter bread slices. Top each with lettuce, cucumber, eggs, salt, pepper, onion and shrimp salad.

Makes 4 servings. PER SERVING: about 472 cal, 34 g pro, 24 g total fat (8 g sat. fat), 29 g carb, 2 g fibre, 556 mg chol, 783 mg sodium, 516 mg potassium. % RDI: 16% calcium, 42% iron, 31% vit A, 25% vit C, 59% folate.

TIP
Sweet onions – with their low levels of tear-causing chemicals – include Spanish, Vidalia, Walla Walla, Texas SuperSweet and Maui.

Steak and Mushroom Baguette

A steak sandwich is a real crowd-pleasing meal. Serve it with a salad, or crudités and dip, such as Herbed Feta Dip (recipe, page 166) or Herb Dip (recipe, page 49).

2 tsp (10 mL) **vegetable oil** (approx)

1 lb (500 g) **beef inside round fast-fry steak,** cut in thin strips

1 **onion,** sliced

3 cups (750 mL) sliced **mushrooms** (8 oz/250 g)

3 cloves **garlic,** minced

1 **sweet yellow pepper,** sliced

½ tsp (2 mL) **dried oregano**

½ tsp (2 mL) each **salt** and **pepper**

1 **baguette** (about 24 inches/60 cm)

1 jar (6 oz/170 mL) **marinated artichoke hearts,** drained

In large skillet, heat oil over medium-high heat; stir-fry beef, in 2 batches and adding more oil if necessary, until browned but still pink inside, about 3 minutes. Transfer to plate.

Add onion, mushrooms, garlic, yellow pepper, oregano, salt and pepper to skillet; sauté until liquid is evaporated, about 5 minutes. Return beef and any accumulated juices to pan; heat through.

Cut baguette lengthwise in half almost but not all the way through. If desired, remove some of the soft centre.

Spoon half of the beef mixture onto bottom of baguette. Top with artichokes and remaining beef mixture. Cover with top. Cut into sections.

Makes 4 servings. PER SERVING: about 427 cal, 35 g pro, 10 g total fat (2 g sat. fat), 49 g carb, 5 g fibre, 49 mg chol, 838 mg sodium. % RDI: 8% calcium, 39% iron, 1% vit A, 83% vit C, 51% folate.

SUBSTITUTIONS

• Replace beef with sliced boneless skinless chicken breast or sliced boneless pork chop.

• Replace marinated artichoke hearts with ½ cup (125 mL) sliced drained oil-packed sun-dried tomatoes.

Chicken Piccata Linguine

Rinsing the brine off capers makes them a little milder and reduces salt. If you like a stronger caper flavour, feel free to skip this step. Serve with sautéed rapini or Lemon Garlic Broccolini (recipe, page 204).

12 oz (375 g) **linguine**

2 **boneless skinless chicken breasts**

2 tbsp (30 mL) **all-purpose flour**

½ tsp (2 mL) each **salt** and **pepper**

1 tbsp (15 mL) each **vegetable oil** and **butter**

1 clove **garlic,** minced

¾ cup (175 mL) **sodium-reduced chicken broth**

¼ cup (60 mL) chopped **fresh parsley**

3 tbsp (45 mL) **lemon juice**

2 tbsp (30 mL) **capers,** drained and rinsed

¼ cup (60 mL) grated **Romano cheese**

In large pot of boiling salted water, cook pasta according to package directions; drain and return to pot.

Meanwhile, slice chicken diagonally into ¼-inch (5 mm) thick strips; sprinkle with flour, salt and pepper.

In large nonstick skillet, heat oil and butter over medium-high heat; cook garlic and chicken until chicken is no longer pink inside, about 5 minutes.

Stir in broth, scraping up any brown bits; bring to boil and boil until slightly thickened, about 2 minutes.

Stir in parsley, lemon juice and capers; add to drained pasta. Add cheese and toss to coat.

Makes 4 servings. PER SERVING: about 493 cal, 29 g pro, 11 g total fat (4 g sat. fat), 68 g carb, 4 g fibre, 53 mg chol, 888 mg sodium, 312 mg potassium. % RDI: 9% calcium, 29% iron, 7% vit A, 12% vit C, 86% folate.

COOKING BASICS

• Read the recipe through before starting.

• The size of fresh food (such as fruits and vegetables), pans and dishes is medium unless otherwise specified.

• All foods requiring washing are washed before preparation or use.

• Fruits and vegetables such as carrots, onions and bananas are peeled.

• Eggs are large and shelled.

• Butter is salted unless otherwise stated.

• Pepper is black and freshly ground.

• All-purpose flour, icing sugar and cocoa powder are not sifted before measuring.

• Dried herbs are crumbled, not ground.

• Ovens are preheated. Items are baked in the centre of the oven unless otherwise noted.

• Saucepans are uncovered unless noted.

• Generic names for ingredients (for example, hot pepper sauce for Tabasco) are used unless a specific brand is essential to the recipe.

Cajun Fillets with Steamed Vegetables

Cajun-style fish is often fried, but this baked version is better for you without giving up the slight heat and spiciness of the Cajun seasoning.

2 tbsp (30 mL) **light mayonnaise**

4 **catfish fillets** or tilapia fillets
   (each 6 oz/175 g)

1 tbsp (15 mL) minced **fresh parsley**

1½ tsp (7 mL) **Cajun seasoning**

1 **lemon,** cut in wedges

STEAMED VEGETABLES:

2 **carrots,** sliced

1 cup (250 mL) **broccoli florets**

1 cup (250 mL) **sugar snap peas,** trimmed

Half **sweet red pepper,** cut in ½-inch
   (1 cm) pieces

VINAIGRETTE:

2 tbsp (30 mL) **extra-virgin olive oil**

1 tbsp (15 mL) **white wine vinegar**

1 tsp (5 mL) minced **fresh basil** or parsley

¾ tsp (4 mL) **grainy mustard**

Pinch each **salt** and **pepper**

On greased baking sheet, spread mayonnaise over fish; sprinkle with parsley and seasoning. Bake in 450°F (230°C) oven until fish flakes easily when tested, about 12 minutes.

STEAMED VEGETABLES: Meanwhile, in steamer basket at least 1 inch (2.5 cm) above boiling water, cover and steam carrots, broccoli, peas and red pepper until tender-crisp, 3 to 4 minutes.

VINAIGRETTE: In large bowl, whisk together oil, vinegar, basil, mustard, salt and pepper; add vegetables and toss to coat. Serve with fish and lemon.

Makes 4 servings. PER SERVING: about 341 cal, 29 g pro, 21 g total fat (4 g sat. fat), 10 g carb, 3 g fibre, 93 mg chol, 241 mg sodium. % RDI: 4% calcium, 16% iron, 82% vit A, 83% vit C, 18% folate.

Squash, Lentil and Chickpea Soup

For a shortcut, look in the produce section for packages of fresh butternut squash that's already peeled and cubed.

1 tbsp (15 mL) **vegetable oil**
1 tsp (5 mL) **cumin seeds** or ground cumin
2 cups (500 mL) chopped peeled **butternut squash**
1 **onion,** chopped
2 cloves **garlic,** minced
½ tsp (2 mL) each **chili powder** and **pepper**
¼ tsp (1 mL) **salt**
3 tbsp (45 mL) **tomato paste**
1 can (19 oz/540 mL) **lentils,** drained and rinsed
1 can (19 oz/540 mL) **chickpeas,** drained and rinsed
4 cups (1 L) **vegetable broth**
1 strip **lemon zest**
¼ cup (60 mL) chopped **fresh parsley**
Lemon wedges

In Dutch oven, heat oil over medium heat; fry cumin seeds for 1 minute. Add squash, onion, garlic, chili powder, pepper and salt; fry, stirring occasionally, until onion is softened, about 4 minutes. Add tomato paste; cook, stirring, for 1 minute.

Add lentils, chickpeas, broth and lemon zest; cover and bring to boil over high heat. Reduce heat and simmer until squash is tender, about 12 minutes. Discard lemon zest. Sprinkle with parsley. Serve with lemon wedges.

Makes 4 servings. PER SERVING: about 349 cal, 16 g pro, 5 g total fat (1 g sat. fat), 62 g carb, 12 g fibre, 0 mg chol, 1,710 mg sodium. % RDI: 10% calcium, 44% iron, 67% vit A, 50% vit C, 123% folate.

Tuna Salad Potatoes

To make Tuna Salad Potato Melts, follow recipe but broil for only 2 minutes. Top each stuffed potato with 1 slice Cheddar cheese; broil until bubbly and golden, about 3 minutes.

4 large **baking potatoes** (about 2 lb/1 kg)
2 cans (each 170 g) **solid white tuna** or chunk light tuna, drained
½ cup (125 mL) diced roasted or fresh **sweet red pepper**
¼ cup (60 mL) sliced **black olives**
¼ cup (60 mL) **light mayonnaise**
¼ cup (60 mL) **light sour cream**
1 rib **celery,** diced
¼ cup (60 mL) diced **red onion**
2 tbsp (30 mL) chopped **fresh parsley**
2 tbsp (30 mL) **lemon juice**
½ tsp (2 mL) **salt**
¼ tsp (1 mL) **pepper**

Prick each potato several times; microwave on high, turning halfway through, until tender, about 12 minutes.

Meanwhile, in bowl, combine tuna, red pepper, olives, mayonnaise, sour cream, celery, onion, parsley, lemon juice, salt and pepper; set aside.

Cut X in top of each potato; squeeze to open and separate. Mound tuna mixture on potatoes.

Place potatoes on rimmed baking sheet; broil 6 inches (15 cm) from heat until heated through and edges of potatoes are crisp and darkened, about 5 minutes.

Makes 4 servings. PER SERVING: about 338 cal, 22 g pro, 8 g total fat (2 g sat. fat), 46 g carb, 4 g fibre, 28 mg chol, 776 mg sodium. % RDI: 7% calcium, 27% iron, 12% vit A, 107% vit C, 14% folate.

Pan-Fried Tofu with Asian Garlic Sauce

Rice is a must-serve side dish for this recipe, and the secret to having everything on the table fast is to put the rice on first. See No-Fail Rice, right, for our tried-and-true method.

1 pkg (350 g) **extra-firm tofu**
2 tbsp (30 mL) **vegetable oil** (approx)
1 **onion,** chopped
3 cloves **garlic,** minced
1 tsp (5 mL) minced **fresh ginger**
   (or ½ tsp/2 mL ground ginger)
¼ tsp (1 mL) **pepper**
¾ cup (175 mL) **vegetable broth** or
   sodium-reduced chicken broth
¼ cup (60 mL) **soy sauce**
1 tbsp (15 mL) **cornstarch**
2 **green onions,** diagonally sliced

Pat tofu dry; cut crosswise into 4 slices. In large skillet, heat half of the oil over medium-high heat; fry tofu, turning once and adding more oil if necessary, until golden, about 8 minutes. Remove to plates and keep warm.

Add remaining oil to pan; fry onion, garlic, ginger and pepper over medium heat, adding more oil if necessary, until onion is softened, about 3 minutes.

Add broth and soy sauce; bring to boil. Stir cornstarch with 1 tbsp (15 mL) water; stir into pan. Boil, stirring, until thickened, 1 minute. Pour over tofu; sprinkle with green onions.

Makes 4 servings. PER SERVING: about 181 cal, 11 g pro, 12 g total fat (1 g sat. fat), 9 g carb, 1 g fibre, 0 mg chol, 1,155 mg sodium. % RDI: 13% calcium, 15% iron, 7% vit C, 15% folate.

Sesame Green Bean Stir-Fry

1 tsp (5 mL) **vegetable oil**
1 lb (500 g) **green beans,** trimmed
1 tsp (5 mL) **sesame seeds**
1 tsp (5 mL) **sesame oil**

In skillet, heat oil over medium-high heat; stir-fry green beans for 2 minutes. Add 1 tbsp (15 mL) water, sesame seeds and sesame oil. Cover and steam until green beans are tender-crisp, about 4 minutes.

Makes 4 servings. PER SERVING: about 56 cal, 2 g pro, 3 g total fat (trace sat. fat), 7 g carb, 3 g fibre, 0 mg chol, 1 mg sodium. % RDI: 4% calcium, 4% iron, 6% vit A, 15% vit C, 14% folate.

NO-FAIL RICE

In covered saucepan, bring 2⅔ cups (650 mL) water and ¼ tsp (1 mL) salt to boil. Stir in 1⅓ cups (325 mL) rice; cover, reduce heat to low and simmer until rice is tender and liquid is absorbed, about 20 minutes for basmati, jasmine or other white long-grain rice; about 45 minutes for brown rice. Fluff with fork and serve.

FLAVOURING SUGGESTIONS

Add a strip of lemon zest, sprig of parsley, bay leaf or a few slices of fresh ginger. Or simmer in chicken or vegetable broth instead of water.

Tomato Baguette Pizza

This pizza gets its smoky flavour from smoked mozzarella. You can use plain mozzarella or provolone – or a smoked Cheddar or Gouda.

1 tbsp (15 mL) **vegetable oil**
2 **onions,** sliced
2 cloves **garlic,** minced
3 cups (750 mL) sliced **mushrooms**
½ tsp (2 mL) each **salt** and **dried Italian herb seasoning**
¼ tsp (1 mL) **pepper**
1 **baguette** (about 24 inches/60 cm)
2 cups (500 mL) shredded **smoked mozzarella cheese**
⅔ cup (150 mL) packed **fresh basil leaves**
2 **tomatoes,** sliced

In skillet, heat oil over medium-high heat; sauté onions, garlic, mushrooms, salt, Italian seasoning and pepper until golden, about 6 minutes.

Halve baguette lengthwise then crosswise; place, cut side up, on rimmed baking sheet. Sprinkle with half of the cheese; top with ½ cup (125 mL) of the basil, mushroom mixture, then tomatoes. Sprinkle with remaining cheese.

Bake in 400°F (200°C) oven until cheese is melted, about 10 minutes. Shred remaining basil; sprinkle over top. Cut into 8 pieces.

Makes 4 servings. PER SERVING: about 449 cal, 21 g pro, 20 g total fat (10 g sat. fat), 48 g carb, 5 g fibre, 51 mg chol, 956 mg sodium. % RDI: 37% calcium, 24% iron, 22% vit A, 30% vit C, 38% folate.

Romaine Wedges

1 **romaine heart,** quartered
4 **radishes,** sliced
1 piece (2 inches/5 cm) **English cucumber,** halved lengthwise and thinly sliced
2 tbsp (30 mL) **vegetable oil**
1 tbsp (15 mL) chopped **fresh parsley**
1 tbsp (15 mL) **red wine vinegar**
1 tsp (5 mL) **Dijon mustard**
Pinch each **salt** and **pepper**

Place each romaine quarter on plate; top with radishes and cucumber. In bowl, whisk together oil, parsley, vinegar, mustard, salt and pepper. Drizzle over salads.

Makes 4 servings. PER SERVING: about 75 cal, 1 g pro, 7 g total fat (1 g sat. fat), 3 g carb, 2 g fibre, 0 mg chol, 24 mg sodium. % RDI: 2% calcium, 5% iron, 30% vit A, 27% vit C, 33% folate.

Family-Size Pan Bagnat

This sandwich has all the flavours of a classic salade Niçoise – olive oil, tuna, eggs, greens and other vegetables – in a fun-to-share, handheld format.

Quarter **sweet onion,** thinly sliced

¼ cup (60 mL) **extra-virgin olive oil**

2 tbsp (30 mL) **red wine vinegar**

2 tbsp (30 mL) **Dijon mustard**

1 tsp (5 mL) **dried thyme**

¼ tsp (1 mL) each **salt** and **pepper**

2 cans (each 7 oz/198 g) **tuna**

¼ cup (60 mL) chopped **black olives**

1 round **French bread** (about 7 inches/ 18 cm, 675 g)

1 **plum tomato,** thinly sliced

1 cup (250 mL) packed **fresh spinach**

2 **hard-cooked eggs,** sliced

2 jarred **roasted red peppers,** drained, rinsed and patted dry

In bowl, cover onion with cold water; let stand for 15 minutes. Drain and pat dry; set aside.

In small bowl, whisk together oil, vinegar, mustard, thyme, salt and pepper; set aside 2 tbsp (30 mL). Toss tuna and olives with remaining dressing mixture to combine.

Cut bread in half horizontally; hollow out loaf, leaving 1-inch (2.5 cm) border. Brush cut side with reserved dressing mixture.

Spread tuna mixture over bottom half of loaf. Top with tomato, spinach, eggs, onion and red peppers. Top with remaining bread. *(Make-ahead: Wrap in plastic wrap and refrigerate for up to 24 hours.)* Cut into wedges.

Makes 4 servings. PER SERVING: about 631 cal, 36 g pro, 22 g total fat (4 g sat. fat), 72 g carb, 5 g fibre, 117 mg chol, 1,470 mg sodium. % RDI: 14% calcium, 43% iron, 27% vit A, 112% vit C, 74% folate.

Gruyère and Ham Pasta

Any short pasta – such as macaroni, penne or shells – is suitable. Get the pasta water boiling before you make the sauce to ensure that everything's on the table in 20 minutes.

2 tbsp (30 mL) **butter**
1 **onion,** chopped
½ tsp (2 mL) **salt**
¼ tsp (1 mL) each **dried thyme** and **pepper**
2 tbsp (30 mL) **all-purpose flour**
2 cups (500 mL) **milk**
1½ cups (375 mL) shredded **Gruyère cheese** or Cheddar cheese
1 tsp (5 mL) **Dijon mustard**
4 cups (1 L) **Scoobi doo pasta**
2 cups (500 mL) chopped **fresh spinach**
2 cups (500 mL) cubed **ham**
1 cup (250 mL) halved **grape tomatoes**

In saucepan, melt butter over medium heat; fry onion, salt, thyme and pepper until onion is softened, about 5 minutes.

Sprinkle with flour; cook, stirring, for 1 minute. Whisk in milk; cook, whisking, until thick enough to coat spoon, about 7 minutes. Stir in cheese and mustard; cook, stirring, until cheese is melted.

Meanwhile, in large pot of boiling salted water, cook pasta until tender but firm, about 8 minutes. Drain and return to pot. Add sauce, spinach, ham and tomatoes; toss to combine.

Makes 4 servings. PER SERVING: about 738 cal, 47 g pro, 28 g total fat (15 g sat. fat), 76 g carb, 5 g fibre, 112 mg chol, 1,732 mg sodium. % RDI: 59% calcium, 38% iron, 49% vit A, 20% vit C, 105% folate.

Spaghetti Carbonara

When it's almost time to go grocery shopping, this is an entrée you can pull off with refrigerator staples. Serve with extra grated Parmesan cheese to sprinkle over top.

4 slices **bacon,** chopped
1 small **onion,** chopped
2 cloves **garlic,** minced
4 **eggs**
¼ cup (60 mL) grated **Parmesan cheese**
2 tbsp (30 mL) chopped **fresh parsley**
¼ tsp (1 mL) each **salt** and **pepper**
12 oz (375 g) **spaghetti**

In large skillet, fry bacon over medium heat until crisp, about 5 minutes. Drain off fat. Add onion and garlic to pan. Fry until softened, about 4 minutes.

Meanwhile, in bowl, whisk together eggs, cheese, parsley, salt and pepper. Set aside.

Meanwhile, in large pot of boiling salted water, cook spaghetti until tender but firm, about 8 minutes. Drain; return to pot over low heat.

Immediately stir in bacon and egg mixtures; heat, stirring, until pasta is coated, about 30 seconds.

Makes 4 servings. PER SERVING: about 482 cal, 22 g pro, 14 g total fat (5 g sat. fat), 66 g carb, 4 g fibre, 200 mg chol, 628 mg sodium. % RDI: 11% calcium, 29% iron, 9% vit A, 5% vit C, 92% folate.

CHAPTER 2

Make It Tonight... in 30 Minutes

Tomato-Topped Beef Patties

If anyone in the family doesn't like onions in patties or burgers, try grating them instead of chopping. It's a little more work, but the onion cooks more evenly, and onion haters won't find any little raw bits.

1 **egg**
¼ cup (60 mL) **dry bread crumbs**
1 small **onion,** grated
2 cloves **garlic,** minced
2 tbsp (30 mL) chopped **fresh parsley**
½ tsp (2 mL) each **salt** and **pepper**
¼ tsp (1 mL) each **hot pepper sauce**
　and **Worcestershire sauce**
1 lb (500 g) **lean ground beef**
2 **plum tomatoes,** thinly sliced
¼ tsp (1 mL) each **dried thyme** and
　oregano

In bowl, beat egg; mix in bread crumbs, onion, garlic, parsley, salt, pepper, hot pepper sauce and Worcestershire sauce. Mix in beef. Shape into four ½-inch (1 cm) thick patties. Place on foil-lined rimmed baking sheet. Top with tomato slices; sprinkle with thyme and oregano.

Roast in 400°F (200°C) oven until digital thermometer inserted sideways registers 160°F (71°C), about 25 minutes.

Makes 4 servings. PER SERVING: about 293 cal, 25 g pro, 17 g total fat (7 g sat. fat), 8 g carb, 1 g fibre, 114 mg chol, 442 mg sodium. % RDI: 4% calcium, 22% iron, 5% vit A, 15% vit C, 10% folate.

Sweet-and-Sour Coleslaw

1 tbsp (15 mL) **light mayonnaise**
1 tbsp (15 mL) **vegetable oil**
1 tbsp (15 mL) **cider vinegar**
1 tsp (5 mL) **granulated sugar**
½ tsp (2 mL) **celery seeds**
¼ tsp (1 mL) each **salt** and **pepper**
3 cups (750 mL) **coleslaw mix** or
　shredded cabbage
⅓ cup (75 mL) thinly sliced **red onion**

In large bowl, whisk together mayonnaise, oil, vinegar, sugar, celery seeds, salt and pepper. Add coleslaw mix and onion; toss to coat.

Makes 4 servings. PER SERVING: about 65 cal, 1 g pro, 5 g total fat (trace sat. fat), 6 g carb, 1 g fibre, 1 mg chol, 182 mg sodium. % RDI: 3% calcium, 4% iron, 12% vit A, 30% vit C, 10% folate.

Lazy Shepherd's Pie

It's not the shepherd who's lazy – it's the smart cook who puts this comforting dish together fast.

4 large **potatoes** (unpeeled), cubed (2 lb/1 kg)

¼ cup (60 mL) **milk** or buttermilk

1 **green onion,** sliced

1 lb (500 g) **lean ground beef**

1 tbsp (15 mL) **vegetable oil**

2½ cups (625 mL) small **mushrooms** (about 8 oz/250 g)

1 **onion,** diced

1 tsp (5 mL) **dried thyme**

¼ tsp (1 mL) each **salt** and **pepper**

1½ cups (375 mL) **sodium-reduced beef broth**

1 tbsp (15 mL) **cornstarch**

1 tbsp (15 mL) **Dijon mustard**

1 cup (250 mL) **frozen peas**

In large saucepan of boiling salted water, cover and cook potatoes until tender, about 12 minutes. Drain and return to pan; shaking pan, dry over low heat, about 1 minute. Mash coarsely; stir in milk and green onion.

Meanwhile, heat skillet over medium-high heat; sauté beef, breaking up with fork, until no longer pink, about 5 minutes. Transfer to plate. Drain fat from skillet.

In same skillet, heat oil over medium heat; fry mushrooms, onion, thyme, salt and pepper, stirring occasionally, until mushrooms are golden, about 8 minutes.

Whisk together broth, cornstarch and mustard; stir into skillet. Add beef and peas; bring to boil. Reduce heat and simmer until thickened and heated through, about 5 minutes. Serve over potatoes.

Makes 4 servings. PER SERVING: about 492 cal, 30 g pro, 19 g total fat (7 g sat. fat), 51 g carb, 6 g fibre, 65 mg chol, 1,045 mg sodium. % RDI: 7% calcium, 39% iron, 8% vit A, 48% vit C, 24% folate.

Beef and Sweet Potato Stir-Fry

When making a stir-fry sauce, stir it together in a 2-cup (500 mL) glass measuring cup.
Then it's easy to pour the well-mixed sauce into the pan when you're ready.

2 tbsp (30 mL) **vegetable oil**

1 lb (500 g) **beef stir-fry strips**

1 **onion,** sliced

3 cloves **garlic,** minced

2 cups (500 mL) cubed peeled
   sweet potatoes (2 small)

1 **sweet yellow pepper** or sweet green
   pepper, sliced

½ cup (125 mL) **beef broth**

¼ cup (60 mL) **oyster sauce**

1 tbsp (15 mL) **cornstarch**

1 tbsp (15 mL) **unseasoned rice vinegar**
   or cider vinegar

1 tsp (5 mL) **sesame oil**

2 **green onions,** thinly sliced

In wok or large skillet, heat 1 tbsp (15 mL) of
the oil over high heat. Stir-fry beef, in
2 batches, until browned but still pink inside,
about 2 minutes. Transfer to plate.

Drain fat from pan; add remaining oil. Fry
onion and garlic over medium heat until onion
is softened, about 2 minutes.

Stir in sweet potatoes, yellow pepper and ½ cup
(125 mL) water; cover and steam until sweet
potatoes are tender, about 10 minutes.

Meanwhile, in measuring cup, whisk together
beef broth, oyster sauce, cornstarch, vinegar
and sesame oil. Return beef and any
accumulated juices to pan.

Add oyster sauce mixture and bring to boil;
boil, stirring, until thickened and glossy, about
1 minute. Sprinkle with green onions.

Makes 4 servings. PER SERVING: about 316 cal, 29 g pro,
11 g total fat (2 g sat. fat), 26 g carb, 2 g fibre, 49 mg chol,
658 mg sodium. % RDI: 4% calcium, 22% iron, 114% vit A,
98% vit C, 16% folate.

EQUIPMENT
WOK 101

For stir-frying, nothing beats the wok. Its unique
bowl shape ensures even heat distribution for
faster cooking, while sloping sides keep food in
the pan (and off the stove). Plus, you can stir-fry,
steam, braise, fry and smoke all in one pan.

SIZE AND SHAPE
Size Matters: Wok sizes vary. For home use, we
recommend a 14-inch (35 cm) wok, which is a
manageable weight with enough surface area
for cooking three or four portions at once.

Nice Bottoms: Traditional round-bottom woks
are unstable on western stove tops, so flat-
bottom woks were designed to sit directly on
electric coils (ceramic cooktops and gas burners,
too).

Handles: Traditional woks have two metal
handles, making it easy to lift the pan on and off
the stove. Most modern household woks have
only one long handle (like a skillet), eliminating
the need for a pot holder while providing
excellent leverage for tilting. Many also have a
small grip at the front, providing better balance
when lifting.

Sweet-and-Sour Halibut with Vegetable Noodle Stir-Fry

This is a lovely layered supper – noodles and vegetables underneath, glazed fish on top.

Half pkg (1-lb/454 g pkg) **rice stick noodles**

1 cup (250 mL) **chicken broth**

¼ cup (60 mL) **orange juice**

3 tbsp (45 mL) **granulated sugar**

2 tbsp (30 mL) each **red wine vinegar** and **tomato paste**

2 tsp (10 mL) **cornstarch**

2 tsp (10 mL) **soy sauce**

1 tsp (5 mL) **ground ginger**

2 cloves **garlic,** minced

2 tbsp (30 mL) **vegetable oil** (approx)

4 **halibut fillets,** or tilapia or catfish fillets (1½ lb/750 g total)

1 **sweet red pepper,** diced

2 cups (500 mL) quartered **mushrooms** (about 5 oz/150 g)

1 **zucchini,** diced

In bowl of boiling water, soak noodles until pliable and tender, about 6 minutes. Drain and chill in cold water; drain and set aside.

Meanwhile, in glass measure, whisk broth, juice, sugar, vinegar, tomato paste, cornstarch, soy sauce, ginger and garlic; set aside.

In large skillet, heat 2 tsp (10 mL) of the oil over medium-high heat; fry halibut, turning once and adding more oil if necessary, until golden and fish flakes easily when tested, about 6 minutes. Add broth mixture and bring to boil; boil until thickened, about 2 minutes.

Meanwhile, in separate skillet, heat remaining oil over medium-high heat; stir-fry red pepper, mushrooms and zucchini, adding more oil if necessary, until tender-crisp, about 2 minutes. Add noodles; stir-fry until hot, about 1 minute. Serve in bowls topped with fish and sauce.

Makes 4 servings. PER SERVING: about 566 cal, 40 g pro, 12 g total fat (1 g sat. fat), 72 g carb, 4 g fibre, 54 mg chol, 506 mg sodium. % RDI: 10% calcium, 21% iron, 21% vit A, 100% vit C, 19% folate.

MATERIALS

Cast Iron/Enamel: Cast-iron woks have been used in China for centuries. They retain heat evenly and cook quickly. Before using, season to prevent sticking. Here's how.
• Using sponge, scrub inside of wok with hot water and a bit of liquid detergent; scrub exterior with scouring pad. Rinse and dry well.
• Using paper towel, rub about 2 tbsp (30 mL) beef fat, lard or coconut oil over wok surface. Heat over medium-low heat for about 10 minutes. Wipe off black residue. Let cool.
• Repeat until no black remains (about 3 times).

Preseasoned Carbon Steel: This natural nonstick surface is easy to clean up and is a good choice for novice wokers. Hand-wash.

WOK ACCESSORIES

If you do a lot of frying, a skimmer-strainer made of brass wire mesh with a long bamboo handle is essential. For stir-frying, a shovel-shaped wok spatula is handy: its curved bowl matches the contours of the wok, and it has a long handle to keep your hands safe.

Vegetable and Tilapia Fajitas

If tilapia isn't available, any mild white fish would be a good substitute.

2 **tilapia fillets** (about 8 oz/250 g total)
3 tbsp (45 mL) **all-purpose flour**
1 tsp (5 mL) **chili powder**
½ tsp (2 mL) each **salt** and **pepper**
2 tbsp (30 mL) **vegetable oil**
2 **sweet yellow peppers,** thinly sliced
1 **zucchini** (about 10 oz/300 g), julienned
1 **red onion,** thinly sliced
1 tsp (5 mL) each **ground cumin**
  and **coriander**
½ tsp (2 mL) **dried oregano**
⅓ cup (75 mL) **salsa**
1 **avocado,** halved, pitted and sliced
4 **whole wheat tortillas,** warmed

Cut tilapia crosswise in ¾-inch (2 cm) wide strips. In resealable plastic bag, shake flour, chili powder and half each of the salt and pepper; add tilapia, shaking gently to coat.

In large nonstick skillet, heat 1 tbsp (15 mL) of the oil over medium-high heat; cook tilapia, turning once, until golden and fish flakes easily when tested, 6 to 8 minutes. Transfer to plate; keep warm.

In same skillet, heat remaining oil over medium heat; cook yellow peppers, zucchini, onion, cumin, coriander, oregano and remaining salt and pepper, stirring occasionally, until tender, 7 to 10 minutes.

Divide fish, vegetables, salsa and avocado among tortillas; roll up.

Makes 4 servings. PER SERVING: about 458 cal, 21 g pro, 20 g total fat (3 g sat. fat), 51 g carb, 10 g fibre, 28 mg chol, 883 mg sodium, 902 mg potassium. % RDI: 8% calcium, 24% iron, 11% vit A, 162% vit C, 54% folate.

Edamame Vegetable Soup

Edamame is the Japanese name for green soybeans. The shelled version is the most convenient to use.

1 tbsp (15 mL) **vegetable oil**
3 **carrots,** sliced
2 ribs **celery,** sliced
1 **onion,** chopped
2 cloves **garlic,** minced
½ tsp (2 mL) **dried thyme**
¼ tsp (1 mL) **pepper**
4 cups (1 L) **vegetable broth**
1 **red-skinned potato** (unpeeled), cubed
Half pkg (454 g pkg) **medium-firm tofu**
1½ cups (375 mL) **frozen shelled edamame**
Dash **hot pepper sauce**
1 tbsp (15 mL) minced **fresh chives** or
  green onion

In large saucepan, heat oil over medium heat; fry carrots, celery, onion, garlic, thyme and pepper, stirring occasionally, until onion is softened, about 5 minutes.

Add broth and potato; bring to boil. Reduce heat, cover and simmer until carrots and potato are tender, about 15 minutes.

Cut tofu into ½-inch (1 cm) cubes. Add to soup along with edamame and hot pepper sauce; heat through.

Serve sprinkled with chives.

Makes 4 servings. PER SERVING: about 291 cal, 18 g pro, 12 g total fat (1 g sat. fat), 32 g carb, 8 g fibre, 0 mg chol, 1,053 mg sodium. % RDI: 22% calcium, 29% iron, 145% vit A, 47% vit C, 71% folate.

33

Jerk Pork Chops

For this menu, start the rice first, then season and roast the chops. Allspice and thyme are the signature flavours of any jerk dish.

4 **pork loin centre chops**
1 tbsp (15 mL) **soy sauce**
1 tbsp (15 mL) **orange juice**
1 tbsp (15 mL) **extra-virgin olive oil**
2 cloves **garlic,** minced
3 **green onions,** minced
1 tsp (5 mL) each **ground allspice** and
   dried thyme
¼ tsp (1 mL) each **salt** and **pepper**
¼ tsp (1 mL) **ground ginger**
Pinch **cayenne pepper**

Slash fat around pork at 1-inch (2.5 cm) intervals; set aside.

In bowl, combine soy sauce, orange juice, oil, garlic, green onions, allspice, thyme, salt, pepper, ginger and cayenne; rub on both sides of chops.

In small roasting pan, roast chops in 375°F (190°C) oven, turning halfway through, until browned, juices run clear when pork is pierced and just a hint of pink remains inside, about 18 minutes.

Makes 4 servings. PER SERVING: about 190 cal, 21 g pro, 10 g total fat (3 g sat. fat), 3 g carb, 1 g fibre, 58 mg chol, 453 mg sodium. % RDI: 3% calcium, 10% iron, 1% vit A, 7% vit C, 5% folate.

Peas, Pepper and Rice

1 tbsp (15 mL) **vegetable oil**
1 small **onion,** chopped
1 **sweet red pepper,** chopped
¾ cup (175 mL) **parboiled rice**
1½ cups (375 mL) **chicken broth**
¼ tsp (1 mL) **cinnamon**
¼ tsp (1 mL) each **salt** and **pepper**
¾ cup (175 mL) **frozen peas**

In saucepan, heat oil over medium-high heat; fry onion until softened. Add red pepper and rice; stir for 1 minute.

Add broth, cinnamon, salt and pepper; bring to boil. Reduce heat, cover and simmer until rice is tender and liquid is absorbed, 20 minutes. With fork, stir in peas; heat through.

Makes 4 servings. PER SERVING: about 207 cal, 6 g pro, 4 g total fat (1 g sat. fat), 35 g carb, 2 g fibre, 0 mg chol, 460 mg sodium. % RDI: 4% calcium, 7% iron, 12% vit A, 87% vit C, 12% folate.

Chicken and Gnocchi Soup

This soup has the kind of grandmother (*nonna, oma;* fill in whatever word you like) touch we crave on a cold evening. It's a very up-to-date grandmother, though, who adds the spinach topping.

8 oz (250 g) **boneless skinless chicken breasts**

1 tbsp (15 mL) **vegetable oil**

1 small **onion,** diced

1 each small **carrot** and rib **celery,** diced

2 cloves **garlic,** minced

1 tsp (5 mL) **dried oregano**

Pinch each **salt** and **pepper**

1 **bay leaf**

1 pkg (900 mL) **sodium-reduced chicken broth**

1 pkg (1 lb/500 g) **fresh gnocchi**

RUSTIC SPINACH GREMOLATA:

1 cup (250 mL) **fresh spinach,** chopped

½ tsp (2 mL) grated **lemon zest**

2 tsp (10 mL) **lemon juice**

2 tsp (10 mL) **extra-virgin olive oil**

1 clove **garlic,** minced

Cut chicken into cubes. In large saucepan, heat oil over medium heat; fry chicken, onion, carrot, celery, garlic, oregano, salt, pepper and bay leaf, stirring occasionally, until onion is softened, about 5 minutes.

Add chicken broth and 1½ cups (375 mL) water; bring to boil. Reduce heat to medium; cover and simmer for 10 minutes. Add gnocchi; simmer, uncovered, until gnocchi float to top and are firm to the touch, about 5 minutes. Discard bay leaf.

RUSTIC SPINACH GREMOLATA: Meanwhile, in bowl, combine spinach, lemon zest and juice, oil and garlic. Sprinkle onto bowls of soup.

Makes 4 servings. PER SERVING: about 399 cal, 22 g pro, 7 g total fat (1 g sat. fat), 63 g carb, 6 g fibre, 34 mg chol, 765 mg sodium. % RDI: 6% calcium, 13% iron, 38% vit A, 95% vit C, 26% folate.

WHAT DO I COOK FIRST?

"It all depends" isn't much help, but it does all depend on what you're cooking. Start by reading the recipes you're serving, then:

•**Start with the dish that takes the longest time.** This is often the starch. To make pasta, for example, it takes about 10 minutes for the covered pot of water to come to a boil. Then it takes up to 10 minutes for most pastas to soften to the al dente stage. Rice and potatoes take about 25 minutes from start to finish.

•**Move on to the quick stuff.** While the starches are cooking, get to work on the quicker dishes: grilled or roasted fish, sautéed chops or chicken, or sauce to serve over pasta.

•**Toss the salad or make veggies and dip.** Serve them while the rest of dinner cooks. It's a healthy first course and kills hunger pangs while you wait.

Pork Tenderloin with Mushroom Sauce

Rich, creamy and perfect for unexpected company, this dish is surprisingly simple to pull together.

1 pkg (14 g) **dried mixed mushrooms**
1 **pork tenderloin** (about 1 lb/500 g)
¼ tsp (1 mL) each **salt** and **pepper**
2 tbsp (30 mL) **vegetable oil**
1 **shallot** (or half small onion), minced
3 cloves **garlic,** minced
2 tbsp (30 mL) **brandy** or chicken broth
2 tbsp (30 mL) **10% cream**

In small heatproof bowl, cover and soak mushrooms in 1 cup (250 mL) boiling water until softened, about 10 minutes. With slotted spoon, remove and pat dry; coarsely chop and set aside. Strain liquid into measure; add enough water to make ¾ cup (175 mL). Set aside.

Sprinkle pork with salt and pepper. In large ovenproof skillet, heat half of the oil over medium-high heat; sear pork all over, about 6 minutes. Roast in 400°F (200°C) oven until juices run clear when pork is pierced and just a hint of pink remains inside, about 15 minutes. Transfer to cutting board and tent with foil; let stand for 5 minutes before carving into 1-inch (2.5 cm) thick slices. Keep warm.

Meanwhile, in same skillet, heat remaining oil over medium-low heat; cook shallot, garlic and mushrooms, stirring occasionally, until softened and golden, about 6 minutes.

Stir in brandy; boil until almost no liquid remains, about 30 seconds. Stir in reserved soaking liquid and cream; simmer until reduced to about ½ cup (125 mL), 10 minutes. Stir in accumulated pork juices. Serve with pork.

Makes 4 servings. PER SERVING: about 235 cal, 28 g pro, 10 g total fat (2 g sat. fat), 4 g carb, 1 g fibre, 69 mg chol, 206 mg sodium. % RDI: 2% calcium, 11% iron, 1% vit A, 2% vit C, 5% folate.

Chicken Caesar Salad with Garlic Croutons

This Caesar-style vinaigrette is made from pantry staples and doesn't require a raw egg like the authentic version.

2 tbsp (30 mL) **extra-virgin olive oil**
¾ tsp (4 mL) **salt**
¾ tsp (4 mL) **dried Italian herb seasoning**
1 large clove **garlic,** minced
4 **boneless skinless chicken breasts**
Half **whole wheat baguette**
6 cups (1.5 L) torn **romaine lettuce**
1 cup (250 mL) halved **grape tomatoes** or cherry tomatoes
¼ cup (60 mL) shaved **Parmesan cheese**
DRESSING:
2 tbsp (30 mL) **white wine vinegar**
2 tsp (10 mL) **anchovy paste**
2 tsp (10 mL) **lemon juice**
1 tsp (5 mL) **Dijon mustard**
1 tsp (5 mL) **Worcestershire sauce**
¼ cup (60 mL) **extra-virgin olive oil**

In bowl, combine oil, salt, Italian herb seasoning and garlic; brush one-third over chicken. Sear in ovenproof skillet over medium-high heat, turning once, until golden. Roast in 400°F (200°C) oven until juices run clear when chicken is pierced, 15 to 20 minutes. Let stand for 5 minutes before slicing diagonally.

Meanwhile, cut baguette into scant 1-inch (2.5 cm) cubes. Add to remaining oil mixture, tossing to coat. Spread on baking sheet and bake in 400°F (200°C) oven until golden and crisp, about 10 minutes.

DRESSING: In separate large bowl, whisk together vinegar, anchovy paste, lemon juice, mustard and Worcestershire sauce; whisk in oil. Add lettuce, tomatoes, croutons and chicken; toss to combine. Sprinkle with cheese.

Makes 4 servings. PER SERVING: about 453 cal. 37 g pro. 25 g total fat (5 g sat. fat), 20 g carb, 4 g fibre, 84 mg chol, 859 mg sodium. % RDI: 12% calcium, 21% iron, 45% vit A, 38% vit C, 53% folate.

Pizza Margherita

Authentic Italian pizza is light on the toppings, which lets their pure, fresh flavours shine.

1 lb (500 g) **pizza dough**
1 can (28 oz/796 mL) **tomatoes,** drained, seeded and chopped
¼ tsp (1 mL) **salt**
3 tbsp (45 mL) **olive oil**
5 oz (150 g) **mozzarella ball,** thinly sliced in about 8 pieces
6 **black olives,** pitted and halved
8 to 10 **fresh basil leaves**

On floured surface, roll out dough to 12 inch (30 cm) circle; transfer to pizza stone or pan.

Spread tomatoes over dough; sprinkle with salt. Drizzle with 2 tbsp (30 mL) of the oil; top with cheese and olives. Bake in 475°F (240°C) oven until golden and bubbly, 15 to 18 minutes. Sprinkle with basil; drizzle with remaining oil.

Makes 4 servings. PER SERVING: about 475 cal, 15 g pro, 23 g total fat (7 g sat. fat), 51 g carb, 2 g fibre, 32 mg chol, 918 mg sodium, 321 mg potassium. % RDI: 23% calcium, 31% iron, 9% vit A, 23% vit C, 74% folate.

EASY PIZZA CRUST

• In food processor, pulse 2 cups (500 mL) all-purpose flour; 1½ tsp (7 mL) quick-rising (instant) dry yeast; and ¾ tsp (4 mL) salt. With motor running, whirl in ¾ cup (175 mL) hot water and 2 tsp (10 mL) olive oil . Whirl until dough forms ball, about 1 minute. Let rest in work bowl until doubled in bulk, about 40 minutes.

• Press dough into ball; on floured surface, roll out or press into circle big enough to fit 12-inch (30 cm) greased pizza pan. (If dough is too elastic, let relax for a few minutes.) Let rise for thick crust, or top and bake right away for thin crust. Makes one 12-inch (30 cm) pizza crust.

Spinach Pesto Fusilli with Peppers

If you don't have any fusilli pasta on hand, you can use penne, rotini or radiatore instead.

5 cups (1.25 L) **fusilli** (12 oz/375 g)
1 small **red onion**
1 each **sweet red** and **yellow pepper**
SPINACH PESTO:
1 pkg (300 g) **frozen spinach,** thawed
3 cloves **garlic,** minced
1 tbsp (15 mL) **pine nuts**
1 tsp (5 mL) **dried basil**
½ tsp (2 mL) each **salt** and **pepper**
¼ cup (60 mL) **extra-virgin olive oil**
¼ cup (60 mL) grated **Parmesan cheese**
4 tsp (20 mL) **balsamic vinegar**

SPINACH PESTO: Squeeze spinach to remove moisture. In food processor, purée together spinach, garlic, pine nuts, basil, salt and pepper until smooth. Pulse in 3 tbsp (45 mL) of the oil; pulse in Parmesan cheese and vinegar. Set aside.

In large pot of boiling salted water, cook pasta until tender but firm, about 8 minutes. Reserving 1½ cups (375 mL) cooking liquid, drain pasta and return to pot. Add spinach pesto and reserved cooking liquid; simmer over medium heat until hot, about 3 minutes.

Meanwhile, thinly slice onion and red and yellow peppers. In skillet, heat remaining oil over medium heat; fry onion and peppers until tender-crisp, about 4 minutes.

Serve pasta topped with pepper mixture.

Makes 4 servings. PER SERVING: about 531 cal, 17 g pro, 18 g total fat (3 g sat. fat), 76 g carb, 7 g fibre, 5 mg chol, 813 mg sodium. % RDI: 18% calcium, 25% iron, 51% vit A, 168% vit C, 85% folate.

Beef Patties with Stout Gravy

Stout beer makes a rich and flavourful gravy that complements the melt-in-your-mouth beef. Serve with mashed potatoes or rolls to soak up every last drop.

1 **egg**
1 clove **garlic,** minced
2 tbsp (30 mL) **Worcestershire sauce**
1 tbsp (15 mL) **prepared hot mustard**
1 lb (500 g) **medium ground beef**
1 tbsp (15 mL) **vegetable oil**
1 cup (250 mL) **sodium-reduced beef broth**
1 cup (250 mL) **stout** or water
1 pkg (10 oz/284 g) **pearl onions,** peeled
1 cup (250 mL) **frozen peas**
1 tbsp (15 mL) **cornstarch**

In bowl, whisk together egg, garlic, half of the Worcestershire sauce and 1 tsp (5 mL) of the mustard. Mix in beef. Shape into 8 patties.

In skillet, heat oil over medium heat; fry patties, turning once, until digital thermometer inserted sideways registers 160°F (71°C), about 10 minutes. Transfer to plate; cover and keep warm.

Whisk together broth, stout and remaining Worcestershire sauce and mustard; add to pan and bring to boil. Add onions and peas; simmer until onions are softened, 3 to 5 minutes.

Mix cornstarch with 1 tbsp (15 mL) water; stir into pan. Return patties to skillet; simmer until gravy is thickened.

Makes 4 servings. PER SERVING: about 394 cal, 26 g pro, 23 g total fat (8 g sat. fat), 16 g carb, 2 g fibre, 114 mg chol, 390 mg sodium, 531 mg potassium. % RDI: 5% calcium, 24% iron, 9% vit A, 12% vit C, 18% folate.

QUICK FIXES

IF YOUR SAUCE OR GRAVY IS TOO THIN

• Uncover pan and boil over medium-high heat for a few minutes. If meat or vegetables are already tender, remove with a slotted spoon and keep warm in the serving bowl.

• If the sauce has a salted base, boiling it down can make it too salty. Try one of the following:

• Stir in beurre manié, 1 tbsp (15 mL) at a time. What's beurre manié? Simply equal parts soft unsalted butter and all-purpose flour mashed together until smooth. Keep a jar of it in the fridge to thicken soups, sauces, stews or anything braised.

• Shake or whisk 2 tbsp (30 mL) all-purpose flour with ⅓ cup (75 mL) cold water. Whisk or stir into liquid and simmer until thickened. This amount should thicken 2 cups (500 mL) sauce or gravy.

IF YOUR SAUCE OR GRAVY IS TOO THICK

• Add a little more of the liquid called for in the recipe. If you've run out of broth, tomato juice or wine, just use water.

Fish and Chips

The roasted potato wedges – a lighter version of french fries – are possible in this 30-minute supper thanks to a quick precooking stint in the microwave.

4 **potatoes** (about 2 lb/1 kg)
2 tbsp (30 mL) **vegetable oil** (approx)
1 tsp (5 mL) **ground cumin**
½ tsp (2 mL) each **salt** and **pepper**
¼ tsp (1 mL) **turmeric**
2 cloves **garlic,** minced
¼ cup (60 mL) **all-purpose flour**
½ tsp (2 mL) **sweet paprika**
4 **tilapia fillets** or catfish fillets
4 cups (1 L) packed **baby spinach**
Lemon wedges

Scrub potatoes; prick in several places. Microwave on high until tender-firm, about 4 minutes. Let cool for 5 minutes. Cut lengthwise into wedges.

In large bowl, toss together potato wedges, half each of the oil, cumin, salt and pepper, and the turmeric and garlic; arrange on greased rimmed baking sheet. Bake in 450°F (230°C) oven, turning once, until crispy and golden brown, about 20 minutes.

Meanwhile, in shallow dish, whisk together flour, paprika and remaining cumin, salt and pepper. Press fish into flour mixture, turning to coat; shake off excess.

In large skillet, heat remaining oil over medium-high heat; fry fish in 2 batches, turning once and adding more oil if necessary, until golden and fish flakes easily when tested, about 7 minutes.

Add spinach; cover and steam until wilted, about 2 minutes. Serve with potato wedges and lemon wedges to squeeze over fish.

Makes 4 servings. PER SERVING: about 417 cal, 39 g pro, 11 g total fat (2 g sat. fat), 44 g carb, 5 g fibre, 71 mg chol, 366 mg sodium. % RDI: 8% calcium, 33% iron, 32% vit A, 38% vit C, 51% folate.

CHAPTER 3

Make It Tonight... with Five or So Ingredients

Beef and Broccoli Stir-Fry

Instead of flank steak, you can use a piece of top sirloin grilling steak and slice thinly across the grain, or use beef stir-fry strips available at the meat counter. This recipe can be your template for other stir-fries. Try lean pork or chicken breasts instead of the beef, or replace the broccoli with an equal amount of other quick-cooking green vegetables: sugar snap peas, green beans, halved brussels sprouts, halved baby bok choy or coarsely shredded cabbage are all excellent.

12 oz (375 g) **flank marinating steak**
3 tbsp (45 mL) **oyster sauce**
1 tbsp (15 mL) **cornstarch**
4 cups (1 L) **broccoli florets**
2 cloves **garlic,** minced
1 tbsp (15 mL) minced **fresh ginger**

Slice beef thinly across the grain; sprinkle with ¼ tsp (1 mL) pepper; set aside.

In small bowl, whisk together ¾ cup (175 mL) water, oyster sauce and cornstarch; set aside.

In wok or skillet, heat 1 tbsp (15 mL) vegetable oil over medium-high heat; stir-fry beef until browned but still pink inside, about 3 minutes. Transfer to plate.

Add 1 tbsp (15 mL) vegetable oil to wok; stir-fry broccoli, garlic and ginger for 1 minute. Cover and steam for 2 minutes.

Return beef and any accumulated juices to wok. Add oyster sauce mixture; stir-fry until slightly thickened, about 3 minutes.

Makes 4 servings. PER SERVING: about 253 cal, 21 g pro, 15 g total fat (4 g sat. fat), 8 g carb, trace fibre, 36 mg chol, 436 mg sodium. % RDI: 4% calcium, 16% iron, 20% vit A, 67% vit C, 19% folate.

TECHNIQUE
STIR-FRYING

1. Heat wok over medium-high to high heat for at least 1 minute; add oil, drizzling over side and bottom of wok. To ensure tender, flavourful meat, sear only small amounts (about 1 cup/250 mL) at a time.

2. When adding sauce, form a well by pushing meat and vegetables up the side of the wok. Pour sauce in the middle, stirring to thicken before tossing with other ingredients.

TIPS
• Have all ingredients prepped and at hand.
• Cut all ingredients about the same size.
• Stir-fry hard vegetables (broccoli, carrots and eggplant) first, followed by softer vegetables (zucchini, snow peas and bean sprouts) and leafy greens (bok choy).

Beef and Pepper Kabobs

Here's a dish you can grill outside or on an indoor electric grill, or even broil in the oven.

1 lb (500 g) **top sirloin grilling steak**
   (about 1 inch/2.5 cm thick)
1 tbsp (15 mL) **lemon juice**
½ tsp (2 mL) **dried rosemary**
1 large **sweet red pepper** (or 2 small)

Trim fat from grilling steak; cut into 1-inch (2.5 cm) cubes.

In glass bowl, whisk together 3 tbsp (45 mL) extra-virgin olive oil, lemon juice, rosemary and ½ tsp (2 mL) each salt and pepper; add beef and stir to coat. Cover and marinate for 10 minutes. (*Make ahead: Refrigerate for up to 8 hours.*)

Meanwhile, core and cut red pepper into 1-inch (2.5 cm) squares. Alternately thread marinated beef and red pepper loosely onto metal or soaked wooden skewers.

Place skewers on greased grill over medium high heat or under broiler; close lid and grill or broil, turning 3 times, until beef is browned but still pink inside, about 10 minutes.

Makes 4 servings. PER SERVING: about 189 cal, 21 g pro, 10 g total fat (3 g sat. fat), 3 g carb, 1 g fibre, 51 mg chol, 185 mg sodium. % RDI: 2% calcium, 18% iron, 15% vit A, 113% vit C, 6% folate.

Parsley Rice

¾ cup (175 mL) **parboiled rice**
¼ cup (60 mL) finely chopped **fresh parsley**

In saucepan, bring 1½ cups (375 mL) water and ¼ tsp (1 mL) salt to boil over medium-high heat; stir in rice. Cover and reduce heat to medium-low; simmer until tender, about 20 minutes.

Remove from heat; let stand until liquid is absorbed, about 5 minutes. Fluff with fork. Stir in parsley.

Makes 4 servings. PER SERVING: about 130 cal, 3 g pro, trace total fat (0 g sat. fat), 28 g carb, 1 g fibre, 0 mg chol, 151 mg sodium. % RDI: 3% calcium, 4% iron, 2% vit A, 7% vit C, 4% folate.

WHAT DOES FIVE OR SO INGREDIENTS MEAN?

The ingredient lists for the recipes in this chapter include about five (sometimes four, sometimes up to seven) ingredients. The only other things you'll need to make them are your pantry staples of oil, salt and pepper. It's that simple!

Pork with Lemon Caper Sauce

This restaurant-style dish, also known as piccata, is deceptively easy. Don't be afraid to dazzle your family and friends!

8 **pork loin centre-cut chops,** boneless fast fry (about 1 lb/500 g)
¼ cup (60 mL) **all-purpose flour**
3 cloves **garlic,** minced
1 tbsp (15 mL) rinsed drained **capers**
½ cup (125 mL) **sodium-reduced chicken broth**
2 tbsp (30 mL) **lemon juice**

Between sheets of plastic wrap, pound pork to scant ¼-inch (5 mm) thickness. In bag, shake together flour and ¼ tsp (1 mL) each salt and pepper. One piece at a time, shake pork in flour mixture to coat.

In large skillet, heat 1 tbsp (15 mL) extra-virgin olive oil over medium-high heat; fry pork, turning once, in 2 batches and adding more oil if necessary, until golden, juices run clear when pork is pierced and just a hint of pink remains inside, about 3 minutes. Transfer to platter; keep warm.

Add 1 tbsp (15 mL) extra-virgin olive oil to pan; fry garlic and capers over medium heat for 1 minute. Add broth and lemon juice; boil for 1 minute, scraping up any brown bits from bottom of pan. Serve over pork.

Makes 4 servings. PER SERVING: about 302 cal, 26 g pro, 18 g total fat (4 g sat. fat), 7 g carb, trace fibre, 73 mg chol, 357 mg sodium. % RDI: 3% calcium, 10% iron, 5% vit C, 7% folate.

Chili-Rubbed Pork Chops

Just wait for a harried suppertime, when this simple recipe will come to your rescue. Check out other rubs you can make at home (see Make-Your-Own Seasonings, opposite) that taste just as delicious on these succulent chops.

4 **pork rib chops**
1 tbsp (15 mL) packed **brown sugar**
2 tsp (10 mL) **ground cumin**
2 tsp (10 mL) **chili powder**

Trim fat from chops; slash edges at 1-inch (2.5 cm) intervals to prevent curling. In small bowl, combine sugar, cumin, chili powder and 1 tsp (5 mL) salt; stir in 1 tbsp (15 mL) vegetable oil. Rub all over chops. (*Make-ahead: Cover and refrigerate for up to 24 hours.*)

Place chops in greased grill pan or on greased grill over medium-high heat; close lid (if using barbecue) and grill, turning once, until juices run clear when pork is pierced and just a hint of pink remains inside, about 8 minutes.

Makes 4 servings. PER SERVING: about 227 cal, 23 g pro, 13 g total fat (4 g sat. fat), 4 g carb, trace fibre, 56 mg chol, 626 mg sodium. % RDI: 3% calcium, 12% iron, 5% vit A, 2% vit C, 2% folate.

TIP

Try buying a family pack of chops. Season and enclose the number you need for each meal in freezer bags. Packed in a single layer, four chops will defrost in the fridge in a day.

MAKE-YOUR-OWN SEASONINGS AND HERB BLENDS

Add a little oil to these blends and rub over fish, chicken, chops, roasts or steaks. Or add them straight to soups, dips, vinaigrettes, stuffings, burgers or pizzas. Be sure to use dried herb leaves, not powdered herbs, and store in airtight jars in a cool, dark drawer for up to 3 months.

HERB SEASONING MIX

• In small bowl, mix together ½ cup (125 mL) dried chopped chives; 2 tbsp (30 mL) dried parsley flakes; 2 tsp (10 mL) each dried basil, dried thyme, garlic powder and onion powder; and 1 tsp (5 mL) pepper. Makes 1 cup (250 mL).

LEMON DILL SEASONING MIX

• Mix together ⅓ cup (75 mL) each dried dillweed and parsley flakes; 4 tsp (20 mL) lemon-and-pepper seasoning; and 1 tbsp (15 mL) each celery salt, dry mustard and garlic salt. Makes about 1 cup (250 mL).

CURRY SEASONING MIX

• Mix together ½ cup (125 mL) dried minced onion; 2 tbsp (30 mL) curry powder; 4 tsp (20 mL) each ground cumin and salt; and 2 tsp (10 mL) each turmeric and pepper. Makes 1 cup (250 mL).

HERBES DE PROVENCE

• Mix together ¼ cup (60 mL) each dried oregano, thyme and savory; 1 tsp (5 mL) each dried basil and rosemary; and ½ tsp (2 mL) dried sage. Makes about ¾ cup (175 mL).

POULTRY SEASONING

• Mix together ¼ cup (60 mL) each dried sage, thyme and oregano. Makes about ¾ cup (175 mL).

ITALIAN HERB SEASONING

• Mix together 2 tbsp (30 mL) each dried basil, thyme, marjoram, oregano, sage and rosemary. Makes about ¾ cup (175 mL).

QUICK DIPS

HERB DIP

• In bowl, whisk together ½ cup (125 mL) plain yogurt; ½ cup (125 mL) cream cheese; ¼ cup (60 mL) light mayonnaise; and 4 tsp (20 mL) Herb Seasoning Mix (recipe, left). Cover and refrigerate for at least 2 hours. *(Make-ahead: Cover and refrigerate for up to 3 days.)* Garnish with 2 tbsp (30 mL) chopped fresh chives. Makes 1¼ cups (300 mL).

PER 1 TBSP (15 mL): about 35 cal, 1 g pro, 3 g total fat (2 g sat. fat), 1 g carb, 0 g fibre, 8 mg chol, 44 mg sodium. % RDI: 1% calcium, 1% iron, 3% vit A, 1% folate.

VARIATIONS

LEMON DILL DIP

• Replace Herb Seasoning Mix with 2 tsp (10 mL) Lemon Dill Seasoning Mix (recipe, left). Replace chives with chopped fresh dill.

CURRY DIP

• Replace Herb Seasoning Mix with 2 tsp (10 mL) Curry Seasoning Mix (recipe, left). Add 1 tbsp (15 mL) mango chutney. Replace chives with chopped fresh cilantro.

Greek-Style Flank Steak

The sunny flavours of lemon, oregano and garlic liven up this humble cut of beef.

1 tsp (5 mL) grated **lemon zest**
1 tbsp (15 mL) **lemon juice**
2 cloves **garlic,** minced
1 tbsp (15 mL) minced **fresh oregano**
1 lb (500 g) **beef flank marinating steak**

In shallow glass dish, whisk together lemon zest and juice, 1 tbsp (15 mL) extra-virgin olive oil, garlic, oregano, and ¼ tsp (1 mL) each salt and pepper; add steak, turning and patting to coat. Refrigerate for at least 15 minutes or up to 4 hours.

Place steak on greased grill over medium-high heat; close lid and grill until medium-rare, about 6 minutes per side. (Or broil for about 4 minutes per side.)

Transfer steak to cutting board and tent with foil; let stand for 5 minutes before carving thinly across the grain.

Makes 4 servings. PER SERVING: about 195 cal, 24 g pro, 10 g total fat (3 g sat. fat), 1 g carb, trace fibre, 48 mg chol, 187 mg sodium. % RDI: 1% calcium, 16% iron, 5% vit C, 3% folate.

Feta Green Pea Orzo

1½ cups (375 mL) **orzo** or other small pasta
½ cup (125 mL) **frozen peas**
¼ cup (60 mL) cubed **feta cheese**
2 tbsp (30 mL) minced **fresh dill**
1 tbsp (15 mL) **lemon juice**

In saucepan of boiling salted water, cook orzo until almost tender, about 5 minutes. Add peas; heat through. Drain and toss with feta, dill, 1 tbsp (15 mL) extra-virgin olive oil, lemon juice, and ¼ tsp (1 mL) each salt and pepper.

Makes 4 servings. PER SERVING: about 302 cal, 10 g pro, 6 g total fat (2 g sat. fat), 50 g carb, 4 g fibre, 8 mg chol, 416 mg sodium. % RDI: 5% calcium, 19% iron, 5% vit A, 3% vit C, 65% folate.

Pork Chops with Balsamic Glaze

The sweet-and-sour taste of balsamic vinegar really tarts up everyday pork chops.

2 tsp (10 mL) **dried Italian herb seasoning**
4 **pork loin centre chops**
2 tbsp (30 mL) **balsamic vinegar**
¾ cup (175 mL) **sodium-reduced chicken broth**
1 tsp (5 mL) **cornstarch**

In small bowl, mix together 2 tbsp (30 mL) extra-virgin olive oil, Italian herb seasoning and pinch salt; brush over chops. In large skillet, fry chops over medium-high heat, adding more oil if necessary, until browned, juices run clear when pork is pierced and just a hint of pink remains inside, about 4 minutes per side. Transfer to plate; keep warm. Drain off any fat in pan.

Add vinegar to pan; simmer over medium heat for 30 seconds. Whisk broth with cornstarch; add to pan and bring to boil, stirring and scraping up any brown bits. Reduce heat and simmer until thickened, about 1 minute. Return chops and any accumulated juices to pan; heat through, turning to coat and glaze.

Makes 4 servings. PER SERVING: about 385 cal, 24 g pro, 16 g total fat (4 g sat. fat), 35 g carb, 3 g fibre, 66 mg chol, 231 mg sodium. % RDI: 6% calcium, 14% iron, 223% vit A, 42% vit C, 10% folate.

SUBSTITUTION

• Wine, cider vinegar and rice vinegar are equally good for glazing the chops. If you substitute one of these, add a pinch of sugar to the cornstarch mixture to make up for the natural sweetness of the balsamic vinegar.

Mashed Sweet Potatoes

4 **sweet potatoes,** peeled and cubed
¼ cup (60 mL) **sodium-reduced chicken broth**
2 **green onions,** sliced

In large saucepan of boiling salted water, cover and cook potatoes until tender, about 10 minutes. Drain and return to pot. Add broth and ½ tsp (2 mL) pepper; mash until smooth. Serve sprinkled with green onions.

Makes 4 servings. PER SERVING: about 141 cal, 2 g pro, trace total fat (0 g sat. fat), 32 g carb, 3 g fibre, 0 mg chol, 56 mg sodium. % RDI: 3% calcium, 6% iron, 222% vit A, 40% vit C, 9% folate.

Five-Spice Roasted Chicken

To ovenproof a skillet that has a wooden or plastic handle, wrap the handle in foil.

2 tbsp (30 mL) **lemon juice**
2 tsp (10 mL) **liquid honey**
1 tsp (5 mL) **five-spice powder**
8 **chicken pieces**

In large bowl, whisk together lemon juice, 1 tbsp (15 mL) vegetable oil, honey, five-spice powder and ¼ tsp (1 mL) each salt and pepper. Remove skin from chicken, if desired. Add chicken to marinade, turning to coat; let stand for 5 minutes. *(Make-ahead: Cover and refrigerate for up to 8 hours.)*

In ovenproof skillet, heat 1 tbsp (15 mL) vegetable oil over medium-high heat; brown chicken, in batches and adding more oil if necessary. Drain fat from skillet.

Return all chicken to skillet. Roast in 425°F (220°C) oven until juices run clear when chicken is pierced, about 30 minutes.

Makes 4 servings. PER SERVING (WITHOUT SKIN): about 275 cal, 26 g pro, 17 g total fat (3 g sat. fat), 5 g carb, trace fibre, 94 mg chol, 226 mg sodium. % RDI: 1% calcium, 9% iron, 3% vit A, 2% vit C, 3% folate.

Ginger Rice

1 cup (250 mL) **jasmine rice** or other long-grain rice
6 slices **fresh ginger**
1 **green onion** (green part only), minced

In saucepan, bring 1½ cups (375 mL) water, rice, ginger and ¼ tsp (1 mL) salt to boil. Reduce heat to low; cover and simmer until rice is tender and no liquid remains, about 20 minutes. Stir in green onion.

Makes 4 servings. PER SERVING: about 172 cal, 4 g pro, trace total fat (trace sat. fat), 37 g carb, 1 g fibre, 0 mg chol, 147 mg sodium. % RDI: 2% calcium, 2% iron, 2% vit C, 3% folate.

THE TOP 10 RECIPES TO KNOW BY HEART

1. **BEST-EVER BURGERS** (recipe, page 150)
2. **SPAGHETTI SAUCE** (recipe, page 120)
3. **BEEF AND BROCCOLI STIR-FRY** (recipe, page 46)
4. **CHUNKY BEEF CHILI** (recipe, page 113)
5. **PORK CHOPS WITH BALSAMIC GLAZE** (recipe, opposite)
6. **SAUCY CHICKEN WITH TOMATOES** (recipe, page 72)
7. **SWISS CHEESE FONDUE** (recipe, page 176)
8. **RAINBOW TROUT WITH DIJON MAYONNAISE** (recipe, page 8)
9. **MAC AND CHEESE** (recipe, page 119)
10. **PIZZA MARGHERITA** (recipe, page 41)

Crispy Cornmeal Chicken

You don't need to buy coating mixes to create crusty, moist chicken. Cornmeal and a few seasonings are the secret.

½ cup (125 mL) **cornmeal**
½ tsp (2 mL) **dried thyme**
¼ cup (60 mL) **buttermilk**
4 **boneless skinless chicken breasts**

In shallow dish, whisk together cornmeal, thyme, ½ tsp (2 mL) salt and ¼ tsp (1 mL) pepper. Pour buttermilk into separate shallow dish. Dip chicken into buttermilk then cornmeal mixture, turning and pressing to coat.

In large skillet, heat 1 tbsp (15 mL) vegetable oil over medium heat; fry chicken, turning once and adding up to 1 tbsp (15 mL) more vegetable oil if necessary, until crisp, golden and no longer pink inside, about 14 minutes.

Makes 4 servings. PER SERVING: about 279 cal, 32 g pro, 9 g total fat (1 g sat. fat), 14 g carb, 1 g fibre, 78 mg chol, 377 mg sodium. % RDI: 3% calcium, 6% iron, 1% vit A, 2% vit C, 5% folate.

Sautéed Cherry Tomatoes

2 cloves **garlic,** minced
2 cups (500 mL) **cherry tomatoes** or grape tomatoes
1 tbsp (15 mL) chopped **fresh parsley** or chives

In skillet, heat 1 tbsp (15 mL) vegetable oil over medium-high heat; sauté garlic and ¼ tsp (1 mL) each salt and pepper until fragrant, about 30 seconds. Add tomatoes; sauté until beginning to soften, about 5 minutes. Sprinkle with parsley.

Makes 4 servings. PER SERVING: about 44 cal, 1 g pro, 4 g total fat (trace sat. fat), 3 g carb, 1 g fibre, 0 mg chol, 150 mg sodium. % RDI: 1% calcium, 3% iron, 4% vit A, 22% vit C, 4% folate.

Roasted Chicken Breasts with Sage and Prosciutto

Instead of sage, you can take your pick of herbs to season this chicken. Thyme, basil and marjoram are delicious choices.

2 tbsp (30 mL) **Dijon mustard**
Dash **hot pepper sauce**
4 **boneless skinless chicken breasts**
1 tsp (5 mL) crumbled **dried sage**
8 thin slices **prosciutto** (5 oz/150 g)

Combine mustard and hot pepper sauce; brush all over chicken. Sprinkle with sage and ¼ tsp (1 mL) pepper.

Wrap prosciutto around chicken, covering as much as possible. Place on foil-lined rimmed baking sheet; brush tops with 1 tsp (5 mL) vegetable oil. (*Make-ahead: Cover and refrigerate for up to 2 hours.*)

Bake in 375°F (190°C) oven until prosciutto is crispy and chicken is no longer pink inside, about 20 minutes.

Makes 4 servings. PER SERVING: about 226 cal, 38 g pro, 7 g total fat (2 g sat. fat), 2 g carb, trace fibre, 99 mg chol, 649 mg sodium. % RDI: 2% calcium, 8% iron, 1% vit A, 2% folate.

TIP

In warm weather, cook these breasts on the barbecue. Instead of using crumbled dried sage, place whole fresh sage leaves on the chicken before wrapping the prosciutto slice around it.

Pork Chops with Mustard Crumb Crust

With a crunchy golden coating, these chops are pleasing to everyone, especially children. Serve with mashed potatoes and green beans or broccoli.

1 tbsp (15 mL) **Dijon mustard**
1 tbsp (15 mL) **light mayonnaise**
2 **green onions,** minced
½ cup (125 mL) **fresh bread crumbs**
2 tbsp (30 mL) minced **fresh parsley** (optional)
2 cloves **garlic,** minced
4 **pork loin centre chops,** boneless or bone in, trimmed

In bowl, combine mustard, mayonnaise and green onions. In another bowl, combine bread crumbs, parsley (if using), 1 tbsp (15 mL) vegetable oil and garlic.

Slash edges of pork chops to prevent curling; sprinkle with ¼ tsp (1 mL) each salt and pepper. In large ovenproof skillet, heat 1 tbsp (15 mL) vegetable oil over medium-high heat; brown chops. Drain off fat, leaving chops in pan.

Spread mayonnaise mixture over chops; top with bread crumb mixture, pressing to adhere. Roast in 425°F (220°C) oven until juices run clear when pork is pierced and just a hint of pink remains inside, and bread crumbs are golden, about 15 minutes.

Makes 4 servings. PER SERVING: about 260 cal, 27 g pro, 15 g total fat (3 g sat. fat), 4 g carb, trace fibre, 72 mg chol, 312 mg sodium. % RDI: 4% calcium, 11% iron, 1% vit A, 7% vit C, 6% folate.

Grilled Lemon Herb Trout for Two

The grilled lemons are so delicious that you may want to grill a few of them.
Serve the fish alongside steamed new potatoes and green beans, sprinkled with lots of
freshly ground black pepper.

1 **whole trout,** cleaned (about 2 lb/1 kg)
1 **lemon**
2 **bay leaves**
10 sprigs **fresh parsley**
2 sprigs **fresh thyme**

Sprinkle inside of fish with ¼ tsp (1 mL) each salt and pepper. Slice half of the lemon; stuff lemon slices, bay leaves, parsley and thyme into fish cavity.

Rub 1½ tsp (7 mL) extra-virgin olive oil all over outside of fish; sprinkle with ¼ tsp (1 mL) each salt and pepper.

Place fish and remaining lemon half on well-greased grill over medium-high heat; close lid and grill, turning once, until fish flakes easily when tested, about 10 minutes per side.

Transfer to platter. Squeeze grilled lemon over top; drizzle with 1½ tsp (7 mL) extra-virgin olive oil.

Makes 2 servings. PER SERVING: about 488 cal, 61 g pro, 25 g total fat (6 g sat. fat), 2 g carb, trace fibre, 170 mg chol, 679 mg sodium, 1,134 mg potassium. % RDI: 20% calcium, 7% iron, 22% vit A, 32% vit C, 29% folate.

Vaguely Coq au Vin

Impressive enough for guests, this browned then wine-simmered chicken is a dish every cook should have in his or her repertoire.

8 **chicken thighs** (2 lb/1 kg total)
¼ cup (60 mL) **all-purpose flour**
2¼ tsp (11 mL) **dried thyme**
6 small **onions,** quartered
1 cup (250 mL) **dry white wine**

Pull skin off chicken. In bag, shake together flour, 2 tsp (10 mL) of the thyme and ½ tsp (2 mL) each salt and pepper. Add chicken, in batches, and shake to coat.

In large skillet or Dutch oven, heat 1 tbsp (15 mL) extra-virgin olive oil over medium-high heat; brown chicken on both sides, adding more oil if necessary. Transfer to plate.

Drain off fat in skillet; reduce heat to medium. Cook onions, stirring occasionally and adding more oil if necessary, until golden and softened, about 5 minutes.

Return chicken to skillet; pour wine over top. Cover and simmer, turning once, until juices run clear when chicken is pierced, about 20 minutes. Transfer to platter and keep warm.

Add remaining thyme and ¼ tsp (1 mL) each salt and pepper to pan juices; boil until thickened, about 5 minutes. Pour over chicken.

Makes 4 servings. PER SERVING: about 262 cal, 24 g pro, 10 g total fat (2 g sat. fat), 16 g carb, 2 g fibre, 95 mg chol, 534 mg sodium. % RDI: 5% calcium, 20% iron, 2% vit A, 13% vit C, 17% folate.

TIP

While the taste will not be exactly the same, you can replace the wine with chicken broth, sodium-reduced if possible, and a splash of vinegar for acidity. Pour 1 tbsp (15 mL) white or red wine vinegar or cider vinegar into liquid measure; fill to 1 cup (250 mL) with chicken broth.

Teriyaki-Glazed Wings

Get the wings in the oven first, then put the rice on to simmer.

2½ lb (1.25 kg) **chicken wings** (about 15)
¾ cup (175 mL) **thick teriyaki sauce**
1 clove **garlic,** minced
1 tsp (5 mL) grated **orange zest**
2 tbsp (30 mL) thinly sliced **green onion**

Cut off wing tips at joint; freeze tips for stock (see Slow Cooker Chicken Stock, page 130). Separate wings at remaining joint; trim off excess skin. Place wings on rack on foil-lined rimmed baking sheet. Bake in 400°F (200°C) oven, turning once, for 20 minutes.

Meanwhile, in large bowl, combine teriyaki sauce, garlic and orange zest; set ¼ cup (60 mL) aside for basting. Add wings to remaining sauce in large bowl; toss to coat well.

Return to rack; bake, turning once, until juices run clear when wings are pierced, about 25 minutes. Brush with reserved sauce. Broil, turning once, until browned, about 4 minutes. Sprinkle with green onion.

Makes 4 servings. PER SERVING: about 361 cal, 32 g pro, 21 g total fat (6 g sat. fat), 9 g carb, trace fibre, 91 mg chol, 2,163 mg sodium. % RDI: 3% calcium, 17% iron, 5% vit A, 2% vit C, 7% folate.

Rice with Peas and Bamboo Shoots

1½ cups (375 mL) **chicken broth**
2 tbsp (30 mL) **soy sauce**
2 cups (500 mL) **short-grain rice**
1 can (8 oz/227 mL) **sliced bamboo shoots,** drained and rinsed
½ cup (125 mL) **frozen peas**
1 **green onion,** thinly sliced
2 tbsp (30 mL) toasted **sesame seeds**

In saucepan, bring broth, ¾ cup (175 mL) water and soy sauce to boil. Add rice and bamboo shoots. Cover and simmer over medium-low heat until rice is tender but still firm, about 15 minutes. Turn off heat.

With fork, gently stir in peas, green onion and sesame seeds. Let stand, covered, until liquid is absorbed and rice is completely tender, about 8 minutes.

Makes 4 servings. PER SERVING: about 425 cal, 12 g pro, 4 g total fat (1 g sat. fat), 84 g carb, 3 g fibre, 0 mg chol, 827 mg sodium. % RDI: 2% calcium, 12% iron, 1% vit A, 3% vit C, 11% folate.

Zucchini Toss with Penne

Year round, zucchini is inexpensive, and in the summer there are countless ways to enjoy this colourful vegetable.

4 cloves **garlic,** slivered
1 tsp (5 mL) **dried Italian herb seasoning**
2 **sweet red peppers,** chopped
3 **zucchini** (1 lb/500 g total)
4 cups (1 L) **penne**
½ cup (125 mL) freshly grated **pecorino cheese,** or Asiago or feta cheese

In skillet, heat 2 tbsp (30 mL) extra-virgin olive oil over medium heat; fry garlic, Italian herb seasoning and ¼ tsp (1 mL) coarsely ground pepper for 4 minutes, stirring occasionally.

Add chopped red peppers; fry for 4 minutes, stirring occasionally.

Meanwhile, shred zucchini coarsely. Increase heat to medium-high; add zucchini to pan and sauté until heated through, about 2 minutes.

Meanwhile, in pot of boiling salted water, cook penne until tender but firm, 8 minutes. Drain.

In large warmed pasta bowl, combine zucchini mixture, penne and cheese; toss to coat.

Makes 4 servings. PER SERVING: about 460 cal, 15 g pro, 13 g total fat (4 g sat. fat), 72 g carb, 6 g fibre, 12 mg chol, 340 mg sodium. % RDI: 14% calcium, 29% iron, 38% vit A, 173% vit C, 90% folate.

BREADS ON THE DOUBLE

Who doesn't like delicious, warm, crusty bread? Here are a couple of quick versions to serve with dinner tonight.

QUICK AND FRESH FLATBREAD

• Pat out 1 lb (500 g) fresh pizza dough onto 12-inch (30 cm) greased pizza pan or small rimmed baking sheet. Brush with extra-virgin olive oil and season as desired below. Bake in centre of 425°F (220°C) oven until golden, about 12 minutes.

• **Herb Flatbread:** Sprinkle with chopped fresh rosemary or dried rosemary (or oregano or dried Italian herb seasoning). If you like, dust with a generous sprinkle of freshly grated Parmesan, Asiago or Romano cheese.

• **Simple Salt-and-Pepper Flatbread:** Sprinkle with coarse sea salt and cracked pepper.

• **Seeded Flatbread:** Sprinkle with sesame, poppy or flaxseeds. A touch of salt is good with the seeds, too.

ROASTED GARLIC BAGUETTE

• In small saucepan, combine 6 cloves garlic with a drizzle of oil. Cover and "roast" over low heat, swirling pan occasionally, until garlic is soft, about 15 minutes. Transfer to bowl and let cool.

• Mash garlic with ¼ cup (60 mL) butter, generous sprinkle dried thyme and rosemary or oregano, and quick grate of pepper.

• Slit baguette lengthwise almost all the way through. Spread cut sides with butter mixture; sprinkle with freshly grated Parmesan, Asiago or Romano cheese if you like. Wrap in foil.

• Bake in 350°F (180°C) oven, turning once, until crust is crisped and butter is melted, about 10 minutes. (Or place on barbecue; close lid and grill over medium heat.)

Bean Burgers with Cilantro Cream

When it comes to cooking for a vegetarian and burgers are on the menu, nothing is easier than these bean-based patties. Mild or medium salsa is plenty hot for most people, especially when salsa is not just a condiment but also the central ingredient that adds moisture and flavour to the patties.

1 can (19 oz/540 mL) **red kidney beans,** or romano or black beans
½ cup (125 mL) **dry bread crumbs**
½ cup (125 mL) mild or medium **salsa**
⅓ cup (75 mL) **light sour cream**
2 tbsp (30 mL) minced **fresh cilantro**

Drain and rinse beans; place in bowl. With potato masher or fork, mash beans until fairly smooth but still with some small lumps.

Stir in bread crumbs and salsa to make fairly firm mixture. With wet hands, form into four ½-inch (1 cm) thick patties; set aside on waxed paper–lined baking sheet.

In small bowl, stir sour cream with cilantro. *(Make-ahead: Cover patties and cream separately and refrigerate for up to 4 hours.)*

In large skillet, heat 2 tsp (10 mL) vegetable oil over medium-high heat; fry patties, turning once and adding more oil if necessary, until crusty outside and piping hot inside, about 10 minutes. Serve topped with cilantro cream.

Makes 4 servings. PER SERVING: about 203 cal, 10 g pro, 4 g total fat (1 g sat. fat), 32 g carb, 9 g fibre, 3 mg chol, 654 mg sodium. % RDI: 9% calcium, 15% iron, 2% vit A, 3% vit C, 30% folate.

TIP

Experiment with all sorts of toppings, such as diced avocado, a generous mound of shredded romaine lettuce or sprouts, or a little cheese, such as Monterey Jack or creamy Fontina.

Tagliatelle with Lemon, Shrimp and Arugula

This standout pasta dish is elegantly simple, letting the flavour of each ingredient sing.

12 oz (375 g) **egg noodle tagliatelle**

1 lb (500 g) raw **large shrimp,** peeled and deveined

2 cloves **garlic,** thinly sliced

1 tsp (5 mL) **fennel seeds,** crushed

1 tsp (5 mL) grated **lemon zest**

6 cups (1.5 L) packed **baby arugula leaves**

2 tbsp (30 mL) **lemon juice**

In large pot of boiling salted water, cook pasta until tender but firm, about 10 minutes. Drain, reserving ½ cup (125 mL) of the cooking liquid.

Meanwhile, in large nonstick skillet, heat ¼ cup (60 mL) extra-virgin olive oil over medium-high heat; cook shrimp, garlic, fennel seeds, lemon zest, and ¼ tsp (1 mL) each salt and pepper, stirring occasionally, until shrimp are pink, about 5 minutes.

Add arugula, lemon juice, pasta and half of the reserved cooking liquid; toss to coat. Add more cooking liquid if desired.

Makes 4 servings. PER SERVING: about 560 cal, 31 g pro, 19 g total fat (3 g sat. fat), 66 g carb, 7 g fibre, 210 mg chol, 741 mg sodium, 557 mg potassium. % RDI: 20% calcium, 54% iron, 23% vit A, 23% vit C, 100% folate.

Havarti Cheese and Pepper Panini

While arugula is usually a salad ingredient, here it lends its distinct peppery flavour to hot, crusty grilled sandwiches.

4 **panini buns,** halved
8 slices plain or jalapeño **Havarti cheese**
1½ cups (375 mL) **arugula leaves** or
    spinach leaves
1 cup (250 mL) sliced **roasted red peppers**

Brush cut sides of panini bottoms with 1 tbsp (15 mL) extra-virgin olive oil; cover with half of the cheese. Top with arugula, red peppers then remaining cheese. Cover with panini tops.

Cook in panini press on medium-low until buns are toasted and cheese is melted, about 6 minutes. (Or cook in skillet, turning once and pressing to flatten.)

Makes 4 servings. PER SERVING: about 403 cal, 17 g pro, 22 g total fat (11 g sat. fat), 37 g carb, 2 g fibre, 51 mg chol, 648 mg sodium. % RDI: 33% calcium, 18% iron, 34% vit A, 100% vit C, 39% folate.

VARIATION
Grilled Havarti Cheese and Pepper Sandwiches
• Substitute 8 slices whole grain bread for the panini buns. Brush vegetable oil or butter over bottom of large skillet or grill pan; heat over medium-low heat. Cook sandwiches, pressing with spatula and turning once, until bread is crusty and cheese is melted.

Yogurt Dill Dip with Carrots and Radishes

½ cup (125 mL) **Balkan-style plain yogurt**
2 tbsp (30 mL) **light mayonnaise**
1 tbsp (15 mL) chopped **fresh dill** (or 1 tsp/
    5 mL dried dillweed)
1 clove **garlic,** minced
Carrot sticks and **radishes**

In small bowl, mix together yogurt, mayonnaise, dill, garlic, and ¼ tsp (1 mL) each salt and pepper. Serve with carrot sticks and radishes.

Makes ⅔ cup (150 mL) dip. PER 1 TBSP (15 mL) DIP: about 21 cal, 1 g pro, 2 g total fat (1 g sat. fat), 1 g carb, 0 g fibre, 3 mg chol, 81 mg sodium. % RDI: 2% calcium, 1% vit A.

Make It Tonight... in One Pot

Meatball Noodle Soup

Have a bowl of cold water handy when forming any raw meat into patties or balls – dipping your hands in the water helps unstick them.

1 lb (500 g) **lean ground beef**

2 cloves **garlic,** minced

1 tsp (5 mL) **dried thyme**

1 tsp (5 mL) each **salt** and **pepper**

2 tsp (10 mL) **vegetable oil**

1 each **onion** and **sweet red pepper,** chopped

2 **carrots,** halved lengthwise and sliced

2 tbsp (30 mL) **tomato paste**

4 cups (1 L) **beef broth**

1½ cups (375 mL) thinly sliced **broccoli florets**

1 cup (250 mL) **egg noodles**

In bowl, combine beef, garlic, thyme and ½ tsp (2 mL) each of the salt and pepper; roll by scant 1 tbsp (15 mL) into balls.

In large saucepan, heat oil over medium-high heat; brown meatballs, in batches and turning often, about 5 minutes. Transfer to plate. Drain fat from pan.

Add onion, red pepper, carrots and remaining salt and pepper to pan; fry over medium heat, stirring occasionally, until softened, about 3 minutes. Stir in tomato paste; cook for 2 minutes. Add broth and bring to boil, stirring and scraping up brown bits from bottom of pan. Return meatballs to pan; reduce heat and simmer for 5 minutes.

Add broccoli and noodles; simmer until noodles are tender and digital thermometer inserted into meatballs registers 160°F (71°C), about 5 minutes.

Makes 4 servings. PER SERVING: about 305 cal, 27 g pro, 14 g total fat (5 g sat. fat), 18 g carb, 3 g fibre, 69 mg chol, 1,450 mg sodium. % RDI: 6% calcium, 28% iron, 106% vit A, 115% vit C, 18% folate.

TIP

During the winter, you can use frozen broccoli. For variety, change the pasta; alphabet shapes are a favourite with kids.

Sausage, Potato and Swiss Chard Soup

If you like it hot, use hot Italian sausage, or use another favourite fresh sausage, such as farmer's or chorizo. Spinach can substitute for the Swiss chard, but heat it just until wilted.

1 lb (500 g) **Italian sausage**

1 tbsp (15 mL) **extra-virgin olive oil**

1 **onion,** chopped

2 cloves **garlic,** minced

3 cups (750 mL) cubed peeled **potatoes**

½ tsp (2 mL) **dried Italian herb seasoning**

½ tsp (2 mL) **pepper**

¼ tsp (1 mL) **hot pepper flakes**

3 cups (750 mL) **water**

1 cup (250 mL) **sodium-reduced chicken broth**

2 cups (500 mL) packed coarsely chopped **Swiss chard leaves**

½ cup (125 mL) shaved **Parmesan cheese**

Cut sausage into 1-inch (2.5 cm) pieces. In large saucepan, heat oil over medium-high heat; brown sausage. Transfer to bowl. Drain fat from pan.

Add onion, garlic, potatoes, Italian herb seasoning, pepper and hot pepper flakes to pan; fry over medium heat, stirring occasionally, until onion is softened, about 5 minutes.

Add water and broth; bring to boil. Return sausage to pan; reduce heat, cover and simmer until potatoes are almost tender, about 7 minutes.

Add Swiss chard; simmer, covered, until tender, about 5 minutes. Top with Parmesan cheese.

Makes 8 servings. PER SERVING: about 203 cal, 12 g pro, 12 g total fat (4 g sat. fat), 13 g carb, 1 g fibre, 29 mg chol, 508 mg sodium. % RDI: 6% calcium, 8% iron, 3% vit A, 10% vit C, 4% folate.

EQUIPMENT
ESSENTIAL KITCHEN TOOLS

ON A DESERT ISLAND, YOU CAN GET BY WITH:

• Paring knife and chef's knife

• Cutting board

• Large and small saucepan

• Skillet (seasoned cast-iron is best)

IF YOU AREN'T PLANNING A ROBINSON CRUSOE EXISTENCE, ADD THE FOLLOWING:

• Dry and liquid measuring cups

• Salad spinner and colander

• Lifter

• Tongs – about 9 inches (23 cm) long

• Pepper mill

• Butcher's steel

• Large sieve for draining and straining

• Wooden spoons

• Silicone spatulas

• Skewers

• Meat thermometer (digital instant-read recommended for ground meats and poultry)

• Rimmed baking sheet

• Small roasting pan with rack

• Grill pan

• Steamer insert

• Kitchen scissors and vegetable peeler

• Dutch oven

• Wok or large, deep skillet

FOR A LITTLE LUXURY, ADD:

• Immersion blender

• Food processor

• Toaster oven

• Slow cooker

• Muffin, loaf and cake pans

• Rice cooker

• Panini press

Quick Sausage Risotto

Sausage makes this creamy weeknight risotto a little heartier. Hot sausage is jazzy, but mild works well, too.

8 oz (250 g) hot or mild **Italian sausage**

2 cloves **garlic,** minced

1 **onion,** chopped

1 **zucchini,** chopped

½ tsp (2 mL) **dried oregano**

¼ tsp (1 mL) each **salt** and **pepper**

1½ cups (375 mL) **short-grain Italian rice,**
   such as arborio

3½ cups (875 mL) **chicken broth**

1 **tomato,** chopped

¼ cup (60 mL) grated **Parmesan cheese**

2 tbsp (30 mL) chopped **fresh parsley**

Remove casings from sausage. In large saucepan, cook sausage meat over medium-high heat, breaking up with spoon, until browned, about 4 minutes. Drain off fat.

Add garlic, onion, zucchini, oregano, salt and pepper; cook over medium heat, stirring often, until vegetables are softened, about 3 minutes. Add rice, stirring to coat.

Add 3 cups (750 mL) of the broth; bring to boil. Reduce heat to medium-low; cover and simmer, stirring once, for 15 minutes. Add remaining broth; simmer, stirring often, until moist and creamy, about 5 minutes. Stir in tomato, Parmesan cheese and parsley.

Makes 4 servings. PER SERVING: about 485 cal, 21 g pro, 14 g total fat (5 g sat. fat), 67 g carb, 2 g fibre, 32 mg chol, 1,302 mg sodium. % RDI: 12% calcium, 15% iron, 6% vit A, 17% vit C, 11% folate.

Pork Chops with Puttanesca Sauce

Serve this hearty dish over Fluffy Couscous (below). If you don't mind dirtying another saucepan, it's also terrific over pasta or Creamy Polenta (see page 72).

4 **pork loin centre chops,** boneless or
   bone in, trimmed
2 tbsp (30 mL) **vegetable oil**
1 **onion,** chopped
2 cloves **garlic,** minced
½ tsp (2 mL) **pepper**
½ tsp (2 mL) **hot pepper flakes**
¼ tsp (1 mL) **salt**
1 can (19 oz/540 mL) **tomatoes**
¼ cup (60 mL) **tomato paste**
½ cup (125 mL) chopped **black olives**
1 tbsp (15 mL) drained **capers**
¼ cup (60 mL) minced **fresh basil** or
   parsley

Slash edges of pork chops to prevent curling. In large skillet, heat 1 tbsp (15 mL) of the oil over medium-high heat; brown pork chops. Transfer to plate.

Drain fat from pan; add remaining oil. Fry onion, garlic, pepper, hot pepper flakes and salt over medium heat until softened, about 4 minutes.

Add tomatoes and tomato paste; mash with potato masher. Add olives and capers; bring to boil, stirring and scraping up brown bits. Reduce heat and simmer until spoon drawn across bottom of pan leaves space that fills in slowly, about 10 minutes.

Return chops and any accumulated juices to pan; add basil. Cover and simmer until juices run clear when pork is pierced and just a hint of pink remains inside, about 10 minutes.

Makes 4 servings. PER SERVING: about 292 cal, 25 g pro, 16 g total fat (2 g sat. fat), 14 g carb, 3 g fibre, 60 mg chol, 980 mg sodium. % RDI: 9% calcium, 19% iron, 14% vit A, 48% vit C, 10% folate.

VARIATION
Veal Chops with Puttanesca Sauce
• Replace pork with veal rib or loin chops. Increase tomato paste to ⅓ cup (75 mL). Increase cooking time to 15 minutes.

FLUFFY COUSCOUS

Measure 1 cup (250 mL) couscous (whole wheat recommended) into heatproof bowl. Stir in ½ tsp (2 mL) salt; stir in 1½ cups (375 mL) boiling water or sodium-reduced chicken or vegetable broth. Cover and let stand for 5 minutes. Fluff with fork and serve.

FLAVOURING SUGGESTIONS
Add chopped fresh herbs, such as parsley or chives, a few currants and/or slivered almonds or other nuts.

Herbed Lamb Chops with Tuscan Beans

Pairing lamb with seasoned white beans is a French classic. Canned white kidney beans make this dish doable on a weeknight.

8 **lamb loin chops** (about 1½ lb/750 g)

1 tsp (5 mL) crumbled **dried rosemary** (or 1 sprig fresh)

½ tsp (2 mL) each **salt** and **pepper**

2 tbsp (30 mL) **extra-virgin olive oil**

1 **onion,** chopped

2 cloves **garlic,** minced

2 tsp (10 mL) **all-purpose flour**

1¼ cups (300 mL) **sodium-reduced chicken broth**

1 can (19 oz/540 mL) **white kidney beans,** drained and rinsed

1 tbsp (15 mL) chopped **fresh parsley**

1 tbsp (15 mL) **lemon juice**

Lemon wedges

Sprinkle lamb chops with half each of the rosemary, salt and pepper. In skillet, heat half of the oil over medium-high heat; fry chops, turning once, until medium-rare, about 5 minutes. Transfer to plate and keep warm. Drain fat from pan.

Add remaining oil to pan; fry onion, garlic and remaining rosemary, salt and pepper, stirring occasionally, until onion is softened, about 5 minutes. Sprinkle flour into pan; whisk in broth and bring to boil over medium heat, whisking and scraping up brown bits, until thickened, about 1 minute.

Add beans; heat through. Mash about ⅓ cup (75 mL) bean mixture in skillet. Stir in parsley and lemon juice; spoon onto plates. Top with lamb chops; drizzle any remaining sauce around beans. Garnish with lemon wedges.

Makes 4 servings PER SERVING: about 539 cal, 30 g pro, 36 g total fat (13 g sat. fat), 23 g carb, 8 g fibre, 93 mg chol, 895 mg sodium. % RDI: 5% calcium, 27% iron, 1% vit A, 10% vit C, 34% folate.

EQUIPMENT
SEASONING A CAST-IRON SKILLET

Seasoning creates a natural nonstick surface. Do this before you use the pan for the first time and reseason if food starts to stick.
• Lightly rub interior of pan with lard or coconut oil; bake in 300°F (150°C) oven for 1 hour. Repeat process several times.
• Cast iron absorbs grease from fatty foods, creating a patina that strengthens the pan's seasoning.

Saucy Chicken with Tomatoes

This is your basic browned-then-skillet-stewed chicken. If you have a handful of mushrooms in the crisper, chop and fry them up with the green pepper. Crusty bread is the ideal no-cook side, but pasta, rice or Creamy Polenta (below) are other tasty partners.

8 **boneless skinless chicken thighs**
2 tbsp (30 mL) **all-purpose flour**
½ tsp (2 mL) **salt**
¼ tsp (1 mL) **pepper**
2 tbsp (30 mL) **vegetable oil** (approx)
1 **onion,** diced
2 cloves **garlic,** minced
1 **sweet green pepper,** chopped
1 tsp (5 mL) **dried Italian herb seasoning**
1 can (28 oz/796 mL) **diced tomatoes**
½ cup (125 mL) **sodium-reduced chicken broth**
⅓ cup (75 mL) **tomato paste**
2 tbsp (30 mL) chopped **fresh parsley**

Toss together chicken, flour, salt and pepper. In large shallow Dutch oven, heat half of the oil over medium-high heat; brown chicken, in 2 batches and adding more oil if necessary. Transfer to plate. Drain fat from pan.

Heat remaining oil in pan over medium heat; fry onion, garlic, green pepper and Italian herb seasoning until onion is softened, about 4 minutes. Stir in tomatoes, broth and tomato paste; bring to boil.

Return chicken and any accumulated juices to pan; reduce heat and simmer until thickened and juices run clear when chicken is pierced, about 20 minutes. Sprinkle with parsley.

Makes 4 servings. PER SERVING: about 298 cal, 26 g pro, 13 g total fat (2 g sat. fat), 21 g carb, 4 g fibre, 95 mg chol, 743 mg sodium. % RDI: 9% calcium, 32% iron, 10% vit A, 98% vit C, 18% folate.

CREAMY POLENTA

In large saucepan, bring 4 cups (1 L) water to boil. Stir in ½ tsp (2 mL) salt. Reduce heat to low; whisk in 1 cup (250 mL) cornmeal. Simmer, whisking almost constantly, until polenta is thick enough to mound on spoon, about 20 minutes.

TIP
For the silkiest texture, use medium cornmeal, not coarse.

TIP
Save a few dollars by buying bone-in skin-on chicken thighs. It's easy to pull off the skin and trim off any fat. Bone-in thighs need to be cooked for about 40 minutes in the sauce.

Paprika Chicken and Rice

Dark meat is always the best choice for braising. Thighs stay moist and are more flavourful than breasts. Trim any fat from thighs before browning.

1 large **onion**

1 lb (500 g) **boneless skinless chicken thighs** or chicken breasts, halved

½ tsp (2 mL) each **salt** and **pepper**

2 tbsp (30 mL) **vegetable oil**

2 cups (500 mL) halved **white mushrooms** or cremini mushrooms

2 tbsp (30 mL) **sweet paprika**

½ tsp (2 mL) **dried dillweed**

1¾ cups (425 mL) **sodium-reduced chicken broth**

1 cup (250 mL) **parboiled rice**

1 large **Cubanelle pepper** or sweet green pepper, chopped

⅓ cup (75 mL) **light sour cream**

Cut onion into ½-inch (1 cm) wide strips; set aside.

Sprinkle chicken with half each of the salt and pepper. In large skillet, heat 1 tbsp (15 mL) of the oil over medium-high heat; brown chicken, about 6 minutes. Transfer to plate. Drain fat from pan.

Add remaining oil to pan; sauté onion and mushrooms until onion is softened and no liquid remains, about 3 minutes. Reduce heat to medium-low. Add paprika, dillweed and remaining salt and pepper; cook, stirring, until fragrant, about 1 minute.

Stir in broth and rice; bring to boil. Return chicken and any accumulated juices to pan, stirring to coat. Reduce heat, cover and simmer until almost all liquid is absorbed, 12 minutes.

Stir in pepper; simmer, covered, until juices run clear when chicken is pierced and pepper is tender, about 4 minutes. Serve with sour cream.

Makes 4 servings. PER SERVING: about 451 cal, 29 g pro, 15 g total fat (3 g sat. fat), 50 g carb, 4 g fibre, 98 mg chol, 675 mg sodium. % RDI: 10% calcium, 26% iron, 20% vit A, 57% vit C, 14% folate.

TIP

The selection of paprika available today has expanded with the arrival of smoked paprika from Spain. Sweet or mild paprika is ideal for this dish, and you can use either smoked or regular, depending on your preference.

Smoky Oyster Chowder

Soup doesn't always have to be long-simmered to have great flavour. This smoky, creamy blend is ready in a weeknight-friendly amount of time.

2 cans (each 133 g) **whole oysters**

4 strips **bacon,** chopped

1 **onion,** chopped

1 rib **celery,** chopped

2 cloves **garlic,** minced

3 small **red-skinned potatoes,** cubed (about 12 oz/375 g)

2 tbsp (30 mL) **all-purpose flour**

½ tsp (2 mL) each **salt** and **pepper**

1 cup (250 mL) **chicken broth** or vegetable broth

2 cups (500 mL) **milk**

1 cup (250 mL) **corn kernels**

2 tbsp (30 mL) chopped **fresh parsley**

Drain oysters, reserving juice; cut oysters in half crosswise. Set aside.

In large saucepan, cook bacon over medium heat for 5 minutes; drain off fat. Add onion, celery and garlic; cook, stirring occasionally, until softened, about 5 minutes. Add potatoes, flour, salt and pepper; stir until vegetables are coated.

Stir in broth and reserved oyster juice; bring to simmer. Cover and cook, stirring occasionally, until potatoes are tender, about 15 minutes.

Add milk, corn and reserved oysters; heat until bubbly and hot, about 3 minutes. Serve garnished with parsley.

Makes 4 servings. PER SERVING: about 327 cal, 16 g pro, 13 g total fat (5 g sat. fat), 39 g carb, 3 g fibre, 56 mg chol, 766 mg sodium. % RDI: 19% calcium, 43% iron, 14% vit A, 30% vit C, 19% folate.

VARIATION
Clam Chowder
• Use 2 cans (5 oz/142 g each) baby clams instead of the oysters, leaving clams whole.

Chicken and Kielbasa Rice Dinner

A good Dutch oven has a thick bottom and a lid that fits snugly. Any large saucepan that fits that description is useful for brown-and-braise dishes like this.

8 **boneless skinless chicken thighs**

½ tsp (2 mL) each **salt** and **pepper**

1 tbsp (15 mL) **vegetable oil**

1 **onion**

1 **sweet red pepper** or sweet green pepper

¾ cup (175 mL) cubed **kielbasa** or ham (about 4 oz/125 g)

1 tsp (5 mL) **dried thyme**

¾ cup (175 mL) **long-grain rice**

1½ cups (375 mL) **sodium-reduced chicken broth**

1 cup (250 mL) **frozen peas**

2 **green onions,** sliced

Sprinkle chicken with half each of the salt and pepper. In Dutch oven, heat oil over medium-high heat; brown chicken, about 4 minutes. Transfer to plate and set aside. Drain fat from pan.

Meanwhile, cut onion and red pepper lengthwise into ¼-inch (5 mm) wide slices.

In same pan, fry kielbasa, onion, red pepper, thyme and remaining salt and pepper over medium heat, stirring occasionally, until onion is softened, about 5 minutes.

Add rice; fry, stirring, for 1 minute to coat; add broth. Nestle chicken into rice and bring to boil. Reduce heat to low; cover and simmer until almost no liquid remains and juices run clear when chicken is pierced, 15 minutes.

Stir in peas; heat through, about 2 minutes. Sprinkle with green onions.

Makes 4 servings. PER SERVING: about 413 cal, 32 g pro, 14 g total fat (3 g sat. fat), 38 g carb, 3 g fibre, 113 mg chol, 887 mg sodium. % RDI: 6% calcium, 21% iron, 15% vit A, 98% vit C, 20% folate.

Chicken with Green Beans and Cherry Tomatoes

You can make this simple dish in your wok or Dutch oven; the green beans steam right in the flavourful sauce. Serve with crusty bread to soak it all up.

8 **boneless skinless chicken thighs**
2 tbsp (30 mL) **vegetable oil**
1 **onion,** chopped
3 cloves **garlic,** minced
1 tsp (5 mL) **dried oregano**
¼ tsp (1 mL) each **salt** and **pepper**
1 cup (250 mL) **chicken broth**
2 cups (500 mL) **green beans,** trimmed
2 tsp (10 mL) **cornstarch**
1 cup (250 mL) **cherry tomatoes,** halved
2 **green onions,** thinly sliced

Cut chicken into 2-inch (5 cm) pieces. In large deep skillet, heat 1 tbsp (15 mL) of the oil over medium-high heat; brown chicken. Transfer to plate. Drain off fat in pan.

Heat remaining oil in pan over medium heat; fry onion, garlic, oregano, salt and pepper until onion is softened, about 3 minutes.

Add broth, chicken and any accumulated juices; bring to boil. Reduce heat, cover and simmer until juices run clear when chicken is pierced, about 10 minutes.

Meanwhile, cut beans into 1-inch (2.5 cm) long pieces; add to pan. Cover and cook until beans are tender-crisp, about 5 minutes.

Whisk cornstarch with 1 tbsp (15 mL) water; stir into pan. Stir in tomatoes. Simmer, stirring, until thickened, about 1 minute. Sprinkle with green onions.

Makes 4 servings. PER SERVING: about 242 cal, 25 g pro, 11 g total fat (2 g sat. fat), 11 g carb, 2 g fibre, 95 mg chol, 443 mg sodium. % RDI: 5% calcium, 18% iron, 8% vit A, 28% vit C, 18% folate.

TIP
Substitute 4 boneless skinless chicken breasts for the thighs; cook until no longer pink inside, about 10 minutes.

Chicken Cauliflower Curry

Don't have fresh jalapeños on hand? Replace them with a pinch of hot pepper flakes, a little cayenne pepper or pickled jalapeño peppers for that desired touch of heat.

12 oz (375 g) **boneless skinless chicken breasts**
2 tbsp (30 mL) **vegetable oil** (approx)
1 **onion,** chopped
1 **jalapeño pepper,** seeded and minced (optional)
¼ tsp (1 mL) **salt**
2 tbsp (30 mL) **mild curry paste**
1 can (28 oz/796 mL) **diced tomatoes**
2 cups (500 mL) **cauliflower florets**
1 **Granny Smith apple,** cored and diced
¼ cup (60 mL) **golden raisins**
1 cup (250 mL) **frozen peas**
¼ cup (60 mL) chopped **fresh cilantro**

Cut chicken crosswise into strips. In large skillet, heat 1 tbsp (15 mL) of the oil over medium-high heat; brown chicken, in 2 batches and adding more oil if necessary. Transfer to bowl. Drain fat from skillet.

In same pan, heat remaining oil over medium heat; fry onion, jalapeño pepper (if using) and salt, stirring occasionally, until onion is softened, about 3 minutes.

Add curry paste; cook, stirring, until fragrant, about 1 minute. Drain tomatoes, reserving juice for another use (see Tip, below). Add diced tomatoes to skillet.

Return chicken to pan. Stir in cauliflower, apple and raisins; cover and simmer until cauliflower is tender, about 10 minutes.

Add peas and half of the cilantro. Simmer, covered, until steaming, about 5 minutes. Sprinkle with remaining cilantro.

Makes 4 servings. PER SERVING: about 313 cal, 24 g pro, 13 g total fat (1 g sat. fat), 28 g carb, 6 g fibre, 49 mg chol, 610 mg sodium. % RDI: 7% calcium, 19% iron, 9% vit A, 77% vit C, 25% folate.

TIP
When you don't need the juice from a can of tomatoes for a recipe, you can refrigerate or freeze it to use in spaghetti sauce or soup. You can even freeze it in ice-cube trays for quick melting.

Skillet Fish with Tomato Zucchini Sauce

One-pot meals are great with easy sides, such as bread or couscous. But red-skinned new potatoes are another delicious accompaniment. No need to peel them – just scrub, quarter if large and cook in covered saucepan of boiling salted water until tender, about 15 minutes.

2 tbsp (30 mL) **butter** or vegetable oil

1 **onion,** chopped

2 cloves **garlic,** minced

2 cups (500 mL) thinly sliced **zucchini** (about 2 small)

½ cup (125 mL) diced **sweet red pepper**

2 tbsp (30 mL) chopped **fresh oregano** (or 1 tsp/5 mL dried)

¾ tsp (4 mL) each **salt** and **pepper**

¼ tsp (1 mL) **hot pepper sauce**

1 can (14 oz/398 mL) **stewed tomatoes**

4 **fish fillets** (such as tilapia or catfish), about 6 oz (175 g) each

1 **lemon,** thinly sliced

In large skillet, melt butter over medium-high heat; sauté onion, garlic, zucchini, red pepper, oregano, ½ tsp (2 mL) each of the salt and pepper and hot pepper sauce until onion is softened, about 5 minutes.

Add tomatoes; break up large pieces with potato masher. Bring to boil; reduce heat and simmer, stirring often, until thick enough to mound on spoon, about 10 minutes.

Place fish in single layer on vegetables; sprinkle with remaining salt and pepper. Cover and simmer until fish flakes easily when tested, about 8 minutes.

Transfer fish to plate; keep warm. Simmer sauce until thickened again, about 2 minutes. Spoon over fish; serve with lemon slices.

Makes 4 servings. PER SERVING: about 275 cal, 32 g pro, 10 g total fat (4 g sat. fat), 15 g carb, 3 g fibre, 96 mg chol, 875 mg sodium. % RDI: 6% calcium, 11% iron, 36% vit A, 87% vit C, 14% folate.

Turkey Black Bean Chili

This chili is the perfect blend of taste, nutrition and convenience – many of the ingredients are simple pantry staples.

2 tbsp (30 mL) **vegetable oil**

1 lb (500 g) **ground turkey** or chicken

1 **onion,** chopped

2 cloves **garlic,** minced

2 tsp (10 mL) **dried oregano**

½ tsp (2 mL) **salt**

¼ tsp (1 mL) **pepper**

2 tbsp (30 mL) **tomato paste**

1 can (28 oz/796 mL) **diced tomatoes**

1 can (19 oz/540 mL) **black beans,**
   drained and rinsed

1 small **zucchini,** cubed

½ cup (125 mL) **corn kernels**

3 tbsp (45 mL) **chili powder**

¼ cup (60 mL) minced **fresh cilantro**
   or parsley

Sour cream and **sliced jalapeño
   peppers** (optional)

In large saucepan, heat 1 tbsp (15 mL) of the oil over medium-high heat; sauté turkey, breaking up, until no longer pink, about 8 minutes. Drain off fat; transfer to bowl.

In same saucepan, heat remaining oil over medium heat; cook onion, garlic, oregano, salt and pepper until onion is softened, about 3 minutes. Stir in tomato paste; cook for 1 minute.

Return turkey to pan. Add tomatoes, black beans, zucchini, corn and chili powder; bring to boil. Reduce heat and simmer for 30 minutes. Stir in cilantro. Serve garnished with sour cream and jalapeño peppers (if using).

Makes 4 to 6 servings. PER EACH OF 6 SERVINGS: about 281 cal, 20 g pro, 12 g total fat (3 g sat. fat), 26 g carb, 9 g fibre, 60 mg chol, 717 mg sodium. % RDI: 9% calcium, 33% iron, 16% vit A, 42% vit C, 30% folate.

Grilled Rosemary Garlic Flank Steak with Potatoes and Carrots

The "one pot" this time is the barbecue. Nothing could be simpler.

¼ cup (60 mL) **vegetable oil**

2 tbsp (30 mL) **balsamic vinegar** or wine vinegar

1 tbsp (15 mL) chopped **fresh rosemary** (or ¾ tsp/4 mL crumbled dried)

2 tsp (10 mL) **Dijon mustard**

2 cloves **garlic,** minced

1 tsp (5 mL) packed **brown sugar**

1 tsp (5 mL) each **salt** and **pepper**

1 **flank steak** (about 1½ lb/750 g)

4 **potatoes** (about 1 lb/500 g), peeled

4 **carrots**

In shallow glass dish, whisk together oil, vinegar, rosemary, mustard, garlic, brown sugar, salt and pepper; remove half and set aside. Add steak to remaining marinade in dish; turn to coat. Let stand for 10 minutes. (*Make-ahead: Cover and refrigerate for up to 12 hours.*)

Meanwhile, cut potatoes into ¼-inch (5 mm) thick rounds. Cut carrots diagonally into ½-inch (1 cm) thick slices. In microwaveable bowl, combine potatoes, carrots and ⅓ cup (75 mL) hot water; cover and microwave at high until tender-crisp, about 5 minutes. Drain. Add reserved marinade; toss to coat.

Arrange steak, potatoes and carrots on greased grill over medium-high heat; close lid and grill, turning once, until steak is medium-rare and vegetables are tender and grill-marked, about 12 minutes.

Transfer steak to cutting board; tent with foil and let stand for 5 minutes. Transfer potatoes and carrots to plates; keep warm. Thinly slice steak across the grain; serve with potatoes and carrots.

Makes 4 servings. PER SERVING: about 497 cal, 42 g pro, 24 g total fat (6 g sat. fat), 28 g carb, 4 g fibre, 69 mg chol, 593 mg sodium. % RDI: 4% calcium, 28% iron, 182% vit A, 27% vit C, 14% folate.

CHAPTER 5

Make It Tonight... from the Pantry

Artichoke Chicken Flatbread

The cooked chicken called for in this recipe could be leftovers from the night before, the remains of a rotisserie chicken from the supermarket or 1 tin (284 g) seasoned chicken chunks.

1 jar (370 mL) **roasted red peppers,** drained

2 cloves **garlic,** smashed

2 tbsp (30 mL) **extra-virgin olive oil**

½ tsp (2 mL) **salt**

1 thin-crust 12-inch (30 cm) **flatbread** or pizza crust

1 cup (250 mL) shredded **mozzarella cheese** or crumbled goat cheese

1¾ cups (425 mL) sliced **cooked chicken**

Half **red onion,** thinly sliced

1 jar (6 oz/170 mL) **marinated artichoke hearts**

¼ cup (60 mL) sliced **black olives** (optional)

½ tsp (2 mL) **dried oregano**

In food processor, purée together roasted red peppers, smashed garlic, olive oil and salt; spread evenly over flatbread.

Sprinkle with half of the cheese. Scatter chicken, onion, artichoke hearts, olives (if using) and oregano over top; sprinkle with remaining cheese.

Bake in bottom third of 500°F (260°C) oven until golden and bubbly, 15 minutes. (Or bake according to flatbread package instructions.)

Makes 4 servings. PER SERVING: about 486 cal, 31 g pro, 23 g total fat (7 g sat. fat), 39 g carb, 4 g fibre, 80 mg chol, 947 mg sodium. % RDI: 19% calcium, 22% iron, 27% vit A, 162% vit C, 16% folate.

Tex-Mex Tomato Rice Soup

Garnish this kid-friendly soup with shredded Cheddar cheese and sour cream. Serve with warmed flour or corn tortillas.

2 tbsp (30 mL) **vegetable oil**

1 **onion,** chopped

2 cloves **garlic,** minced

1 fresh or pickled **jalapeño pepper,** seeded and minced

½ tsp (2 mL) each **salt** and **pepper**

½ tsp (2 mL) **ground cumin**

¼ tsp (1 mL) **chili powder**

2 **carrots,** chopped

¼ cup (60 mL) **long-grain rice**

1 can (28 oz/796 mL) **diced tomatoes**

¼ cup (60 mL) minced **fresh cilantro** (optional)

1 tbsp (15 mL) **lime juice**

In large saucepan, heat oil over medium heat; fry onion, garlic, jalapeño, salt, pepper, cumin and chili powder, stirring occasionally, until onion is softened, about 5 minutes.

Add carrots, rice, tomatoes and 4 cups (1 L) water; bring to boil. Reduce heat and simmer until rice and carrots are tender, about 20 minutes. (*Make-ahead: Let cool for 30 minutes; refrigerate until cold. Refrigerate in airtight container for up to 3 days.*) Add cilantro (if using) and lime juice.

Makes 6 servings. PER SERVING: about 116 cal, 2 g pro, 5 g total fat (trace sat. fat), 17 g carb, 2 g fibre, 0 mg chol, 409 mg sodium. % RDI: 5% calcium, 9% iron, 70% vit A, 40% vit C, 7% folate.

Salmon Wraps

It takes just 10 minutes to put these fresh-tasting wraps together.

¼ cup (60 mL) minced **fresh mint**
   (or ½ tsp/2 mL dried)
¼ cup (60 mL) **light mayonnaise**
1 tbsp (15 mL) **lime juice** or lemon juice
1 tsp (5 mL) minced **fresh ginger**
   (or ¾ tsp/4 mL ground ginger)
1 **green onion,** minced
¼ tsp (1 mL) each **salt** and **pepper**
2 cans (each 7½ oz/213 g) **sockeye salmon,**
   drained
4 large **whole wheat tortillas**
2 cups (500 mL) shredded **lettuce**

In bowl, stir together mint, mayonnaise, lime juice, ginger, green onion, salt and pepper. Add salmon; mash to combine.

Place tortillas on work surface; top with lettuce. Spoon one-quarter of the salmon mixture onto centre of each tortilla. Fold in sides and roll up from bottom; cut in half, if desired.

Makes 4 servings. PER SERVING: about 352 cal, 27 g pro, 12 g total fat (2 g sat. fat), 44 g carb, 5 g fibre, 43 mg chol, 913 mg sodium. % RDI: 21% calcium, 22% iron, 7% vit A, 5% vit C, 21% folate.

TIME-SAVING TIPS

• Plan a week's worth of menus at one time. Try two weeks if that suits you better.

• Make a shopping list from your menus and organize it according to the store's layout (produce, dairy, meat – you get the picture). This cuts back on missed items and return visits to the supermarket.

• Shop when the store is not busy and stick with the supermarket you like so you're not constantly looking for items in a new layout.

• Grocery shop online. It's a great time saver, especially for items you regularly purchase.

• Make at least one meal a week that creates leftovers. Reheat them or get creative: roasted chicken one night, then chicken pizza the next.

• Double and freeze your favourite dishes. Don't forget to label them with name, date and reheating instructions – otherwise, you'll be facing a freezer full of UFOs (unidentified frozen objects).

• Try prepared items in the produce department. More and more items come peeled (pineapple), destalked (broccoli), premixed (salad greens) and cubed (squash).

• Don't freeze out frozen vegetables and fruit. They are just as nutritious as fresh, and you'll save a bundle of time not having to scrape the kernels off the cob, trim the beans or broccoli, or shell the peas.

• Wash greens and herbs as soon as you get home (see How to Wash and Store Greens, Herbs and Vegetables, page 193).

• Organize the week's food in a way that other family members find easy to understand. That means no excuses for not taking their turn with the cooking or prep.

Soy-Braised Tofu

A well-stocked Asian pantry and fridge set you up for a dish that's faster to the table than takeout or delivery. To make it even easier, buy minced ginger and garlic in jars and keep them at the ready in the fridge.

2 tbsp (30 mL) **cornstarch**

2 tbsp (30 mL) **sodium-reduced soy sauce**

2 tbsp (30 mL) **black bean garlic sauce**

2 tbsp (30 mL) **oyster sauce** or hoisin sauce

¼ tsp (1 mL) **hot pepper sauce**

1 tbsp (15 mL) **vegetable oil**

2 **carrots,** diced

6 **green onions** (green and white parts separated), sliced

3 cloves **garlic,** minced

1 tbsp (15 mL) minced **fresh ginger**

⅛ tsp (0.5 mL) each **ground cloves** and **pepper**

1 pkg (12 oz/340 g) **precooked ground soy protein mixture**

1 pkg (454 g) **medium-firm tofu,** drained and cut into ¾-inch (2 cm) cubes

1 can (10 oz/300 g) sliced **mushrooms,** drained

¾ cup (175 mL) **frozen peas** or cut green beans

In small bowl, whisk together cornstarch, soy sauce, black bean sauce, oyster sauce and hot pepper sauce; set aside.

In wok, heat oil over medium-high heat; stir-fry carrots, white parts of green onions, garlic, ginger, cloves and pepper until vegetables are tender, about 6 minutes. Add soy protein; heat through, about 1 minute.

Stir in cornstarch mixture and 1¾ cups (425 mL) water; bring to boil. Add tofu and mushrooms; cover and cook over low heat until thickened, about 10 minutes.

Stir in peas and green parts of green onions; cook for 1 minute.

Makes 4 servings. PER SERVING: about 289 cal, 27 g pro, 8 g total fat (1 g sat. fat), 28 g carb, 10 g fibre, 0 mg chol, 1,280 mg sodium. % RDI: 21% calcium, 49% iron, 71% vit A, 13% vit C, 40% folate.

Tortellini Casserole

Even a baked casserole is possible if you stock your fridge or freezer with a package or two of cheese- or meat-filled tortellini.

12 oz (375 g) fresh or frozen **cheese tortellini** or meat tortellini
1 tbsp (15 mL) **butter**
¼ cup (60 mL) **all-purpose flour**
3 cups (750 mL) **1% milk,** warmed
1 cup (250 mL) grated **Parmesan cheese**
¼ tsp (1 mL) each **salt** and **pepper**
Pinch **ground nutmeg**
½ cup (125 mL) **fresh bread crumbs**
   (or ⅓ cup/75 mL dry bread crumbs)
¼ cup (60 mL) chopped **fresh parsley**

In pot of boiling salted water, cook tortellini until tender, about 8 minutes; drain.

Meanwhile, in saucepan, melt butter over medium heat; stir in flour and cook, stirring, until light golden, about 1 minute. Gradually whisk in milk; simmer, stirring constantly, just until thick enough to coat back of spoon, about 7 minutes.

Stir in ¾ cup (175 mL) of the Parmesan cheese, salt, pepper and nutmeg. Stir in tortellini. Scrape into 8-inch (2 L) square baking dish.

In small bowl, mix together bread crumbs, parsley and remaining cheese; sprinkle over tortellini mixture. Bake in 400°F (200°C) oven until bubbly and browned, about 10 minutes.

Makes 4 servings. PER SERVING: about 504 cal, 29 g pro, 18 g total fat (10 g sat. fat), 56 g carb, 2 g fibre, 91 mg chol, 1,249 mg sodium. % RDI: 64% calcium, 17% iron, 22% vit A, 8% vit C, 19% folate.

Spinach Salad

¼ cup (60 mL) coarsely chopped **roasted red peppers**
2 tbsp (30 mL) each **extra-virgin olive oil** and **wine vinegar**
¼ tsp (1 mL) each **salt** and **pepper**
4 cups (1 L) **baby spinach**
1 cup (250 mL) sliced **mushrooms**

In large bowl, whisk together red peppers, oil, vinegar, salt and pepper. Add spinach and mushrooms; toss to coat.

Makes 4 servings. PER SERVING: about 75 cal, 2 g pro, 7 g total fat (1 g sat. fat), 3 g carb, 1 g fibre, 0 mg chol, 195 mg sodium. % RDI: 3% calcium, 8% iron, 33% vit A, 48% vit C, 29% folate.

THE WELL-STOCKED KITCHEN
ESSENTIAL GRAINS

• **Rice:** Parboiled long grain (white and whole grain), basmati and short grain (arborio or other kinds)
• **Cornmeal:** Medium and coarse
• **Couscous:** Regular and whole wheat
• **Pasta:** Short (macaroni, fusilli, rigatoni and penne) and long (spaghetti, linguine and fettuccine) – try whole wheat for a nutritional boost
• **Bread products:** Croutons, dry bread crumbs and crackers

Shrimp and Pea Risotto

To make this a supereasy weeknight meal option, use frozen deveined zipperback shrimp.
All you have to do is defrost them under cold water and pop off the shells.

1 tbsp (15 mL) **extra-virgin olive oil**

1 **onion,** finely diced

2 cloves **garlic,** minced

1 tsp (5 mL) grated **lemon zest**

¼ tsp (1 mL) each **salt** and **pepper**

1 cup (250 mL) **arborio rice** or other
short-grain rice

¼ cup (60 mL) **dry white wine** or
sodium-reduced chicken broth

2½ cups (625 mL) hot **sodium-reduced
chicken broth**

10 oz (300 g) peeled deveined
large raw shrimp

1 cup (250 mL) **frozen peas** or frozen
shelled edamame

2 tbsp (30 mL) chopped **fresh mint**
or parsley

In large saucepan, heat oil over medium heat;
fry onion, garlic, lemon zest, salt and pepper,
stirring occasionally, until softened, about
3 minutes.

Add rice, stirring to coat. Add wine; boil until
evaporated, about 1 minute.

Stir in broth and bring to boil. Reduce heat to
low; cover and simmer, stirring once, for
10 minutes. Stir vigorously for 15 seconds.
Simmer, covered, for 5 minutes.

Stir in shrimp and peas; simmer, covered, until
shrimp are pink, peas are tender and rice is
creamy and slightly firm to the bite, about
3 minutes. Sprinkle with mint.

Makes 4 servings. PER SERVING: about 338 cal, 22 g pro,
5 g total fat (1 g sat. fat), 49 g carb, 3 g fibre, 108 mg chol,
652 mg sodium. % RDI: 6% calcium, 21% iron, 11% vit A,
10% vit C, 15% folate.

THE WELL-STOCKED KITCHEN
ESSENTIAL FLAVOURINGS

• **Sauces:** Soy, oyster, hoisin, black bean and
garlic, ketchup, salsa, Worcestershire,
barbecue and hot pepper

• **Pastes and butters:** Indian curry paste (mild
or hot), Thai red curry paste, anchovy
paste, tahini and nut butters (peanut, almond
and others)

• **Mustards:** Dijon, Russian, honey and grainy

• **Prepared horseradish**

Red Pepper Pasta

A pasta shape such as radiator or rotini is best because it will hold every last bit of this robust sauce. Sprinkle each serving with a little freshly grated hard cheese, such as Parmesan, grana Padano, pecorino or Asiago.

2 tbsp (30 mL) **extra-virgin olive oil**
4 cloves **garlic,** minced
1 small **onion,** finely chopped
1 jar (313 mL) **roasted red peppers**
1 can (19 oz/540 mL) **tomatoes**
2 tsp (10 mL) crumbled **dried basil** or mint
½ tsp (2 mL) each **salt** and **pepper**
5 cups (1.25 L) **radiatore** or rotini
   (1 lb/500 g)

In large skillet, heat oil over medium heat; fry garlic and onion, stirring occasionally, until softened, about 3 minutes.

Reserving liquid, drain peppers. In food processor or blender, purée peppers with tomatoes until almost smooth.

Add pepper mixture to pan along with basil, salt and pepper; bring to boil. Reduce heat and simmer, stirring often, until thick enough to mound on spoon, about 10 minutes.

Meanwhile, in large pot of boiling salted water, cook pasta until tender but firm, about 8 minutes. Drain and return to pot. Add sauce and toss, adding some of the reserved pepper liquid, if desired.

Makes 4 servings. PER SERVING: about 532 cal, 16 g pro, 9 g total fat (1 g sat. fat), 97 g carb, 8 g fibre, 0 mg chol, 891 mg sodium. % RDI: 8% calcium, 44% iron, 22% vit A, 188% vit C, 114% folate.

THE WELL-STOCKED KITCHEN
ESSENTIAL PANTRY STAPLES

- **Legumes:** Beans, lentils and chickpeas (always drain and rinse before using)
- **Sodium-reduced broths:** Chicken, beef and vegetable
- **Tomatoes:** Whole, diced and stewed (try healthy no-salt-added varieties)
- **Tomato paste:** Freeze any extra in ice-cube trays; wrap cubes separately and bag
- **Pasta sauce:** Tomato-based (freeze leftovers in handy amounts; for example, 2 cups/500 mL for a pizza) and pesto
- **Antipasti:** Roasted peppers and artichoke hearts (plain or marinated)
- **Meat and fish:** Salmon, tuna, sardines, anchovies, clams, and chicken and turkey chunks
- **Milks:** Dairy (evaporated or dried) and nondairy (soy, rice and coconut milk)
- **Veggies:** Baby beets and corn
- **Oils:** Extra-virgin olive, sesame, and canola or other neutral oil with a high smoke point
- **Vinegars:** Red or white wine, balsamic, cider and rice
- **Sun-dried tomatoes:** Packed in oil (use the oil in dressings or marinades) and made into pesto; dried are OK if they're pliable and softened in hot water for 20 minutes before using

Fettuccine with Green Olives, Capers and Parsley

A few pantry staples and just 10 minutes of cooking give you this stellar pasta dish.

10 oz (300 g) **fettuccine** or spaghetti
2 tbsp (30 mL) **extra-virgin olive oil**
2 cloves **garlic,** thinly sliced
¼ tsp (1 mL) **hot pepper flakes**
1 cup (250 mL) sliced **green olives**
⅓ cup (75 mL) chopped **fresh parsley**
2 tbsp (30 mL) **capers,** drained, rinsed
and coarsely chopped
1 tsp (5 mL) grated **orange zest**
1 tbsp (15 mL) **orange juice**
1 tsp (5 mL) **anchovy paste** (optional)

In large pot of boiling salted water, cook pasta until tender but firm, about 8 minutes. Reserving ½ cup (125 mL) of the cooking liquid, drain and return to pot.

Meanwhile, in large skillet, heat oil over medium heat; fry garlic and hot pepper flakes until fragrant, about 1 minute.

Add olives, half of the parsley, the capers, orange zest and juice, and anchovy paste (if using); cook, stirring, until heated through, 2 minutes. Add to pasta and toss to coat, adding enough of the reserved cooking liquid to moisten, if necessary. Stir in remaining parsley.

Makes 4 servings. PER SERVING: about 378 cal, 10 g pro, 13 g total fat (2 g sat. fat), 56 g carb, 5 g fibre, 0 mg chol, 834 mg sodium. % RDI: 4% calcium, 23% iron, 6% vit A, 13% vit C, 70% folate.

TIP
If you're avoiding gluten in your diet, it's easy to substitute gluten-free alternatives to regular wheat-flour pasta in your favourite dishes. For this recipe, try brown rice fettuccine or white or brown rice spaghetti.

Rigatoni with Sausage and Artichoke

Stash a few links of Italian sausage in the freezer so you're ready to make this pantry-friendly dish at a moment's notice.

2 tbsp (30 mL) **extra-virgin olive oil**

4 mild or hot **Italian sausages,** casings removed

1 **onion,** chopped

2 cloves **garlic,** minced

¼ tsp (1 mL) each **salt** and **pepper**

¼ tsp (1 mL) **hot pepper flakes**

1½ cups (375 mL) **bottled strained tomatoes** (passata)

¼ cup (60 mL) **dry red wine**

¼ tsp (1 mL) **dried Italian herb seasoning**

Pinch **granulated sugar**

2 jars (6 oz/170 mL each) **marinated artichoke hearts,** drained and rinsed

12 oz (375 g) **rigatoni**

¼ cup (60 mL) chopped **fresh parsley**

In skillet, heat oil over medium heat; cook sausages, onion, garlic, salt, pepper and hot pepper flakes until sausage is browned, about 5 minutes. Drain off any fat.

Add tomatoes, wine, herb seasoning and sugar; bring to boil, scraping up any brown bits. Reduce heat and simmer for 15 minutes. Add artichokes; simmer for 10 minutes.

Meanwhile, in large pot of boiling salted water, cook pasta until tender but firm, about 10 minutes. Drain and return to pot.

Stir parsley into sauce. Add to pasta; toss to coat.

Makes 4 to 6 servings. PER EACH OF 6 SERVINGS: about 452 cal, 19 g pro, 18 g total fat (4 g sat. fat), 53 g carb, 5 g fibre, 28 mg chol, 821 mg sodium, 316 mg potassium. % RDI: 5% calcium, 34% iron, 3% vit A, 15% vit C, 65% folate.

PERFECT PASTA

It's important to have enough boiling water in the pot that it circulates freely around the pasta. For 1 lb (500 g) pasta, bring 20 cups (5 L) water to boil in large pot, covered. Add 2 tbsp (30 mL) salt, letting it dissolve for about 2 minutes. Add pasta; stir gently with wooden spoon. Boil until tender but firm (al dente). Drain; return to pot and add the sauce. Heat through if necessary.

TIP
For 12 oz (375 g) pasta, reduce water to 16 cups (4 L) and salt to 4 tsp (20 mL).

Easy Cheese Soufflé

A simple baking-dish soufflé like this is one of the easiest pantry suppers ever.

8 **eggs,** separated
1 cup (250 mL) **milk**
¼ cup (60 mL) chopped **fresh parsley**
3 tbsp (45 mL) **all-purpose flour**
¼ tsp (1 mL) each **salt** and **pepper**
Pinch **ground nutmeg**
1 cup (250 mL) shredded **Swiss cheese**
  or Cheddar cheese

In large bowl, whisk together egg yolks, milk, parsley, flour, salt, pepper and nutmeg. Stir in cheese; set aside.

In separate bowl, beat egg whites until stiff peaks form. Whisk one-third into egg yolk mixture; fold in remaining whites. Pour into 8-inch (2 L) square baking dish.

Bake in centre of 400°F (200°C) oven until puffed and dark golden, and top is firm to the touch, about 30 minutes.

Makes 4 servings. PER SERVING: about 301 cal, 22 g pro, 19 g total fat (9 g sat. fat), 10 g carb, trace fibre, 402 mg chol, 344 mg sodium. % RDI: 31% calcium, 12% iron, 26% vit A, 7% vit C, 31% folate.

VARIATION
Easy Ham and Cheese Soufflé
• Stir in ¼ cup (60 mL) shredded cooked ham.

Spaghetti with Tuna and Tomatoes

Canned tuna gets a dash of Italian flair in a simple homemade spaghetti sauce.

1 tbsp (15 mL) **extra-virgin olive oil**
1 **onion,** chopped
2 cloves **garlic,** minced
1 tsp (5 mL) **dried oregano**
½ tsp (2 mL) **pepper**
1 can (28 oz/796 mL) **tomatoes**
2 tbsp (30 mL) **tomato paste**
½ tsp (2 mL) grated **lemon zest**
2 cans (each 170 g) **solid white tuna**
    or chunk light tuna, drained
⅓ cup (75 mL) **oil-cured black olives,**
    pitted and quartered (approx)
12 oz (375 g) **spaghetti**
¼ cup (60 mL) chopped **fresh parsley**
¼ tsp (1 mL) **hot pepper flakes** (optional)

In large skillet, heat oil over medium heat; fry onion, garlic, oregano and pepper, stirring occasionally, until onion is softened, about 3 minutes.

Mash in tomatoes, tomato paste and lemon zest. Reduce heat; simmer until thickened, about 14 minutes. With fork, break tuna into chunks; add to sauce along with olives. Heat through, about 2 minutes.

Meanwhile, in large pot of boiling salted water, cook pasta until tender but firm, about 8 minutes. Drain and return to pot. Add sauce and parsley; toss to coat. Sprinkle with hot pepper flakes (if using) and more olives (if desired).

Makes 4 servings. PER SERVING: about 529 cal, 30 g pro, 11 g total fat (2 g sat. fat), 78 g carb, 7 g fibre, 28 mg chol, 1,085 mg sodium. % RDI: 10% calcium, 41% iron, 16% vit A, 63% vit C, 89% folate.

Garlic Bread Crumb Pasta

Here's the perfect dish for leftover baguette.

8 oz (250 g) **spaghetti**
1 piece (6 inches/15 cm) **baguette,** cubed
¼ cup (60 mL) **extra-virgin olive oil**
3 cloves **garlic,** minced
¼ cup (60 mL) chopped drained **capers**
¼ cup (60 mL) chopped **fresh parsley**
2 tbsp (30 mL) **lemon juice**
½ cup (125 mL) grated **Parmesan cheese**

In large pot of boiling salted water, cook pasta until tender but firm, about 8 minutes. Reserving ½ cup (125 mL) of the cooking liquid, drain and return to pot.

Meanwhile, in food processor, chop baguette until in pea-size pieces; set aside.

In skillet, heat oil over medium heat; fry crumbs and garlic until garlic is golden, about 4 minutes. Stir in capers, parsley and lemon juice. Add to pasta along with reserved cooking liquid; heat through. Sprinkle with cheese.

Makes 4 servings. PER SERVING: about 456 cal, 15 g pro, 19 g total fat (4 g sat. fat), 57 g carb, 4 g fibre, 11 mg chol, 788 mg sodium. % RDI: 16% calcium, 24% iron, 5% vit A, 10% vit C, 64% folate.

CHAPTER 6

Make It Tonight... in the Toaster Oven

Sun-Dried Tomato Meat Loaf

A classic favourite gets updated with shiitake mushrooms and sun-dried tomatoes. Leftovers make great sandwiches.

1 tbsp (15 mL) **vegetable oil**

1½ cups (375 mL) thinly sliced **shiitake mushroom caps** or white mushrooms

½ cup (125 mL) minced **onion**

1 rib **celery,** finely chopped

2 cloves **garlic,** minced

2 tbsp (30 mL) **balsamic vinegar** or wine vinegar

1 **egg**

½ cup (125 mL) **dry bread crumbs**

⅓ cup (75 mL) chopped drained **oil-packed sun-dried tomatoes**

½ tsp (2 mL) **dried thyme**

¼ tsp (1 mL) each **salt** and **pepper**

1 lb (500 g) **lean ground pork** or beef

TOPPING:

3 tbsp (45 mL) **chili sauce** or ketchup

1 tbsp (15 mL) **Dijon mustard**

¼ tsp (1 mL) **dried thyme**

In skillet, heat oil over medium-high heat; fry mushrooms, onion, celery and garlic, stirring occasionally, until softened, about 5 minutes. Stir in vinegar; cook until evaporated, about 30 seconds. Let cool slightly.

Meanwhile, in large bowl and using fork, beat egg; blend in bread crumbs, tomatoes, thyme, salt and pepper. Mix in mushroom mixture and pork. Pack into 8- x 4-inch (1.5 L) loaf pan, mounding top.

TOPPING: In small bowl, combine chili sauce, mustard and thyme; spread over loaf. (*Make-ahead: Cover and refrigerate for up to 12 hours.*)

Bake in 350°F (180°C) toaster oven or oven until meat thermometer registers 170°F (75°C), 45 to 50 minutes. Let stand for 5 minutes. Drain off fat.

Makes 4 servings. PER SERVING: about 382 cal, 26 g pro, 21 g total fat (6 g sat. fat), 21 g carb, 3 g fibre, 116 mg chol, 592 mg sodium. % RDI: 7% calcium, 22% iron, 4% vit A, 23% vit C, 15% folate.

EASY BOILED OR MASHED POTATOES

Count on 1 potato per person and an extra for the pan. Peel, if desired, or scrub and trim; cut into quarters. Place in saucepan; cover with boiling water and add 1 tsp (5 mL) salt. Cover and bring to boil. Reduce heat and simmer until fork-tender, about 15 minutes. Drain and return to pan; dry briefly over low heat.

SERVING SUGGESTIONS

Serve as is with a drizzle of olive oil or melted butter and a good grate of pepper. Or, for 4 large potatoes (about 2 lb/1 kg), mash or smash until creamy, adding 1 tbsp (15 mL) butter and up to 1 cup (250 mL) hot milk or cold buttermilk. Season with salt and pepper.

Baked Curried Chicken

You can also use bone-in chicken breasts or legs; increase baking time to 45 minutes.

⅓ cup (75 mL) **2% plain yogurt**
3 tbsp (45 mL) **liquid honey**
2 tbsp (30 mL) mild or medium **curry paste**
2 tbsp (30 mL) **soy sauce**
1 tbsp (15 mL) **vegetable oil**
2 tsp (10 mL) **Dijon mustard**
¼ tsp (1 mL) **pepper**
4 **boneless skinless chicken breasts**

In large bowl, whisk together yogurt, honey, curry paste, soy sauce, oil, mustard and pepper. Add chicken and turn to coat all over. Scrape into toaster oven pan or 11- x 7-inch (2 L) baking dish.

Bake in 375°F (190°C) toaster oven or oven, basting occasionally, until sauce is thickened and chicken is browned and no longer pink inside, about 30 minutes.

Makes 4 servings. PER SERVING: about 288 cal, 32 g pro, 10 g total fat (1 g sat. fat), 16 g carb, 1 g fibre, 79 mg chol, 846 mg sodium. % RDI: 4% calcium, 6% iron, 1% vit A, 3% vit C, 3% folate.

Green Beans with Almonds

1 lb (500 g) **green beans,** trimmed
1 tbsp (15 mL) **butter**
2 tbsp (30 mL) **slivered almonds**
1 tbsp (15 mL) **lemon juice**

In large saucepan of boiling salted water, cook beans until tender-crisp, about 7 minutes. Drain well.

Meanwhile, in skillet, melt butter over medium heat; fry almonds until light brown, about 3 minutes. Add lemon juice and beans; toss to coat.

Makes 4 servings. PER SERVING: about 87 cal, 3 g pro, 5 g total fat (2 g sat. fat), 9 g carb, 4 g fibre, 9 mg chol, 273 mg sodium. % RDI: 5% calcium, 8% iron, 10% vit A, 18% vit C, 16% folate.

Broiled Cumin Chicken with Zucchini and Carrot Salad

This recipe is loosely based on one 4-oz (125 g) chicken breast per person. If you get only two or three breasts to a pound (500 g), just slice the chicken after cooking and divide it into four portions.

1 tbsp (15 mL) **lemon juice**

2 tsp (10 mL) **vegetable oil**

1 tsp (5 mL) **ground cumin**

1 tsp (5 mL) **chili powder**

½ tsp (2 mL) **salt**

¼ tsp (1 mL) **pepper**

1 lb (500 g) **boneless skinless chicken breasts**

1½ cups (375 mL) each shredded **zucchini** and **carrots** (2 each)

1 **green onion,** finely chopped

In small bowl, mix 1 tsp (5 mL) each of the lemon juice and oil; stir in cumin, chili powder and half each of the salt and pepper to form thin paste.

Place chicken on greased toaster oven or oven broiler pan; brush with half of the paste. Turn and brush with remaining paste. Broil, turning once, until burnished brown outside and no longer pink inside, about 12 minutes. Transfer to cutting board and tent with foil; let stand for 10 minutes before slicing.

In large bowl, combine remaining lemon juice, oil, salt and pepper. Add zucchini, carrots and green onion; toss to coat. Mound on plates; top with chicken.

Makes 4 servings. PER SERVING: about 175 cal, 27 g pro, 4 g total fat (1 g sat. fat), 7 g carb, 2 g fibre, 67 mg chol, 369 mg sodium. % RDI: 3% calcium, 10% iron, 120% vit A, 17% vit C, 10% folate.

EQUIPMENT
TOASTER OVEN 101

CAPACITY
As well as the usual toast capacity, large models can cook a chicken or 12-inch (30 cm) pizza. The larger the unit, the more room it will occupy, so choose the size that suits your needs and space.

SETTINGS
Most ovens bake, toast and keep food warm, but some don't broil. Often newer models are convection, which circulates heat for even temperature and fast results.

TIMER
Some models turn off automatically when the timer bell sounds.

TRAYS AND PANS
Most ovens come with trays and pans, but additional toaster-oven-size pans are available in houseware stores.

RACKS
Adjustable, multiposition and reversible racks accommodate everything from roasts to cookies. Some models have an auto-advance feature, which means that the rack slides out when the door opens.

COOL TOUCH
Many models have the safety feature of insulated walls so handles and exterior surfaces stay cool.

Penne Vegetable Bake

Individual baking dishes are just right for a meal for two. Double the recipe for four, with the option of making the casserole in an 8-inch (2 L) square baking dish.

1 cup (250 mL) **penne**
2 tsp (10 mL) **extra-virgin olive oil**
1 small **onion,** chopped
1 cup (250 mL) chopped **carrot**
1 cup (250 mL) **cauliflower florets**
¼ tsp (1 mL) each **salt** and **pepper**
3 tbsp (45 mL) **prepared pesto**
1 **egg**
1 tub (250 g) **2% cottage cheese**
1 **plum tomato,** sliced
2 tbsp (30 mL) grated **Parmesan cheese**

In pot of boiling salted water, cook pasta until tender but firm, about 10 minutes. Drain; set aside.

In same pot, heat oil over medium heat; fry onion, carrot, cauliflower, salt and pepper, stirring occasionally, until vegetables are tender-crisp, about 5 minutes. Add pasta and pesto; toss to coat.

In bowl, whisk egg with cottage cheese; stir into pasta mixture and toss to coat. Divide between two 2-cup (500 mL) baking dishes; press gently. Arrange tomato over top; sprinkle with cheese. Bake in 375°F (190°C) toaster oven or oven until golden and bubbly, about 30 minutes.

Makes 2 servings. PER SERVING: about 512 cal, 31 g pro, 22 g total fat (7 g sat. fat), 49 g carb, 6 g fibre, 117 mg chol, 1,296 mg sodium. % RDI: 26% calcium, 24% iron, 151% vit A, 53% vit C, 68% folate.

Piri-Piri Cornish Hen

Cornish hen is a simple yet elegant dinner for two.

1 **frozen Cornish hen,** thawed

1 tbsp (15 mL) chopped **pimiento** or roasted red pepper

2 cloves **garlic**

½ tsp (2 mL) **salt**

2 tbsp (30 mL) **extra-virgin olive oil**

1 tsp (5 mL) **sweet paprika**

1 tsp (5 mL) **hot pepper sauce**

½ tsp (2 mL) finely grated **orange zest**

¼ tsp (1 mL) each **dried thyme** and **pepper**

Using scissors, cut along each side of backbone of hen; discard backbone. Cut hen in half; set aside.

On cutting board, finely mince together pimiento, garlic and salt; scrape into small bowl. Add half of the oil, paprika, hot pepper sauce, orange zest, thyme and pepper; mix well. Rub all over each half of hen. Refrigerate for 10 minutes to marinate. (*Make-ahead: Cover and refrigerate for up to 24 hours.*)

In small ovenproof skillet, heat remaining oil over medium-high heat; brown hen, skin side down, about 5 minutes. Turn over; bake in 400°F (200°C) toaster oven or oven, basting once, until juices run clear when hen is pierced, 20 to 25 minutes.

Makes 2 servings. PER SERVING: about 427 cal, 26 g pro, 35 g total fat (8 g sat. fat), 2 g carb, 1 g fibre, 150 mg chol, 664 mg sodium. % RDI: 3% calcium, 13% iron, 11% vit A, 12% vit C, 2% folate.

COOKING FOR TWO

THERE ARE TWO SCHOOLS OF THOUGHT:

1. Make family-size amounts. Enjoy a portion or two, then divide and freeze what's left in one- or two-serving amounts. This works well for saucy dishes, marinating meat or chicken, or burgers.

2. Make just enough for one or two. If you shop for one or two, this already sets the limit for amounts. Keep leftovers at bay by cooking in smaller saucepans, skillets and roasting pans and using smaller appliances (a toaster oven instead of a regular oven) or smaller versions of appliances (such as a slow cooker).

Lemon Dill Trout

Other mild fish, such as catfish or tilapia, are also excellent for this dish.

1 tbsp (15 mL) **extra-virgin olive oil**
1 **shallot,** minced (or 2 tbsp/30 mL minced onion)
1 tbsp (15 mL) minced **fresh dill** (or 1 tsp/ 5 mL dried dillweed)
1 tsp (5 mL) finely grated **lemon zest**
2 tsp (10 mL) **lemon juice**
1 tsp (5 mL) chopped drained **capers** (optional)
Pinch each **salt** and **pepper**
2 **rainbow trout fillets** (about 12 oz/ 375 g total)

In small bowl, combine oil, shallot, dill, lemon zest and juice, capers (if using), salt and pepper.

Arrange fish, skin side down, on greased toaster oven or oven broiler pan; brush with lemon mixture. Broil, watching closely, until fish is golden and flakes easily when tested, about 10 minutes.

Makes 2 servings. PER SERVING: about 263 cal, 29 g pro, 15 g total fat (3 g sat. fat), 1 g carb, trace fibre, 80 mg chol, 50 mg sodium. % RDI: 10% calcium, 4% iron, 11% vit A, 13% vit C, 14% folate.

BROCCOLI BASICS

Serve the fish with nutritious broccoli. Trim and peel stalks; in saucepan, cover and cook broccoli in about 1 inch (2.5 cm) of boiling water for 4 minutes. Or steam until vivid green and tender-crisp, about 7 minutes. Drain; toss with extra-virgin olive oil or oil from a jar of sun-dried tomatoes.

Roasted Fish with Artichokes and Sun-Dried Tomatoes

You can use dry-packed sun-dried tomatoes instead of oil-packed. Just soak in boiling water for 20 minutes, then drain, slice and use as for the oil-packed variety.

4 **halibut fillets** or tilapia fillets (about 1½ lb/750 g)
2 cloves **garlic,** minced
¼ tsp (1 mL) each **salt** and **pepper**
⅓ cup (75 mL) drained **oil-packed sun-dried tomatoes**
1 jar (6 oz/170 mL) **marinated artichoke hearts,** drained
1 tbsp (15 mL) **extra-virgin olive oil**
1 tbsp (15 mL) chopped **fresh parsley**
1 **lemon,** cut in wedges

Place fish on greased toaster oven pan, in small roasting pan or on parchment paper–lined rimmed baking sheet. Spread garlic over top of fish; sprinkle with salt and pepper. Finely slice tomatoes; arrange over each fillet. Cut artichokes in half; place on tomatoes. Drizzle with oil.

Roast in 400°F (200°C) toaster oven or oven until fish flakes easily when tested, about 12 minutes. Sprinkle with parsley. Serve with lemon wedges.

Makes 4 servings. PER SERVING: about 276 cal, 37 g pro, 11 g total fat (2 g sat. fat), 7 g carb, 2 g fibre, 54 mg chol, 288 mg sodium. % RDI: 9% calcium, 16% iron, 9% vit A, 32% vit C, 17% folate.

Glazed Catfish

Mayonnaise, like oil or butter, lends tons of taste to mild fish, keeps the fillets moist and effortlessly creates a glaze.

4 **catfish fillets** or tilapia fillets (about 6 oz/175 g each)
2 tbsp (30 mL) **light mayonnaise**
2 tsp (10 mL) **lemon juice**
1 tsp (5 mL) **dried Italian herb seasoning**
¼ tsp (1 mL) each **salt** and **pepper**

Pat fish dry; place on greased toaster oven or oven broiler pan.

In small bowl, combine mayonnaise, lemon juice, Italian herb seasoning, salt and pepper; spread over fillets.

Broil until fish flakes easily when tested, about 8 minutes.

Makes 4 servings. PER SERVING: about 204 cal, 21 g pro, 13 g total fat (3 g sat. fat), 1 g carb, trace fibre, 65 mg chol, 264 mg sodium. % RDI: 2% calcium, 6% iron, 2% vit A, 2% vit C, 5% folate.

Boston Lettuce and Radicchio Salad

2 tbsp (30 mL) **extra-virgin olive oil**
1 tbsp (15 mL) **red wine vinegar**
½ tsp (2 mL) **Dijon mustard**
Pinch each **granulated sugar, salt** and **pepper**
6 cups (1.5 L) torn **Boston lettuce leaves**
1 cup (250 mL) torn **radicchio leaves**
½ cup (125 mL) sliced **celery**

In large bowl, whisk together oil, vinegar, mustard, sugar, salt and pepper.

Add lettuce, radicchio and celery; toss to coat.

Makes 4 servings. PER SERVING: about 76 cal, 1 g pro, 7 g total fat (1 g sat. fat), 3 g carb, 1 g fibre, 0 mg chol, 27 mg sodium. % RDI: 3% calcium, 3% iron, 9% vit A, 13% vit C, 33% folate.

Miso-Marinated Salmon

This simple Japanese-style sauce caramelizes as it broils, creating a tasty crust over the soft, meaty fish. Baby Bok Choy with Shiitake Mushrooms (right) is a terrific partner.

¼ cup (60 mL) **miso**
1 tbsp (15 mL) **vegetable oil**
1 tbsp (15 mL) each **granulated sugar** and
  mirin (or 2 tbsp/30 mL granulated sugar)
1 tbsp (15 mL) **sake** (optional)
2 tsp (10 mL) minced **fresh ginger**
4 **centre-cut salmon fillets,** skin-on
  (about 6 oz/175 g each)

In bowl, whisk together miso, oil, sugar, mirin, sake (if using) and ginger; add salmon, turning to coat. Let stand for 10 minutes or cover and refrigerate for up to 8 hours.

Place salmon on greased foil-lined baking sheet. Roast in 400°F (200°C) toaster oven until fish flakes easily when tested, 10 to 12 minutes. Broil until crusty and browned.

Makes 4 servings. PER SERVING: about 328 cal, 28 g pro, 19 g total fat (3 g sat. fat), 9 g carb, 1 g fibre, 74 mg chol, 712 mg sodium, 495 mg potassium. % RDI: 3% calcium, 6% iron, 2% vit A, 7% vit C, 20% folate.

Baby Bok Choy with Shiitake Mushrooms

12 oz (375 g) **baby bok choy**
2 cups (500 mL) **shiitake mushrooms**
1 tbsp (15 mL) **butter**
1 clove **garlic,** minced
¼ cup (60 mL) **water**
4 tsp (20 mL) **soy sauce**
1 tsp (5 mL) **sesame oil**
Pinch **hot pepper flakes**
Sesame seeds

Cut bok choy in half lengthwise; rinse between leaves. Blanch in boiling water until darkened, about 2 minutes. Drain and pat dry. Trim stems off mushrooms; thickly slice caps.

In skillet, melt butter over medium-high heat; sauté mushrooms and garlic until softened, about 3 minutes.

Add bok choy, water, soy sauce, sesame oil and hot pepper flakes; sauté until no liquid remains, about 5 minutes. Sprinkle with sesame seeds to taste.

Makes 4 servings. PER SERVING: about 61 cal, 3 g pro, 4 g total fat (2 g sat. fat), 4 g carb, 2 g fibre, 8 mg chol, 353 mg sodium, 430 mg potassium. % RDI: 8% calcium, 9% iron, 41% vit A, 40% vit C, 19% folate.

Swiss Chard Gratin

This gratin is a delicious way to incorporate greens into your diet.

1 **potato** (5 oz/150 g), peeled and quartered
2 tbsp (30 mL) **butter**
¼ cup (60 mL) diced **onion**
1 clove **garlic,** minced
¼ cup (60 mL) **all-purpose flour**
1¾ cups (425 mL) **milk**
¼ tsp (1 mL) **cayenne pepper**
Pinch each **salt** and **pepper**
Pinch **ground nutmeg**
⅓ cup (75 mL) shredded **Gruyère cheese**
3 tbsp (45 mL) grated **Parmesan cheese**
2½ cups (625 mL) shredded **Swiss chard**

In small saucepan of boiling salted water, cook potato until tender, 10 to 12 minutes. Drain; let cool for 5 minutes. Thinly slice and overlap in greased 3-cup (750 mL) shallow gratin dish.

Meanwhile, in small saucepan, heat butter over medium heat; cook onion and garlic until softened, about 3 minutes. Stir in flour; cook for 1 minute. Whisking constantly, add milk, ½ cup (125 mL) at a time. Whisk in cayenne, salt, pepper and nutmeg. Reduce heat to low; simmer, whisking occasionally, until thickened, 5 to 7 minutes. Stir in Gruyère and Parmesan.

Pour ½ cup (125 mL) sauce over potato. Top with Swiss chard, pressing to compact. Pour remaining sauce over top. Bake in 400°F (200°C) toaster oven or oven until bubbly and browned, 20 to 25 minutes.

Makes 2 servings. PER SERVING: about 475 cal, 21 g pro, 25 g total fat (15 g sat. fat), 43 g carb, 3 g fibre, 77 mg chol, 657 mg sodium. % RDI: 53% calcium, 16% iron, 41% vit A, 25% vit C, 25% folate.

Asian Pork Chops with Green Onions

A jar of hoisin sauce in the fridge is an instant source of Asian flavour. Serve the chops with steamed baby bok choy or broccoli alongside noodles or rice.

¼ cup (60 mL) **hoisin sauce**
2 tbsp (30 mL) **soy sauce**
2 tbsp (30 mL) **lime juice**
2 cloves **garlic,** minced
1 tsp (5 mL) minced **fresh ginger**
   (or ¼ tsp/1 mL ground ginger)
¼ tsp (1 mL) **pepper**
4 **pork loin centre chops,** boneless or
   bone in, trimmed
2 **green onions,** thinly sliced

In shallow dish, combine hoisin sauce, soy sauce, lime juice, garlic, ginger and pepper. Slash edges of pork chops to prevent curling. Add to marinade, turning to coat; let stand for 30 minutes. (*Make-ahead: Cover and refrigerate, turning occasionally, for up to 24 hours.*)

Reserving marinade, place chops on foil-lined toaster oven or oven broiler pan or greased grill; spoon marinade over top. Broil or close lid and grill, turning once, until juices run clear when pork is pierced and just a hint of pink remains inside, about 8 minutes. Sprinkle with green onions.

Makes 4 servings. PER SERVING: about 213 cal, 27 g pro, 7 g total fat (2 g sat. fat), 10 g carb, 1 g fibre, 72 mg chol, 837 mg sodium. % RDI: 4% calcium, 11% iron, 1% vit A, 5% vit C, 6% folate.

Tortilla Pizzas

These toppings are just a starting point. Use your imagination to customize these quick and tasty tortilla or pita pizzas.

Two 6-inch (15 cm) **flour tortillas** or pitas
3 tbsp (45 mL) **prepared pesto**
¼ cup (60 mL) crumbled **goat cheese**
2 tbsp (30 mL) chopped drained
   oil-packed sun-dried tomatoes
6 **Kalamata olives,** pitted and halved

Place tortillas on toaster oven broiler pan or rimmed baking sheet; spread each with pesto. Sprinkle with goat cheese, tomatoes and olives.

Bake in 400°F (200°C) toaster oven or oven until base is crisp and toppings are hot, 8 to 10 minutes.

Makes 2 servings. PER SERVING: about 264 cal, 7 g pro, 17 g total fat (4 g sat. fat), 22 g carb, 3 g fibre, 8 mg chol, 722 mg sodium. % RDI: 8% calcium, 14% iron, 10% vit A, 12% vit C, 19% folate.

VARIATION

Hot and Classic Pizzas
• Replace pesto with pizza sauce; goat cheese with shredded mozzarella cheese; tomatoes with 6 slices pepperoni or 3 slices Genoa salami, halved; and olives with pickled hot pepper rings.

SHOPPING FOR TWO

• **Meat, poultry and fish:** Unless you love leftovers, say goodbye to family-pack trays. Attendants at the meat and seafood counters can portion one or more servings to suit your needs. Look for 1-lb (500 g) quick-cook roasts.

• **Dairy:** Look for half-pounds (250 g) of butter and single servings of yogurt and cottage cheese. The deli counter will slice cheese to order. Buy six- or eight-packs of eggs.

• **Produce:** Only buy as much as you'll eat. Loose mixed salad or spinach is better than packaged – you get exactly what you need. Buy loose vegetables instead of prebagged ones. Also, consider buying storage containers with air vents that keep produce fresh longer, rather than relying on your crisper drawer.

• **Frozen foods:** Resealable bags of individually quick frozen (IQF) fruit and vegetables mean you can take out and use only enough for one meal without any waste.

• **Bulk foods:** Whether it's a single serving of pasta or a spoonful of herbs or spices you don't usually use, the bulk food store is a great place to buy exactly how much you need.

• **Salad and antipasto bars:** When you need only a little of an ingredient for a special recipe, take a look at these offerings.

• **When you have extras:** Freeze canned tomatoes; chicken, beef or vegetable broth; or tomato juice in airtight containers in amounts that suit your recipes. Freeze unused tomato sauce, tomato paste and chipotle peppers in adobo sauce in ice-cube trays; wrap frozen cubes in plastic wrap and enclose in an airtight container.

CHAPTER 7

Make It Tonight... in the Slow Cooker

Slow Cooker Spanish Pot Roast

In Spanish cooking, ground almonds are often used to thicken sauces. The bonus: the extra mellowness they lend to the dish.

3 lb (1.5 kg) **boneless beef cross rib pot roast**

¼ tsp (1 mL) each **salt** and **pepper**

2 tbsp (30 mL) **vegetable oil** (approx)

1 **onion,** thinly sliced

2 cloves **garlic,** minced

½ cup (125 mL) **prosciutto,** diced (4 oz/125 g)

½ tsp (2 mL) **dried marjoram** or oregano

1 cup (250 mL) **sodium-reduced beef broth**

½ cup (125 mL) **sherry** or sodium-reduced beef broth

1 can (28 oz/796 mL) **tomatoes,** drained

1 cup (250 mL) sliced **roasted red peppers**

2 tbsp (30 mL) **all-purpose flour**

¼ cup (60 mL) **ground almonds**

2 tbsp (30 mL) **tomato paste**

1 **sweet green pepper,** thinly sliced

Sprinkle beef with salt and pepper. In large Dutch oven, heat half of the oil over medium-high heat; brown beef, adding more oil if necessary. Transfer to slow cooker.

Drain fat from pan. Add remaining oil; fry onion, garlic, prosciutto and marjoram over medium heat until onion is softened, about 5 minutes. Add broth and sherry; bring to boil, scraping up brown bits. Pour into slow cooker.

Add tomatoes and red peppers; cover and cook on low until beef is tender, 6 to 8 hours. Transfer beef to cutting board; tent with foil and let stand for 15 minutes before slicing.

Meanwhile, whisk flour with 3 tbsp (45 mL) water; whisk into slow cooker. Whisk in almonds and tomato paste. Add green pepper; cover and cook on high until thickened, about 15 minutes. Serve with beef.

Makes 8 servings. PER SERVING: about 397 cal, 36 g pro, 23 g total fat (7 g sat. fat), 12 g carb, 2 g fibre, 110 mg chol, 565 mg sodium. % RDI: 6% calcium, 38% iron, 9% vit A, 90% vit C, 12% folate.

VARIATION
Stove Top Spanish Pot Roast

• In large Dutch oven, brown beef as directed. Transfer to plate.

• Fry onion, garlic, prosciutto and marjoram as directed. Add broth and sherry; bring to boil, scraping up brown bits. Add tomatoes and red peppers; return to boil. Return beef to pan; cover and simmer until beef is tender, about 2 hours. Transfer to cutting board; tent with foil and let stand for 15 minutes before slicing.

• Add almonds, tomato paste and green pepper to pan; bring to boil and cook for 10 minutes. Whisk flour with 3 tbsp (45 mL) water; whisk into pan. Bring to boil and cook, stirring, until thickened, about 5 minutes. Serve with beef.

TIP

The juice drained from the tomatoes is an enriching addition to soups and chilis. Freeze it if you can't use it right away.

Slow Cooker Chunky Beef Chili

Stewing beef is handy but can vary in tenderness. A pot roast, especially a boneless cross rib, is a fine alternative.

2 lb (1 kg) **stewing beef cubes**

2 tbsp (30 mL) **vegetable oil**

2 **onions,** diced

2 large **carrots,** diced

2 ribs **celery,** diced

3 cloves **garlic,** minced

1 tbsp (15 mL) **dried oregano**

1 can (28 oz/796 mL) **stewed tomatoes**

1 can (5½ oz/156 mL) **tomato paste**

2 cans (each 19 oz/540 mL) **red kidney beans,** drained and rinsed

2 tbsp (30 mL) **chili powder**

½ tsp (2 mL) **salt**

1 **sweet green pepper,** diced

1 tsp (5 mL) **hot pepper sauce** (optional)

Cut beef into ½-inch (1 cm) cubes. In large skillet, heat oil over medium-high heat; brown beef, in 4 batches. With slotted spoon, transfer to slow cooker.

Pour off any fat in skillet. Fry onions, carrots, celery, garlic and oregano over medium heat until softened, about 5 minutes. Scrape into slow cooker.

Add tomatoes, tomato paste, beans, chili powder and salt to slow cooker. Cover and cook on low until beef is tender, about 6 hours.

Skim off any fat. Stir in green pepper, and hot pepper sauce (if using). Cover and cook for 30 minutes.

Makes 8 to 12 servings. PER EACH OF 12 SERVINGS: about 252 cal, 23 g pro, 8 g total fat (2 g sat. fat), 23 g carb, 8 g fibre, 37 mg chol, 497 mg sodium. % RDI: 6% calcium, 29% iron, 33% vit A, 37% vit C, 24% folate.

VARIATION

Stove Top Chunky Beef Chili

• Cube and brown beef as directed in Dutch oven. Transfer to plate.

• Drain off fat; in same pan, fry onions, carrots, celery, green pepper, garlic and oregano as directed.

• Add stewed tomatoes, tomato paste, beans, chili powder, salt, hot pepper sauce and beef and any accumulated juices to pan; stir well to combine. Bring to boil.

• Reduce heat, cover and simmer, stirring occasionally, until beef is tender, about 1½ hours.

TECHNIQUE
SEARING

Searing creates a richly flavoured and coloured crust on the outside of meats, poultry and fish. This is technically called the Maillard reaction, and is based on the combination of sugars and protein.

• Pat meat dry and season.

• Preheat pan; if pan is too cool, the meat will stick and tear. Add required fat and heat until ripples form. Add meat. Let cook until browned and turns easily.

• After meat is browned, you can add liquid, such as broth, wine or water, to pan and stir as you scrape up the brown bits on the bottom (this is called deglazing) and create a lip-smacking sauce or jus.

Slow Cooker Mushroom Pot Roast

The slow cooker makes this Sunday dinner classic doable for a Friday night feast. It takes a little hands-on time in the morning, but dinner will be ready and waiting when you get home.

3 lb (1.5 kg) **boneless beef cross rib pot roast**

½ tsp (2 mL) each **salt** and **pepper**

2 tbsp (30 mL) **vegetable oil**

1 **onion,** diced

2 each **carrots** and ribs **celery,** sliced

3 cloves **garlic,** minced

1 tsp (5 mL) each **dried marjoram** and **oregano**

4 cups (1 L) **button mushrooms,** quartered

⅓ cup (75 mL) **sodium-reduced beef broth**

2 tbsp (30 mL) **tomato paste**

2 tsp (10 mL) **Worcestershire sauce**

3 tbsp (45 mL) **all-purpose flour**

WHAT SIZE SLOW COOKER?

Slow cookers are available in a variety of shapes and sizes, so choose one that best suits your needs.
- For 4 to 8 servings, choose a 20- to 24-cup (5 to 6 L) slow cooker.
- For 2 to 4 servings, choose a 10- to 16-cup (2.5 to 4 L) slow cooker.
- For smaller amounts, such as dips, sauces and appetizers, choose a 2-cup (500 mL) or 6-cup (1.5 L) slow cooker.

Sprinkle beef with salt and pepper. In large skillet, heat half of the oil over medium-high heat; brown beef all over, adding more oil if necessary. Transfer to slow cooker.

Drain any fat from pan; add remaining oil. Fry onion, carrots, celery, garlic, marjoram and oregano over medium heat until softened, about 5 minutes. Add mushrooms; cook until tender, about 5 minutes. Scrape into slow cooker.

Stir broth into pan, scraping up brown bits; boil for 1 minute and pour into slow cooker. Add tomato paste and Worcestershire sauce to slow cooker; cover and cook on low until beef is tender, 5 to 7 hours.

Transfer meat to cutting board; tent with foil and let stand for 15 minutes before thinly slicing across the grain.

Meanwhile, whisk flour with ¼ cup (60 mL) water; whisk into slow cooker. Cover and cook on high until thickened, about 15 minutes. Serve with beef.

Makes 4 to 6 servings. PER EACH OF 6 SERVINGS: about 454 cal, 47 g pro, 23 g total fat (8 g sat. fat), 11 g carb, 2 g fibre, 114 mg chol, 347 mg sodium. % RDI: 4% calcium, 42% iron, 44% vit A, 8% vit C, 15% folate.

Slow Cooker Beef and Mushroom Stew

When browning meat, it's vital to do so in batches – each no larger than what fits without touching in the pan.

2 lb (1 kg) **stewing beef cubes**
½ cup (125 mL) **all-purpose flour**
¾ tsp (4 mL) **salt**
¼ tsp (1 mL) **pepper**
2 tbsp (30 mL) **vegetable oil** (approx)
2 cups (500 mL) **sodium-reduced beef broth**
1 **onion,** sliced
2 slices **bacon,** chopped
1 tsp (5 mL) **dried thyme**
4 cups (1 L) **button mushrooms,** halved (12 oz/375 g)
2 ribs **celery,** chopped
3 cups (750 mL) cubed peeled **potatoes**
1 pkg (14 g) **dried porcini mushrooms**
1 **bay leaf**
1 cup (250 mL) **frozen peas**

Trim and cut beef into 1-inch (2.5 cm) cubes; toss with ¼ cup (60 mL) of the flour. Sprinkle with salt and pepper. In large skillet, heat half of the oil over medium-high heat; brown meat, in batches and adding more oil if necessary. Transfer to slow cooker.

Add broth to skillet and bring to boil, scraping up any brown bits; pour into slow cooker.

In same skillet, heat remaining oil over medium heat; fry onion, bacon and thyme for 1 minute. Add button mushrooms; fry until softened and almost no liquid remains, about 8 minutes. Add to slow cooker.

Add celery, potatoes, porcini mushrooms, bay leaf and 1 cup (250 mL) water to slow cooker; stir to combine. Cover and cook on low until meat and vegetables are tender, about 6 hours.

Whisk remaining flour with ¼ cup (60 mL) water; whisk into slow cooker. Add peas. Cover and cook on high until thickened, about 15 minutes. Discard bay leaf.

Makes 8 servings. PER SERVING: about 344 cal, 30 g pro, 14 g total fat (5 g sat. fat), 23 g carb, 3 g fibre, 60 mg chol, 503 mg sodium. % RDI: 3% calcium, 28% iron, 4% vit A, 12% vit C, 22% folate.

VARIATION
Stove Top Beef and Mushroom Stew
• Reduce flour to ¼ cup (60 mL) and use only for browning meat.

• In Dutch oven, brown beef as directed; transfer to plate. Deglaze with broth as directed; set aside.

• Fry onion, bacon, thyme and button mushrooms as directed.

• Stir in celery, potatoes, porcini mushrooms, bay leaf, broth mixture, 1 cup (250 mL) water and beef; bring to boil. Reduce heat, cover and simmer until beef is tender, about 1 hour.

• Add peas; simmer until heated through. Discard bay leaf. (*Make-ahead: Let cool for 30 minutes. Refrigerate, uncovered, in airtight container until cold; cover and refrigerate for up to 2 days or freeze for up to 1 month.*)

Slow Cooker Short Ribs in Red Wine Sauce

Short ribs are a trendy cut nowadays. The meat on the bone is so rich in flavour, and because short ribs are fairly fatty, they are always moist.

1 pkg (14 g) **dried porcini mushrooms** or dried shiitake mushrooms

3 lb (1.5 kg) **beef simmering short ribs**

1 tbsp (15 mL) **vegetable oil**

2 cups (500 mL) **button mushrooms**

2 **onions,** chopped

3 cloves **garlic,** minced

2 **carrots,** diced

1 tbsp (15 mL) crumbled **dried rosemary**

¾ tsp (4 mL) **salt**

½ tsp (2 mL) **pepper**

1 can (28 oz/796 mL) **diced tomatoes**

¾ cup (175 mL) **red wine** (or ¾ cup/ 175 mL beef broth and 1 tbsp/15 mL wine vinegar)

2 tbsp (30 mL) **tomato paste**

¼ cup (60 mL) **all-purpose flour**

2 tbsp (30 mL) **balsamic vinegar** or wine vinegar

2 tbsp (30 mL) chopped **fresh parsley**

In measuring cup, pour 1 cup (250 mL) boiling water over porcini mushrooms; let stand for 20 minutes. Strain, reserving liquid. Set mushrooms and liquid aside.

Cut ribs into 2-bone pieces. Broil, turning once, until browned, 5 minutes. Place in slow cooker.

In skillet, heat oil over medium-high heat; sauté porcini and button mushrooms, onions, garlic, carrots, rosemary, salt and pepper until softened, about 5 minutes. Scrape into slow cooker. Add tomatoes.

Whisk together reserved soaking liquid, wine and tomato paste; pour into slow cooker. Cover and cook on low until meat is tender, 7 to 8 hours. Skim off fat.

In small bowl, whisk together flour, vinegar and ⅓ cup (75 mL) water; whisk into slow cooker. Cover and cook on high until thickened, about 15 minutes. Stir in parsley.

Makes 6 to 8 servings. PER EACH OF 8 SERVINGS: about 468 cal, 20 g pro, 36 g total fat (15 g sat. fat), 17 g carb, 3 g fibre, 69 mg chol, 441 mg sodium. % RDI: 6% calcium, 21% iron, 53% vit A, 33% vit C, 14% folate.

VARIATION
Stove Top Short Ribs in Red Wine Sauce
• Follow recipe as directed, using Dutch oven instead of slow cooker; cover and simmer over medium-low heat until ribs are tender, about 2 hours. Skim off fat. Reduce flour to 2 tbsp (30 mL) and water to ¼ cup (60 mL); whisk into pan and simmer until thickened, about 5 minutes. Stir in parsley.

Slow Cooker Chicken Chili

This tomato-less chili is a lighter-tasting alternative to a traditional red chili.

2 tbsp (30 mL) **vegetable oil**
8 **boneless skinless chicken thighs**
1 **onion,** chopped
3 cloves **garlic,** minced
2 tsp (10 mL) **ground coriander**
1½ tsp (7 mL) **ground cumin**
1 tsp (5 mL) **chipotle chili powder**
¼ tsp (1 mL) each **salt** and **pepper**
1 can (19 oz/540 mL) **white kidney beans,** drained and rinsed
2 cans (each 4½ oz/127 mL) **chopped green chilies**
2 tbsp (30 mL) **all-purpose flour**
⅓ cup (75 mL) chopped **fresh cilantro**
2 tbsp (30 mL) **lime juice**

In large skillet, heat half of the oil over medium-high heat; brown chicken all over. Transfer to slow cooker.

Drain any fat from pan; add remaining oil. Fry onion, garlic, coriander, cumin, chili powder, salt and pepper, stirring occasionally, until onion is softened, about 6 minutes. Scrape into slow cooker. Stir in beans and green chilies; cover and cook on low for 5 hours.

Remove chicken from sauce; cube and set aside. In small bowl, whisk flour with 3 tbsp (45 mL) water; whisk into slow cooker. Cover and cook on high until thickened, 15 minutes.

Stir in chicken, cilantro and lime juice; heat through.

Makes 4 servings. PER SERVING: about 352 cal, 30 g pro, 14 g total fat (2 g sat. fat), 28 g carb, 9 g fibre, 95 mg chol, 708 mg sodium. % RDI: 8% calcium, 29% iron, 5% vit A, 32% vit C, 35% folate.

Slow Cooker Mac and Cheese

This family-pleaser fits everyone's busy schedule.

2 tbsp (30 mL) **butter**
1 **onion,** chopped
⅓ cup (75 mL) **all-purpose flour**
3 cups (750 mL) **milk**
3 cups (750 mL) shredded **old Cheddar cheese**
2 tsp (10 mL) **Dijon mustard**
¾ tsp (4 mL) **salt**
½ tsp (2 mL) **pepper**
2 cups (500 mL) **macaroni**
¼ cup (60 mL) chopped **fresh parsley**

In saucepan, melt butter over medium heat; fry onion, stirring, until softened, about 3 minutes.

Add flour; cook, whisking, for 1 minute. Whisk in milk; cook, whisking, until thickened, about 8 minutes. Add Cheddar cheese, mustard, salt and pepper. Scrape into slow cooker.

Meanwhile, in pot of boiling salted water, cook macaroni until tender but firm, about 8 minutes. Drain; add to slow cooker, stirring to coat. Cover; cook on low until bubbly, about 3 hours. Stir in parsley.

Makes 4 to 6 servings. PER EACH OF 6 SERVINGS: about 487 cal, 24 g pro, 26 g total fat (16 g sat. fat), 40 g carb, 2 g fibre, 81 mg chol, 854 mg sodium. % RDI: 52% calcium, 13% iron, 26% vit A, 7% vit C, 35% folate.

VARIATION
Baked Crusty-Topped Mac and Cheese
• Boil macaroni and make cheese sauce as directed. Combine in 8-inch (2 L) square baking dish. Sprinkle ¼ cup (60 mL) dry bread crumbs over top. Bake in 350°F (180°C) oven until crusty, about 30 minutes.

Slow Cooker Spaghetti Sauce

This classic spaghetti sauce is designed for you to serve a bunch of friends, have leftovers for a quick dinner within three days, or freeze for later. Try switching the ground beef to chicken or lean pork.

1½ lb (750 g) **lean ground beef**
2 cans (each 28 oz/796 mL) **tomatoes**
1 can (5½ oz/156 mL) **tomato paste**
1½ cups (375 mL) sliced **mushrooms**
2 **carrots,** chopped
2 ribs **celery,** chopped
1 large **onion,** chopped
1 **sweet red pepper** or sweet yellow pepper, chopped
4 cloves **garlic,** minced
1 tbsp (15 mL) each **dried basil** and **oregano**
1 tsp (5 mL) each **dried thyme** and **salt**
½ tsp (2 mL) **pepper**
¼ tsp (1 mL) **cayenne pepper**
4 tsp (20 mL) **balsamic vinegar**

In large skillet, sauté beef over medium-high heat, breaking up with fork, until no longer pink, 5 to 8 minutes. Drain off fat.

Place tomatoes in slow cooker; mash until slightly chunky. Stir in tomato paste, beef, mushrooms, carrots, celery, onion, red pepper, garlic, basil, oregano, thyme, salt, pepper and cayenne pepper.

Cover and cook on low until thickened and vegetables are tender, 8 to 10 hours. Stir in vinegar.

Makes 10 cups (2.5 L), enough for 8 servings.
PER SERVING: about 243 cal, 20 g pro, 10 g total fat (4 g sat. fat), 20 g carb, 4 g fibre, 44 mg chol, 706 mg sodium. % RDI: 9% calcium, 31% iron, 68% vit A, 93% vit C, 14% folate.

VARIATION
Stove Top Spaghetti Sauce
• In Dutch oven, brown beef as directed.

• Drain off fat; in same pan, fry mushrooms, carrots, celery, onion, red pepper, garlic, basil, oregano, thyme, salt, pepper and cayenne pepper until onions are softened, about 8 minutes.

• Add tomatoes, tomato paste and beef and any accumulated juices to pan; stir well to combine. Bring to boil.

• Reduce heat, cover and simmer, stirring occasionally, until sauce is thickened, about 1 hour. Stir in vinegar.

Slow Cooker Port and Prune Pork Roast

A pork shoulder blade roast is well marbled and, unlike leaner cuts, stays succulent and moist even after six hours in the slow cooker.

2 **sweet potatoes,** cut in ¾-inch (2 cm) thick rounds

1 pkg (10 oz/300 g) **pearl onions,** peeled

3 lb (1.5 kg) **boneless pork shoulder blade roast**

½ tsp (2 mL) **pepper**

¼ tsp (1 mL) **salt**

1 tbsp (15 mL) **vegetable oil** (approx)

1½ cups (375 mL) **sodium-reduced chicken broth**

½ cup (125 mL) **Port** or sodium-reduced chicken broth (or ½ cup/125 mL dry red wine and 1 tsp/5 mL granulated sugar)

1 cup (250 mL) **pitted prunes**

2 **bay leaves**

½ tsp (2 mL) each **dried sage, thyme** and **dry mustard**

⅓ cup (75 mL) **all-purpose flour**

In slow cooker, mix sweet potatoes with pearl onions.

Trim fat from pork; sprinkle with pepper and salt. In large skillet, heat oil over medium-high heat; brown pork, adding more oil if necessary. Transfer to slow cooker.

Drain fat from pan. Add broth and Port; bring to boil, scraping up brown bits from bottom of pan. Add to slow cooker.

Add prunes, bay leaves, sage, thyme and mustard to slow cooker. Cover and cook on low until meat is tender, about 6 hours. Transfer meat and vegetables to platter; tent with foil and keep warm. Discard bay leaves.

Whisk flour with ⅓ cup (75 mL) water; whisk into slow cooker. Cover and cook on high until thickened, about 15 minutes. Slice meat; serve with sauce and vegetables.

Makes 8 servings. PER SERVING: about 357 cal, 29 g pro, 12 g total fat (4 g sat. fat), 35 g carb, 4 g fibre, 89 mg chol, 308 mg sodium. % RDI: 5% calcium, 20% iron, 114% vit A, 20% vit C, 11% folate.

VARIATION

Stove Top Port and Prune Pork Roast

• In Dutch oven, brown pork as directed. Transfer to plate.

• Drain all but 1 tbsp (15 mL) fat from pan. Reduce heat to medium and fry pearl onions, sage, thyme and mustard until onions are golden, 5 minutes. Add broth and Port; bring to boil, stirring and scraping up brown bits.

• Return pork to pan. Add sweet potatoes, prunes and bay leaves; cover and simmer until meat is tender, about 2 hours. Transfer meat and vegetables to platter; tent with foil and keep warm. Discard bay leaves.

• Whisk flour with 3 tbsp (45 mL) water; whisk into pan. Bring to boil and cook, stirring, until thickened, about 4 minutes. Serve pork with sauce and vegetables.

TIP

No time to peel pearl onions? Quarter 4 cooking onions instead.

Slow Cooker Fennel and Tomato Pork Stew

This Mediterranean-inspired stew is richly flavoured with a simple, sunny combination of fennel seeds, olives and tomatoes.

2 lb (1 kg) **boneless pork shoulder blade roast**

½ tsp (2 mL) each **salt** and **pepper**

2 tbsp (30 mL) **vegetable oil**

1 **onion,** chopped

2 each **carrots** and ribs **celery,** chopped

4 cloves **garlic**

2 tsp (10 mL) **fennel seeds,** crushed

½ cup (125 mL) **sodium-reduced chicken broth**

2 cups (500 mL) **bottled strained tomatoes** (passata)

3 sprigs **fresh thyme** (or 1 tsp/5 mL dried)

1 tbsp (15 mL) **all-purpose flour**

⅓ cup (75 mL) chopped **black olives**

¼ cup (60 mL) chopped **fresh parsley**

Trim pork and cut into 1-inch (2.5 cm) cubes; sprinkle with half each of the salt and pepper. In large shallow Dutch oven, heat half of the oil over medium-high heat; brown pork, in batches and adding more oil if necessary. Transfer to slow cooker.

Drain any fat from pan; add remaining oil. Fry onion, carrots, celery, garlic, fennel seeds and remaining salt and pepper over medium heat until softened and lightly golden, about 8 minutes. Add broth, scraping up brown bits from bottom of pan. Pour into slow cooker.

Add tomatoes and thyme to slow cooker. Cover and cook on low until pork is tender, 6 to 7 hours.

In small bowl, whisk flour with 2 tbsp (30 mL) water; whisk into slow cooker. Stir in olives; cover and cook on high until thickened, about 15 minutes. Stir in parsley.

Makes 4 servings. PER SERVING: about 355 cal, 37 g pro, 15 g total fat (3 g sat. fat), 17 g carb, 3 g fibre, 104 mg chol, 640 mg sodium. % RDI: 10% calcium, 36% iron, 77% vit A, 33% vit C, 18% folate.

Slow Cooker Sausage and Seafood Ragout

This rich stew contains the best of surf and turf: well-spiced chorizo, delicate briny mussels and earthy catfish. The broth is divine to sip or soak up with crusty French bread.

1 tbsp (15 mL) **extra-virgin olive oil**

1 lb (500 g) **chorizo** or mild Italian sausages, cut in chunks

1 **onion,** diced

2 cloves **garlic,** minced

½ cup (125 mL) diced **celery**

½ tsp (2 mL) **dried thyme**

1 small **eggplant,** cut in 1-inch (2.5 cm) cubes

1 can (28 oz/796 mL) **diced tomatoes**

¾ cup (175 mL) **dry white wine**

¼ cup (60 mL) **tomato paste**

1 tbsp (15 mL) **sweet paprika**

2 lb (1 kg) **mussels**

12 oz (375 g) **catfish fillets** or grouper fillets

2 tbsp (30 mL) chopped **fresh parsley**

In large skillet, heat oil over medium-high heat; brown sausages, in batches. Transfer to slow cooker.

Drain fat from pan. Fry onion, garlic, celery and thyme, stirring often, until softened, about 5 minutes. Add to slow cooker. Add eggplant, tomatoes, wine, tomato paste and paprika to slow cooker. Cover and cook on low until eggplant is tender, about 6 hours.

Meanwhile, scrub mussels; trim off any beards. Discard any that do not close when tapped. Cut catfish into 2-inch (5 cm) pieces. Nestle mussels and fish into liquid in slow cooker. Cover and cook on high until mussels open, about 20 minutes. Discard any that do not open. Sprinkle with parsley.

Makes 8 to 10 servings. PER EACH OF 10 SERVINGS: about 313 cal, 22 g pro, 20 g total fat (7 g sat. fat), 11 g carb, 2 g fibre, 63 mg chol, 781 mg sodium. % RDI: 5% calcium, 23% iron, 11% vit A, 27% vit C, 11% folate.

VARIATION

Stove Top Sausage and Seafood Ragout

• In large shallow Dutch oven, brown sausages as directed. Transfer to plate.

• Drain fat from pan; fry onion, garlic, celery and thyme as directed. Add wine; bring to boil, stirring and scraping up brown bits. Add eggplant, tomatoes, tomato paste and paprika; bring to boil. Return sausage to pan; cover and simmer, stirring occasionally, until eggplant is tender, about 40 minutes.

• Nestle mussels and fish into liquid; cover and cook, gently stirring once, until mussels open, about 10 minutes. Discard any that do not open. Sprinkle with parsley.

TIP

Cultivated mussels are so clean that all they usually need is a good rinse.

Slow Cooker Squash and Chickpea Curry

Cashew butter – or good old peanut butter – enriches this aromatic dish.

2 cups (500 mL) cubed peeled **butternut squash**

2 cups (500 mL) diced peeled **potato**

1 can (19 oz/540 mL) **chickpeas,** drained and rinsed

1 tbsp (15 mL) **vegetable oil**

1 **onion,** diced

2 cloves **garlic,** minced

1 tbsp (15 mL) minced **fresh ginger**

3 tbsp (45 mL) **mild curry paste**

1 can (400 mL) **light coconut milk**

1 cup (250 mL) **vegetable broth**

¼ cup (60 mL) **natural cashew butter** or peanut butter

¼ tsp (1 mL) **salt**

2 cups (500 mL) packed shredded **Swiss chard**

1 cup (250 mL) **frozen peas**

2 tbsp (30 mL) chopped **fresh cilantro**

In slow cooker, combine squash, potato and chickpeas.

In large skillet, heat oil over medium heat; fry onion, garlic and ginger, stirring occasionally, until onion is light golden, about 7 minutes. Add curry paste; cook, stirring, until fragrant, about 1 minute. Add to slow cooker.

Add coconut milk and broth to slow cooker; stir in cashew butter and salt. Cover and cook on low until vegetables are tender, 4 hours.

Stir in Swiss chard and peas. Cover and cook on high until Swiss chard wilts, about 15 minutes. Sprinkle with cilantro.

Makes 6 to 8 servings. PER EACH OF 8 SERVINGS: about 217 cal, 6 g pro, 8 g total fat (3 g sat. fat), 32 g carb, 5 g fibre, 0 mg chol, 543 mg sodium. % RDI: 4% calcium, 11% iron, 50% vit A, 23% vit C, 25% folate.

VARIATION
Stove Top Squash and Chickpea Curry

• In Dutch oven, fry onion, garlic and ginger as directed. Add curry paste; cook, stirring, until fragrant, about 1 minute.

• Add squash, potato and chickpeas; stir to coat. Add coconut milk, broth, cashew butter and salt; bring to boil. Cover and simmer, stirring twice, until vegetables are tender, about 30 minutes.

• Gently stir in Swiss chard and peas; cook, stirring, until Swiss chard wilts, about 5 minutes. Sprinkle with cilantro.

Slow Cooker Chicken and Sausage Gumbo

Okra may not be on your menu very often, but it's delightful in this classic thick Cajun soup.

2 tbsp (30 mL) **vegetable oil**

4 **boneless skinless chicken thighs,** cubed

4 **chorizo sausages** or mild Italian sausages, sliced

2 each **onions** and ribs **celery,** diced

1 **sweet red pepper,** diced

4 cloves **garlic,** minced

1 tsp (5 mL) each **sweet paprika** and **dried thyme**

2 **bay leaves**

¼ tsp (1 mL) each **salt** and **pepper**

½ cup (125 mL) **dry white wine** or sodium-reduced chicken broth

1 can (28 oz/796 mL) **diced tomatoes**

½ cup (125 mL) **sodium-reduced chicken broth**

3 tbsp (45 mL) **tomato paste**

1 pkg (250 g) **frozen okra,** thawed and sliced

¼ cup (60 mL) chopped **fresh parsley**

In large skillet, heat half of the oil over medium-high heat; brown chicken and sausages. Transfer to slow cooker.

Drain any fat from pan. Add remaining oil; fry onions, celery, red pepper, garlic, paprika, thyme, bay leaves, salt and pepper until light golden, about 8 minutes. Add to slow cooker.

Add wine to pan; bring to boil, scraping up any brown bits. Add to slow cooker. Add tomatoes, broth, tomato paste and ½ cup (125 mL) water; cover and cook on low until chicken is no longer pink inside but cubes are still whole, about 6 hours. Discard bay leaves.

Stir in okra and parsley; cover and cook on high for 15 minutes.

Makes 4 to 6 servings. PER EACH OF 6 SERVINGS: about 344 cal, 20 g pro, 22 g total fat (7 g sat. fat), 17 g carb, 4 g fibre, 67 mg chol, 869 mg sodium. % RDI: 10% calcium, 26% iron, 17% vit A, 103% vit C, 35% folate.

Slow Cooker Curried Chicken

Bone-in thighs are best for this aromatic dish because they have more flavour. In The Test Kitchen, we've found that chicken has a better texture if the skin stays on in the slow cooker. However, the flabby skin itself is not appealing, so we recommend removing it before serving. Serve with basmati rice and wafer-thin pappadams.

1 tbsp (15 mL) **vegetable oil**

12 **chicken thighs**

4 cups (1 L) thinly sliced **onions**

½ cup (125 mL) each **orange juice** and **sodium-reduced chicken broth**

2 tbsp (30 mL) **mild curry paste**

3 cloves **garlic,** minced

1 tbsp (15 mL) grated **fresh ginger**

3 tbsp (45 mL) **all-purpose flour**

TOPPING:

⅔ cup (150 mL) thinly sliced **red onion**

½ tsp (2 mL) **salt**

2 tbsp (30 mL) **lime juice** or lemon juice

¾ cup (175 mL) **plain yogurt**

2 tbsp (30 mL) chopped **fresh cilantro**

In Dutch oven, heat oil over medium-high heat; brown chicken. Transfer to slow cooker.

Drain fat from pan; fry onions, stirring occasionally, until almost softened, about 10 minutes; scrape over chicken.

Whisk together orange juice, broth, curry paste, garlic and ginger; pour into slow cooker. Cover and cook on low until juices run clear when chicken is pierced, 4 to 6 hours.

Scrape onions off chicken. Remove skin. With slotted spoon, transfer chicken to platter; cover and keep warm. Whisk flour with ¼ cup (60 mL) water; whisk into slow cooker. Cover and cook on high until thickened, about 15 minutes. Pour over chicken.

TOPPING: Meanwhile, sprinkle onion with salt; let stand for 15 minutes. Rinse in cold water; pat dry. In small bowl, toss onion with lime juice. Top each serving with yogurt then red onion mixture. Sprinkle with cilantro.

Makes 6 servings. PER SERVING: about 276 cal, 26 g pro, 12 g total fat (2 g sat. fat), 17 g carb, 2 g fibre, 98 mg chol, 321 mg sodium. % RDI: 8% calcium, 12% iron, 3% vit A, 25% vit C, 17% folate.

VARIATIONS

Small-Batch Curried Chicken

• Use 10-cup (2.5 L) slow cooker. Halve recipe; cook until juices run clear when chicken is pierced, about 4 hours. Makes 2 to 4 servings.

Stove Top Curried Chicken

• Use skinless chicken thighs. Fry onions as directed; transfer to bowl. Brown chicken; top with onions. Add broth mixture; cover and simmer until juices run clear when chicken is pierced, about 45 minutes.

• Transfer chicken to platter; keep warm. Reduce flour to 1 tbsp (15 mL) and whisk with 2 tbsp (30 mL) water; whisk into pan and bring to boil. Reduce heat and simmer until thickened, about 2 minutes. Pour over chicken. Prepare topping as directed.

Slow Cooker No-Fuss Goulash

While the goulash is thickening, there's enough time to cook egg noodles, the traditional partner for this saucy dish. We recommend using sweet Hungarian paprika.

2 **onions,** sliced
2 cloves **garlic,** minced
2 lb (1 kg) **stewing beef cubes**
½ cup (125 mL) **chili sauce**
2 tbsp (30 mL) packed **brown sugar**
2 tbsp (30 mL) **Worcestershire sauce**
1 tbsp (15 mL) **sweet paprika**
1 tsp (5 mL) **dried marjoram**
½ tsp (2 mL) each **dry mustard** and **salt**
¼ tsp (1 mL) **pepper**
3 tbsp (45 mL) **all-purpose flour**

Place onions and garlic in slow cooker. Trim and cut beef into 1-inch (2.5 cm) cubes; place on onions.

Combine 1 cup (250 mL) water, chili sauce, brown sugar, Worcestershire sauce, paprika, marjoram, mustard, salt and pepper; pour into slow cooker. Cover and cook on low until meat is tender, 8 to 10 hours.

Whisk flour with ¼ cup (60 mL) water; whisk into slow cooker. Cover and cook on high until thickened, 10 to 15 minutes.

Makes 4 servings. PER SERVING: about 480 cal, 54 g pro, 17 g total fat (6 g sat. fat), 27 g carb, 3 g fibre, 111 mg chol, 975 mg sodium. % RDI: 5% calcium, 44% iron, 13% vit A, 15% vit C, 15% folate.

FROM STOVE TOP OR OVEN TO SLOW COOKER

It's easy to adapt your favourite braising recipes for the slow cooker if you keep these basics in mind.

• Because root vegetables often take longer to cook than meat, cut them into pieces no larger than 1 inch (2.5 cm) and place them under meat or poultry, where it is hotter.

• Liquid doesn't evaporate from the slow cooker as in oven or stove-top braising. Most slow-cooker recipes require about half the liquid. Stir in thickening agents near the end.

• The flavour of dried herbs and spices dilutes in the slow cooker. Try increasing them by half or sprinkling with more at the end.

• Green peppers turn bitter when cooked for a long time, so add them near the end.

Slow Cooker Chicken Stock

The slow cooker makes fabulous stock – effortlessly.

2 lb (1 kg) **chicken backs, necks** and **wing tips**
2 **onions** (unpeeled), chopped
2 large ribs **celery** (with leaves), chopped
1 **carrot,** chopped
1 **leek** (optional), chopped
6 sprigs **fresh parsley**
2 sprigs **fresh thyme**
2 **bay leaves**
½ tsp (2 mL) **black peppercorns**

Place chicken in slow cooker. Add onions, celery, carrot, leek (if using), parsley, thyme, bay leaves and peppercorns. Pour in 8 cups (2 L) water. Cover and cook on low for 12 hours.

Discard chicken. Strain stock through cheesecloth-lined sieve into large bowl, pressing vegetables to extract liquid. Refrigerate until fat congeals on surface, about 8 hours. Lift off fat and discard. (*Make-ahead: Cover and refrigerate for up to 3 days or freeze for up to 1 month.*)

Makes 8 cups (2 L). PER 1 CUP (250 mL): about 39 cal, 5 g pro, 1 g total fat (trace sat. fat), 1 g carb, 0 g fibre, 1 mg chol, 32 mg sodium. % RDI: 1% calcium, 4% iron, 2% folate.

VARIATION
Stove Top Chicken Stock
•In stockpot, combine chicken, onions, celery, carrot, leek (if using), parsley, thyme, bay leaves and peppercorns. Pour in 14 cups (3.5 L) water; bring to boil. Reduce heat and simmer, skimming occasionally, for about 4 hours. Continue as directed after cooking.

Slow Cooker Smoked Turkey and Noodle Soup

If you can only find a large turkey leg, use 2 cups (500 mL) meat for this soup and the rest in pastas, salads or sandwiches.

1 **smoked turkey leg** (about 1 lb/500 g)
1½ cups (375 mL) each chopped **carrots** and **celery**
1 cup (250 mL) sliced **mushrooms**
1 **onion,** diced
2 sprigs **fresh parsley**
1 **bay leaf**
½ tsp (2 mL) each **dried thyme** and **pepper**
3 cups (750 mL) **sodium-reduced chicken broth**
1 **sweet red pepper,** diced
½ cup (125 mL) **frozen peas**
2 cups (500 mL) **small pasta,** cooked

Remove skin and meat from turkey leg. Reserve bone; discard skin. Cut meat into bite-size pieces; set aside in refrigerator.

In slow cooker, combine carrots, celery, mushrooms, onion, parsley, bay leaf, thyme and pepper. Add turkey bone, broth and 3 cups (750 mL) water. Cover and cook on low until vegetables are tender, about 6 hours.

Add red pepper, peas and turkey meat. Cover and cook on high until vegetables are tender-crisp, about 15 minutes. Discard turkey bone, bay leaf and parsley. Stir in pasta.

Makes 8 to 10 servings. PER EACH OF 10 SERVINGS: about 108 cal, 10 g pro, 2 g total fat (1 g sat. fat), 13 g carb, 2 g fibre, 23 mg chol, 266 mg sodium. % RDI: 3% calcium, 10% iron, 36% vit A, 37% vit C, 17% folate.

CHAPTER 8

Make It Tonight... and Freeze for Later

Saucy Barbecue Meatballs

Meatballs are basic – some might even call them humble. But they are transformed once they hit a flavourful sauce. Below is a fine barbecue sauce, but a favourite pasta sauce, curry sauce or sweet-and-sour sauce – or even store-bought barbecue sauce – give you lots of flavour options.

⅔ cup (150 mL) **fresh bread crumbs**

1 **egg**

1 clove **garlic,** minced

¼ cup (60 mL) chopped **fresh parsley**

2 tsp (10 mL) **Dijon mustard**

1 tsp (5 mL) **Worcestershire sauce**

½ tsp (2 mL) each **salt** and **pepper**

1 lb (500 g) **lean ground beef**

SAUCE:

1 tbsp (15 mL) **vegetable oil**

1 **onion,** finely chopped

1 clove **garlic,** minced

1 can (28 oz/796 mL) **ground tomatoes**

¼ cup (60 mL) packed **brown sugar**

¼ cup (60 mL) **cider vinegar**

1 tbsp (15 mL) **Dijon mustard**

1 tbsp (15 mL) **Worcestershire sauce**

Dash **hot pepper sauce**

In bowl, combine bread crumbs with ½ cup (125 mL) water; let stand until absorbed, about 5 minutes. Beat in egg, garlic, parsley, mustard, Worcestershire sauce, salt and pepper. Mix in beef; roll by rounded tablespoonfuls (15 mL) into balls.

Place, 1 inch (2.5 cm) apart, on foil-lined rimmed baking sheet; bake in 450°F (230°C) oven until no longer pink inside, 20 minutes.

SAUCE: Meanwhile, in large skillet, heat oil over medium heat; fry onion and garlic, stirring often, for 3 minutes. Add tomatoes, brown sugar, vinegar, mustard, Worcestershire sauce and hot pepper sauce; simmer, stirring occasionally, until slightly thickened, about 25 minutes.

Let cool for 30 minutes. Refrigerate, uncovered, in shallow container until cold. Cover and freeze for up to 1 month.

Let meatballs cool on sheet on rack. Refrigerate until chilled. Transfer to freezer bags; freeze in single layer until solid. Freeze for up to 1 month. Thaw meatballs and sauce in refrigerator.

In large skillet or saucepan, combine meatballs and sauce; simmer, turning meatballs occasionally, until sauce is thickened, about 20 minutes.

Makes 4 servings. PER SERVING: about 430 cal, 28 g pro, 18 g total fat (6 g sat. fat), 38 g carb, 5 g fibre, 110 mg chol, 605 mg sodium. % RDI: 12% calcium, 44% iron, 18% vit A, 38% vit C, 22% folate.

TONIGHT'S DINNER
Follow first 3 paragraphs as directed. Cook as directed in last paragraph.

Top and Bottom Crust Pizza

This double-crust pizza freezes well, so you don't have to wait for the delivery guy when you want a slice. You can wrap and freeze it whole or cut it into wedges and wrap each individually.

1 tbsp (15 mL) **vegetable oil**

1 **onion,** chopped

2 cloves **garlic,** minced

1 **sweet green pepper,** chopped

¼ tsp (1 mL) each **salt** and **pepper**

1 lb (500 g) **pizza dough**

2 **eggs**

1 cup (250 mL) shredded **mozzarella cheese**

1 cup (250 mL) shredded **Cheddar cheese**

6 oz (175 g) **salami,** ham or smoked turkey, diced

2 tbsp (30 mL) minced **fresh parsley**

1 **egg yolk**

In skillet, heat oil over medium heat; fry onion, garlic, green pepper, salt and pepper until softened, about 4 minutes. Let cool.

Meanwhile, on floured surface, roll out half of the dough into 10-inch (25 cm) circle. Place on greased pizza pan or rimless baking sheet. Set aside.

In bowl, whisk eggs; stir in mozzarella and Cheddar cheeses, salami, parsley and onion mixture. Spread over dough on pan, leaving 1-inch (2.5 cm) border around edge.

Roll out remaining dough into 10-inch (25 cm) circle. In bowl, whisk egg yolk with 1 tsp (5 mL) water; lightly brush some over border on bottom crust. Place top crust over filling; with fork, press edge to seal. Brush with remaining egg yolk mixture; cut 3 slits in top crust.

Bake in 375°F (190°C) oven until golden, about 45 minutes.

Let baked pizza cool for 30 minutes. Refrigerate until cold. Wrap whole pizza or individual wedges and overwrap with heavy-duty foil; freeze for up to 1 month. Thaw in refrigerator. Place on greased baking sheet; bake in 400°F (200°C) oven until crisp and hot, about 12 minutes.

Makes 6 to 8 servings. PER EACH OF 8 SERVINGS: about 353 cal, 16 g pro, 18 g total fat (8 g sat. fat), 31 g carb, 1 g fibre, 116 mg chol, 733 mg sodium. % RDI: 20% calcium, 16% iron, 12% vit A, 22% vit C, 16% folate.

TONIGHT'S DINNER

Follow first 5 paragraphs. Serve immediately.

Mini-Lasagnas

Because these individual lasagnas use light cheeses, they are lower in calories and fat than many store-bought versions. If you want to freeze one big pan rather than four individual ones, follow the instructions for Tonight's Dinner (below), increasing thawing time and upping baking time to 45 minutes.

12 oz (375 g) **lean ground beef**

1 tsp (5 mL) each **fennel seeds** and **dried oregano**

2 cups (500 mL) sliced **mushrooms**

1 **onion,** chopped

6 cloves **garlic,** minced

¾ tsp (4 mL) each **salt** and **pepper**

½ tsp (2 mL) **hot pepper flakes**

1 can (5½ oz/156 mL) **tomato paste**

1 can (19 oz/540 mL) **tomatoes**

6 **lasagna noodles**

2 cups (500 mL) **light ricotta cheese**

1 **egg,** lightly beaten

Pinch **nutmeg**

1 cup (250 mL) shredded **part-skim mozzarella cheese**

2 tbsp (30 mL) grated **Parmesan cheese**

1 tbsp (15 mL) chopped **fresh parsley**

In large skillet, sauté ground beef over medium-high heat until no longer pink, about 8 minutes; drain off fat. Crush fennel seeds and oregano. Add to pan along with mushrooms, onion, garlic, half each of the salt and pepper and the hot pepper flakes; sauté until onion is softened, about 5 minutes.

Add tomato paste and tomatoes, breaking up with potato masher and scraping up any brown bits. Bring to boil; reduce heat and simmer until sauce is thick enough to mound on spoon, about 15 minutes.

Meanwhile, in large pot of boiling salted water, cook lasagna noodles until tender but firm, about 7 minutes; drain and lay on damp tea towel. Using scissors, cut each in half crosswise.

In small bowl, combine ricotta cheese, egg, nutmeg and remaining salt and pepper.

Spread 1 tbsp (15 mL) sauce in each of 4 metal or foil 5¾- x 3¼-inch (625 mL) loaf pans. Lay 1 noodle half in each pan. Top each with scant ¼ cup (60 mL) of the sauce. Spread half of the ricotta cheese mixture over sauce; sprinkle with half of the mozzarella. Cover with second noodle half. Spread each with scant ¼ cup (60 mL) of the sauce, then remaining ricotta. Top with remaining noodles, sauce and mozzarella. Sprinkle with Parmesan and parsley. Refrigerate until cold. Cover with foil, overwrap with heavy-duty foil and freeze for up to 1 month. Thaw in refrigerator; remove heavy-duty foil.

Bake in 400°F (200°C) oven or toaster oven until cheese is bubbly and knife inserted in centre for 5 seconds feels hot, 30 minutes. Uncover and broil until golden, 3 minutes.

Makes 4 servings. PER SERVING: about 686 cal, 50 g pro, 30 g total fat (15 g sat. fat), 55 g carb, 6 g fibre, 150 mg chol, 1,191 mg sodium. % RDI: 63% calcium, 44% iron, 39% vit A, 70% vit C, 44% folate.

TONIGHT'S DINNER

Follow first 4 paragraphs. Spread 1 cup (250 mL) of the sauce in 8-inch (2 L) square baking dish. Top with 4 noodle halves, then 1 cup (250 mL) of the sauce, 1 cup (250 mL) of the ricotta mixture and ½ cup (125 mL) of the mozzarella. Repeat with noodles and sauce. Layer remaining ricotta mixture, noodles, sauce and mozzarella over top. Sprinkle with Parmesan and parsley. Bake as directed in last paragraph.

Vegetarian Tomato Sauce

This quick-cooking sauce makes 4 cups (1 L), which is perfect for 1 lb (500 g) of spaghetti. Double or triple it and make a freezerful.

2 tbsp (30 mL) **vegetable oil**
1 small **onion,** chopped
1 each **carrot** and rib **celery,** diced
1 **sweet green pepper,** diced
¾ tsp (4 mL) each **salt** and **dried basil**
Pinch **hot pepper flakes**
¼ cup (60 mL) **tomato paste**
1 can (28 oz/796 mL) **diced tomatoes**

In saucepan, heat oil over medium heat; fry onion, carrot, celery, green pepper, salt, basil and hot pepper flakes, stirring occasionally, until softened, about 8 minutes.

Add tomato paste and tomatoes; bring to boil. Reduce heat and simmer, uncovered, until thick enough to mound on spoon, about 30 minutes.

Let cool for 30 minutes. Refrigerate, uncovered, in airtight container until cold. Cover and refrigerate for up to 2 days or freeze for up to 2 months. Thaw in refrigerator. Reheat to serve with pasta (see Tonight's Dinner, below).

Makes 4 cups (1 L). PER ⅔ CUP (150 ML): about 91 cal, 2 g pro, 5 g total fat (trace sat. fat), 12 g carb, 2 g fibre, 0 mg chol, 506 mg sodium. % RDI: 5% calcium, 9% iron, 42% vit A, 63% vit C, 8% folate.

TONIGHT'S DINNER

Follow first 2 paragraphs. In large pot of boiling salted water, cook 1 lb (500 g) spaghetti until tender but firm, about 8 minutes. Drain and return to pot; add sauce and toss to coat. Makes 4 or 5 servings.

FREEZE!

CASEROLES
•Line baking dishes with heavy-duty foil before filling. Let casserole cool and chill completely before freezing. Once frozen, lift block out using foil as handles.
•Rewrap block tightly in plastic wrap or foil then overwrap in heavy-duty foil or place in freezer bag, pressing out air and sealing.
•Label and date the package for easy identification, and include heating directions.
•To use, unwrap and return frozen block to same baking dish. Cover and thaw in refrigerator for up to 48 hours, depending on density of food.

STEWS, CHILIS AND CURRIES
•Let cool for 30 minutes.
•Scoop into shallow airtight freezer containers and refrigerate, uncovered, until cold. Seal, label and date the container, then freeze. Include the reheating information, especially if someone else is going to reheat.
•Thaw in the refrigerator or microwave.

Hint of Jamaica Pork Stew

This saucy Jamaican-inspired dish is excellent with plain rice or Peas, Pepper and Rice (recipe, page 34). You can buy cubed pork shoulder in many grocery stores. Or buy pork shoulders when they're on special and trim, cube and freeze them in handy 1-lb (500 g) portions – perfect for this recipe.

3 **green onions**
¼ cup (60 mL) **all-purpose flour**
1 tsp (5 mL) **dried thyme**
½ tsp (2 mL) **ground allspice**
¼ tsp (1 mL) **cayenne pepper**
1 lb (500 g) **pork shoulder,** trimmed and cubed, or pork stewing cubes
3 tbsp (45 mL) **vegetable oil**
6 cloves **garlic,** minced
1 tbsp (15 mL) minced **fresh ginger**
2 cups (500 mL) **chicken broth**
2 tbsp (30 mL) **soy sauce**
1 tbsp (15 mL) packed **brown sugar**

Chop green onions, keeping white and green parts separate; set aside.

In plastic bag, combine flour, thyme, allspice and cayenne. Add pork and shake to coat, reserving remaining flour mixture.

In Dutch oven, heat 2 tbsp (30 mL) of the oil over medium heat; brown pork, in 2 batches, about 5 minutes. Remove to plate. Add remaining oil to pan; fry white parts of green onions, garlic and ginger until fragrant, about 2 minutes. Add reserved flour mixture; stir for 1 minute. Add broth and 1 cup (250 mL) water; bring to boil, scraping up brown bits.

Return pork and any accumulated juices to pan; stir in soy sauce and brown sugar. Reduce heat, cover and simmer, stirring occasionally, until pork is tender, about 45 minutes. Add green parts of green onions; simmer for 5 minutes.

Let cool for 30 minutes. Refrigerate, uncovered, until cold. Cover and refrigerate in airtight container for up to 2 days or freeze for up to 1 month. Thaw in refrigerator; reheat to serve.

Makes 4 servings. PER SERVING: about 337 cal, 27 g pro, 19 g total fat (4 g sat. fat), 14 g carb, 1 g fibre, 76 mg chol, 995 mg sodium. % RDI: 4% calcium, 20% iron, 1% vit A, 5% vit C, 10% folate.

TONIGHT'S DINNER
Follow first 4 paragraphs; serve immediately.

Pork Tenderloin with Lime-Beer Marinade

Marinated pork tenderloin is a handy item to keep in the freezer. With this recipe, you can grill one or both tenderloins, depending on the number of people you're serving.

½ cup (125 mL) **beer** or nonalcoholic beer
⅓ cup (75 mL) **lime juice**
2 cloves **garlic,** minced
2 tbsp (30 mL) minced **fresh parsley**
1 tsp (5 mL) **chili powder**
½ tsp (2 mL) **ground cumin**
¼ tsp (1 mL) **ground coriander**
¼ tsp (1 mL) each **salt** and **pepper**
2 **pork tenderloins** (about 12 oz/
   375 g each)

In large bowl, whisk together beer, lime juice, garlic, parsley, chili powder, cumin, coriander, salt and pepper. Add pork; turn to coat.

Transfer each tenderloin to large resealable plastic freezer bag; pour marinade over pork. Press out air and seal bags. Freeze for up to 1 month. Thaw in refrigerator.

Place pork on greased grill over medium high heat; brush with any remaining marinade. Close lid and grill, turning occasionally, until juices run clear when pork is pierced and just a hint of pink remains inside, about 18 minutes.

Transfer to cutting board; tent with foil and let stand for 5 minutes before slicing.

Makes 4 to 6 servings. PER EACH OF 6 SERVINGS: about 157 cal, 28 g pro, 3 g total fat (1 g sat. fat), 2 g carb, trace fibre, 61 mg chol, 154 mg sodium. % RDI: 1% calcium, 12% iron, 2% vit A, 5% vit C, 4% folate.

TONIGHT'S DINNER
Follow first paragraph. Cover and marinate in refrigerator for 4 hours. Grill and serve as directed in last 2 paragraphs.

EASY LEFTOVER SOLUTIONS

• **Hot barbecue sandwiches:** Shred beef or pork and heat in barbecue sauce to stack on a bun.

• **Meaty Caesar:** Top Caesar salad with sliced cooked chicken or ham.

• **Panini:** Layer cheese, sliced cooked meat or poultry, mustard and sun-dried tomatoes in panini buns then grill.

• **Ham, turkey or chicken sandwich filling:** Pulse cooked ham, turkey or chicken in food processor until chunky; combine with light mayonnaise, mustard, minced celery, green onion, and finely diced roasted red pepper or sun-dried tomatoes.

• **Pasta salad:** Combine cooked pasta, chopped vegetables, meat or poultry, cheese and favourite salad dressing.

• **Ham and eggs:** Cube cooked ham and add to scrambled eggs.

• **Meat or poultry and salad wraps:** Try sliced cooked meat or poultry, torn lettuce, halved cherry tomatoes, grated carrot, sliced radishes, croutons and a drizzle of dressing.

• **Subs:** Use thinly sliced cooked meat or poultry, torn lettuce, sliced tomatoes, peppers, onions, cheese and mayonnaise.

Chipotle Pork Burritos

Chipotles add just the right amount of smokiness to the well-spiced pork filling.

1½ lb (750 g) **lean ground pork**

4 tsp (20 mL) **vegetable oil**

1 large **onion,** finely diced

1 large **sweet green pepper,** diced

3 cloves **garlic,** minced

1½ tsp (7 mL) each **ground cumin**
   and **coriander**

½ tsp (2 mL) each **salt** and **pepper**

2 cups (500 mL) **mild salsa**

3 **canned chipotle peppers,** minced
   (or ¾ tsp/4 mL chipotle chili powder
   or hot pepper sauce)

½ cup (125 mL) chopped **fresh cilantro**
   or parsley

8 **large flour tortillas**

2 cups (500 mL) shredded **Cheddar cheese**

1 **tomato,** diced

In large nonstick skillet, fry pork over medium heat, breaking up with wooden spoon, until no longer pink, about 8 minutes. Drain off fat; remove pork and set aside.

Add oil to pan; fry onion, green pepper, garlic, cumin, coriander, salt and pepper, stirring occasionally, until onion is softened, about 5 minutes. Return pork to pan. Add salsa and chipotle peppers; simmer, stirring, until thickened, about 4 minutes. Stir in cilantro; let cool.

Spoon one-eighth of the pork mixture down centre of each tortilla; sprinkle evenly with cheese and tomato. Fold bottom, then sides over filling; roll up.

Refrigerate until cold. Wrap individually in plastic wrap; overwrap with foil and freeze for up to 1 month.

Remove foil and plastic wrap; rewrap burritos in foil. Bake from frozen on baking sheet in 400°F (200°C) oven, turning over once, until hot, about 45 minutes.

Makes 8 servings. PER SERVING: about 427 cal, 28 g pro, 20 g total fat (9 g sat. fat), 36 g carb, 3 g fibre, 75 mg chol, 1,178 mg sodium, 626 mg potassium. % RDI: 22% calcium, 23% iron, 15% vit A, 32% vit C, 34% folate.

TONIGHT'S DINNER

Follow first 3 paragraphs. Bake on rimmed baking sheet in 400°F (200°C) oven until golden, about 7 minutes.

Pea Soup with Ham

This chunky soup simmers away when you're relaxing or puttering around the house. If you cook a bone-in ham, save the bone to use in this soup instead of the smoked hock. Another substitute for the hock is smoked turkey leg or thigh.

1 **smoked ham hock** (about 1 lb/500 g)
1 tbsp (15 mL) **vegetable oil**
1 large **onion,** finely chopped
2 each **carrots** and ribs **celery,**
  finely chopped
2 cloves **garlic,** minced
2 **bay leaves**
½ tsp (2 mL) each **salt** and **pepper**
4 cups (1 L) **sodium-reduced chicken broth**
2 cups (500 mL) **dried green split peas**
  or dried yellow split peas
GARNISH:
3 **green onions,** thinly sliced

Using paring knife, pare off and discard skin from ham hock. Trim off and discard fat.

In Dutch oven, heat oil over medium-low heat; fry onion, carrots, celery, garlic, bay leaves, salt, pepper and ham hock, stirring occasionally, until vegetables are softened, about 5 minutes.

Add broth, peas and 2 cups (500 mL) water; bring to boil over medium-high heat, skimming off any foam. Cover and simmer over medium-low heat until peas break down and meat is tender enough to fall off hock, about 1¾ hours.

Remove ham hock; pull off and shred meat. Set aside. Discard bone and bay leaves. In blender, purée half of the soup; return to pot with meat.

Let cool for 30 minutes. Transfer to airtight container and refrigerate, uncovered, until cold. Cover and refrigerate for up to 2 days or freeze for up to 1 month. Thaw in refrigerator. Reheat.

GARNISH: Ladle soup into bowls; top with green onions.

Makes 8 servings. PER SERVING: about 232 cal, 16 g pro, 3 g total fat (trace sat. fat), 36 g carb, 5 g fibre, 6 mg chol, 594 mg sodium. % RDI: 4% calcium, 17% iron, 46% vit A, 8% vit C, 49% folate.

TONIGHT'S DINNER

Follow first 4 paragraphs. Garnish with green onions and serve immediately.

SOUP TOPPERS

Dress up a simple bowl of soup with a sprinkle or drizzle of drama. These give homemade flair to high-quality store-bought soups, too.
• Diced avocado, tomato or roasted red pepper
• Chopped sweet red or green pepper
• Chopped fresh herbs
• Sliced green onions or chives
• Crushed tortilla or other chips
• Popcorn
• Croutons
• Shredded cheese
• Crumbled feta cheese
• Yogurt
• Sour cream
• Pesto
• Balsamic vinegar
• Salsa
• Paprika
• Hot pepper flakes

TIP
After removing the ham hock, you can also use an immersion blender to blend soup to a half-chunky stage while still in the pot.

Spaghetti Bake

This recipe is as good as a lasagna but a lot easier. When you're freezing a pasta dish, undercook the noodles slightly so that they won't end up mushy, and use plenty of sauce since some will be absorbed by the thawing noodles. If you're feeding a crowd, make the whole recipe in a 13- x 9-inch (3 L) baking dish.

2 lb (1 kg) **mild Italian sausage,** casings removed
2 **onions,** chopped
6 cloves **garlic,** minced
1 tbsp (15 mL) **dried basil**
4 cups (1 L) sliced **mushrooms**
2 cans (each 28 oz/796 mL) **tomatoes,** chopped
1 can (5½ oz/156 mL) **tomato paste**
½ tsp (2 mL) **pepper**
6 cups (1.5 L) chopped **fresh spinach**
12 oz (375 g) **spaghetti**
TOPPING:
2 tbsp (30 mL) **butter**
⅓ cup (75 mL) **all-purpose flour**
3 cups (750 mL) **milk**
¾ cup (175 mL) shredded **mozzarella cheese**
¼ tsp (1 mL) each **salt** and **pepper**
½ cup (125 mL) grated **Parmesan cheese**

In Dutch oven, sauté sausage over medium-high heat, breaking up with fork, until no longer pink, about 5 minutes. Drain off fat. Add onions, garlic and basil; fry, stirring, for 5 minutes. Add mushrooms; cook until liquid is evaporated, about 5 minutes.

Add tomatoes, tomato paste and pepper; bring to boil. Reduce heat and simmer until most of the liquid is evaporated, about 15 minutes. Add spinach.

TOPPING: Meanwhile, in saucepan, melt butter over medium heat; whisk in flour and cook, whisking, for 1 minute. Whisk in milk; cook, whisking constantly, until thickened, 12 to 15 minutes. Add mozzarella, salt and pepper.

Meanwhile, in large pot of boiling salted water, cook spaghetti until tender but firm, about 5 minutes. Drain and add to meat sauce; toss to coat. Spread in 2 greased 8-inch (2 L) square baking dishes; pour topping over spaghetti mixture. Sprinkle with Parmesan.

Let cool for 30 minutes. Cover and refrigerate for up to 2 days or overwrap with heavy-duty foil and freeze for up to 1 month. Thaw in refrigerator for 48 hours.

Bake in 375°F (190°C) oven until bubbly and golden, 50 to 60 minutes.

Makes 8 servings. PER SERVING: about 614 cal, 35 g pro, 27 g total fat (12 g sat. fat), 61 g carb, 7 g fibre, 77 mg chol, 1,501 mg sodium. % RDI: 38% calcium, 46% iron, 61% vit A, 62% vit C, 70% folate.

TONIGHT'S DINNER

Follow first 4 paragraphs. Bake as directed in last paragraph, decreasing baking time to 30 to 40 minutes.

TIPS
• **When making casseroles such as Spaghetti Bake, make extra and fill pans that suit your family members' schedules. Chill, wrap in heavy-duty foil and freeze. Thaw in refrigerator. Reheat in oven or toaster oven.**
• **Trade cooking chores with a friend – plan to each make double batches of a favourite recipe, then share your wares. You'll both end up with two meals ready for busy nights.**

Chicken with Mango Chutney and Brie

Just because it's from your freezer doesn't mean it has to be an everyday meal. This chicken is fancy enough to make you feel like you're dining out.

4 **boneless skinless chicken breasts**
¼ cup (60 mL) **Dijon mustard**
2 cloves **garlic,** minced
¼ tsp (1 mL) **dried thyme**
¼ tsp (1 mL) each **salt** and **pepper**
⅔ cup (150 mL) **dry bread crumbs**
2 tbsp (30 mL) **vegetable oil** (approx)
¼ cup (60 mL) **mango chutney,** warmed
4 oz (125 g) **Brie cheese,** sliced

Place chicken between waxed paper; pound to scant ½-inch (1 cm) thickness. In bowl, mix mustard, garlic, thyme, salt and pepper; brush all over chicken. In shallow dish, press chicken into bread crumbs, turning to coat.

In large skillet, heat oil over medium heat; fry chicken, adding more oil if necessary, until golden and no longer pink inside, about 4 minutes per side.

Transfer chicken to four 8- x 5-inch (20 x 12 cm) baking dishes or foil pans, or 13- x 9-inch (3 L) baking dish. Drizzle with mango chutney; top with Brie.

Cover and refrigerate for up to 24 hours or overwrap with heavy-duty foil and freeze for up to 1 month. Thaw in refrigerator and remove heavy-duty foil.

Bake in 400°F (200°C) oven until hot and cheese is bubbly, about 18 minutes.

Makes 4 servings. PER SERVING: about 416 cal, 39 g pro, 19 g total fat (6 g sat. fat), 22 g carb, 1 g fibre, 106 mg chol, 929 mg sodium. % RDI: 11% calcium, 15% iron, 7% vit A, 3% vit C, 11% folate.

TONIGHT'S DINNER
Follow first 3 paragraphs, using 13- x 9-inch (3 L) baking dish. Cover with foil; bake in 400°F (200°C) oven until hot, about 15 minutes.

THE WELL-STOCKED KITCHEN
ESSENTIAL FRIDGE AND FREEZER STAPLES
• **Dairy:** Milk, butter, plain yogurt (regular and/ or Balkan-style), large eggs, Parmesan cheese (a fresh wedge is tastiest), old Cheddar cheese, mozzarella cheese and other favourites
• **Fruit:** Fresh (oranges, lemons, apples and anything else you like) and frozen (blueberries, strawberries, raspberries and/or a mixed-berry blend)
• **Vegetables:** Fresh (carrots and celery) and frozen (peas, corn, edamame or your favourites)
• **Light mayonnaise**
• **Pasta:** Frozen tortellini and gnocchi

Burnished Hoisin Chicken

When you're freezing the chicken in the marinade, you can divide it into individual servings so you only have to thaw as many portions as you need at one time.

½ cup (125 mL) **hoisin sauce**

2 tbsp (30 mL) **soy sauce**

2 tbsp (30 mL) **unseasoned rice vinegar**

2 cloves **garlic,** minced

1 tbsp (15 mL) minced **fresh ginger**
  (or 1 tsp/5 mL ground ginger)

¼ tsp (1 mL) each **salt** and **pepper**

2 lb (1 kg) **chicken pieces**

GARNISH:

1 tbsp (15 mL) **sesame seeds,** toasted

In large bowl, whisk together hoisin sauce, soy sauce, rice vinegar, garlic, ginger, salt and pepper. Add chicken; turn to coat. Cover and marinate in refrigerator for 4 hours.

Divide chicken between 2 large resealable plastic freezer bags; pour marinade over chicken. Press out air and seal bags. Freeze for up to 1 month. Thaw in refrigerator.

Heat 1 burner of 2-burner barbecue, or 2 outside burners of 3-burner barbecue, to medium. Brush grill over unlit burner with oil. Place chicken, bone side down, on greased grill. Close lid and grill until bottom is marked, 25 minutes. Turn and grill until juices run clear when chicken is pierced, 20 minutes. Move any pieces that need more crisping or colouring over direct medium heat. Close lid and grill until golden brown, 5 minutes. (Or place chicken, bone side down, in large roasting pan; brush with any remaining marinade. Roast in 425°F/220°C oven until golden, crisp and juices run clear when chicken is pierced, 30 minutes.)

GARNISH: Sprinkle with sesame seeds.

Makes 4 servings. PER SERVING (WITH SKIN): about 366 cal, 32 g pro, 19 g total fat (5 g sat. fat), 17 g carb, 1 g fibre, 111 mg chol, 1,272 mg sodium. % RDI: 2% calcium, 12% iron, 5% vit A, 2% vit C, 8% folate.

TONIGHT'S DINNER

Follow first paragraph. Cook and garnish as directed in last paragraph.

TIP

Toast sesame seeds in a small dry skillet over medium heat. Swirl the pan often to brown the seeds evenly.

Greek-Style Macaroni and Cheese

Rich with spinach and feta, this macaroni and cheese is a dressed-up version of the ultimate comfort food.

2 bags (8 oz/250 g each) **fresh spinach**

⅓ cup (75 mL) **butter,** melted

1 **onion,** finely chopped

2 cloves **garlic,** minced

2 tbsp (30 mL) chopped **fresh oregano** (or 2 tsp/10 mL dried)

¼ cup (60 mL) **all-purpose flour**

4 tsp (20 mL) **Dijon mustard**

4 cups (1 L) **milk**

¼ tsp (1 mL) each **salt** and **pepper**

¼ tsp (1 mL) **nutmeg**

2 cups (500 mL) shredded **provolone cheese**

1¼ cups (300 mL) crumbled **feta cheese**

1 cup (250 mL) grated **Romano cheese**

4 cups (1 L) **Scoobi doo pasta**

1½ cups (375 mL) **fresh bread crumbs**

In large pot, cook spinach with 2 tbsp (30 mL) water over medium-high heat, stirring once, until wilted, about 3 minutes. Transfer to sieve; press out moisture. Chop and set aside.

In saucepan, melt ¼ cup (60 mL) of the butter over medium heat; cook onion, stirring often, until softened, about 5 minutes. Add garlic and oregano; cook for 1 minute. Sprinkle with flour; cook, stirring, for 1 minute. Stir in mustard.

Whisk in milk until smooth; bring to simmer and cook, stirring frequently, until thickened, about 6 minutes. Sprinkle with salt, pepper and nutmeg. Stir in provolone, ⅓ cup (75 mL) of the feta and the Romano cheese until smooth.

Meanwhile, in large pot of boiling salted water, cook pasta until still slightly firm in centre, 6 minutes. Drain, reserving ½ cup (125 mL) of the cooking liquid. Return pasta to pot. Stir in milk mixture, liquid and spinach. Transfer to greased 13- x 9-inch (3 L) baking dish.

Combine bread crumbs with remaining butter; sprinkle over pasta. Sprinkle with remaining feta cheese.

Let cool. Wrap dish in plastic wrap, then overwrap in heavy-duty foil. Freeze for up to 1 month. Let thaw in refrigerator overnight.

Remove plastic wrap and foil. Bake on baking sheet in 375°F (190°C) oven until bubbly and golden, 40 to 45 minutes.

Makes 6 to 8 servings. PER EACH OF 8 SERVINGS: about 548 cal, 27 g pro, 28 g total fat (17 g sat. fat), 49 g carb, 3 g fibre, 84 mg chol, 1,056 mg sodium, 583 mg potassium. % RDI: 65% calcium, 33% iron, 81% vit A, 10% vit C, 89% folate.

TONIGHT'S DINNER

Follow first 5 paragraphs. Bake on baking sheet in 375°F (190°C) oven until bubbly and golden, 30 to 35 minutes.

Big-Batch Bean and Lentil Soup

This substantial three-bean soup takes away the cold-weather chill. It's also great to come home to if you make the slow-cooker version. Though the recipe calls for three different kinds of beans, you can use all one kind – whatever type your family likes.

2 tsp (10 mL) **vegetable oil**

2 **onions,** chopped

2 cloves **garlic,** minced

1 tbsp (15 mL) **chili powder**

1 can (28 oz/796 mL) **tomatoes**

6 cups (1.5 L) **vegetable broth** or
　chicken broth

2 cups (500 mL) **water**

¾ cup (175 mL) **red lentils**

1 each can (19 oz/540 mL) **chickpeas,
　red kidney beans** and **black beans,**
　drained and rinsed

GARNISH:

1 tbsp (15 mL) chopped **fresh cilantro**

1 tsp (5 mL) **lemon juice**

½ tsp (2 mL) **salt**

¼ tsp (1 mL) **pepper**

In large saucepan or Dutch oven, heat oil over medium heat; fry onions, garlic and chili powder, stirring occasionally, until softened, about 5 minutes.

Add tomatoes, mashing with potato masher. Add broth, water and lentils; bring to boil. Reduce heat to medium-low; simmer until lentils are softened, about 20 minutes.

Add chickpeas, red kidney beans and black beans; cook until heated through, about 15 minutes.

Let cool for 30 minutes. Refrigerate in shallow airtight containers for up to 2 days or freeze for up to 2 weeks. Reheat.

GARNISH: Stir in cilantro, lemon juice, salt and pepper.

Makes 16 cups (4 L), or 10 servings. PER SERVING: about 246 cal, 14 g pro, 4 g total fat (trace sat. fat), 41 g carb, 10 g fibre, 0 mg chol, 922 mg sodium. % RDI: 6% calcium, 26% iron, 5% vit A, 18% vit C, 80% folate.

TONIGHT'S DINNER

Follow first 3 paragraphs. Stir in cilantro, lemon juice, salt and pepper. Serve immediately.

VARIATION

Slow Cooker Big-Batch Bean and Lentil Soup

• Omit oil. To 16-cup (4 L) slow cooker, add onions, garlic, chili powder, tomatoes, broth, water and lentils. Cook on low for 8 hours. Add chickpeas, red kidney beans and black beans; cook on high until heated through, 30 minutes. Stir in cilantro, lemon juice, salt and pepper.

Make It Tonight... on the Barbecue

Rib Eye Steaks

Rib eyes are one of the top butcher-recommended steaks. Garlic and a touch of heat via the hot pepper flakes are all a good steak needs.

2 **rib eye grilling steaks,** each 1 inch (2.5 cm) thick (about 1 lb/500 g)

MARINADE:

¼ cup (60 mL) **extra-virgin olive oil**

3 cloves **garlic,** minced

½ tsp (2 mL) each **salt** and **pepper**

¼ tsp (1 mL) **hot pepper flakes**

MARINADE: In baking dish, combine oil, garlic, salt, pepper and hot pepper flakes. Add steaks; turn and rub marinade all over. Cover and refrigerate for 4 hours. (*Make-ahead: Refrigerate for up to 24 hours.*)

Place steaks on greased grill over medium-high heat; brush with remaining marinade. Close lid and grill, turning once, until medium-rare, about 10 minutes. Transfer to cutting board; tent with foil and let stand for 5 minutes. Cut each in half to serve.

Makes 4 servings. PER SERVING: about 319 cal, 24 g pro, 24 g total fat (6 g sat. fat), 1 g carb, trace fibre, 57 mg chol, 337 mg sodium. % RDI: 1% calcium, 14% iron, 1% vit A, 2% vit C, 3% folate.

BBQ GOLDEN RULES

THE CLEAN PLATE RULE

Place cooked meat, poultry or seafood on a clean plate – not the one you used to carry the raw food to the barbecue.

THE MARINADE RULE

Throw away marinade left over from flavouring and tenderizing raw meat, poultry or seafood. Never brush it over cooked food.

THE BRUSH RULE

When brushing a glaze or sauce over cooked food just before taking it off the grill, be sure to use a clean brush.

Ginger Beef Kabobs

You can buy grilling steaks and marinating steaks. The grilling ones are the most tender and marbled, so when we marinate or rub them with seasoning, it's strictly for flavour. Marinating steaks need – you guessed it – marinating to improve tenderness.

3 cloves **garlic,** minced
2 tbsp (30 mL) grated **fresh ginger**
   (or 1 tsp/5 mL ground ginger)
2 tbsp (30 mL) **soy sauce**
2 tsp (10 mL) **unseasoned rice vinegar**
   or cider vinegar
2 tsp (10 mL) **sesame oil**
½ tsp (2 mL) **granulated sugar**
1 **top sirloin grilling steak** or sirloin tip
   marinating steak, 1 inch (2.5 cm) thick
   (1 lb/500 g)
10 **green onions,** white parts only

In large bowl, whisk together garlic, ginger, soy sauce, vinegar, sesame oil and sugar. Trim fat from steak; cut into 1-inch (2.5 cm) cubes. Add to marinade and turn to coat; let stand for 10 minutes. (*Make-ahead: Cover and refrigerate for up to 8 hours.*)

Meanwhile, cut onions into 2-inch (5 cm) lengths. Alternately thread onions and beef onto metal or soaked wooden skewers; brush with remaining marinade. Place on greased grill over medium-high heat; close lid and grill, turning 3 times, until browned but still pink inside, about 10 minutes.

Makes 4 servings. PER SERVING: about 179 cal, 22 g pro, 7 g total fat (2 g sat. fat), 6 g carb, 1 g fibre, 51 mg chol, 563 mg sodium. % RDI: 4% calcium, 21% iron, 1% vit A, 8% vit C, 11% folate.

Tangy Snow Peas

1 tbsp (15 mL) **white vinegar**
1 tsp (5 mL) **granulated sugar**
1 tsp (5 mL) **sesame oil**
1 clove **garlic,** minced
¼ tsp (1 mL) **hot pepper sauce**
2 cups (500 mL) steamed **snow peas**

In bowl, whisk together vinegar, sugar, sesame oil, garlic and hot pepper sauce. Add snow peas; toss to coat.

Makes 4 servings. PER SERVING: about 49 cal, 3 g pro, 1 g total fat (trace sat. fat), 7 g carb, 2 g fibre, 0 mg chol, 5 mg sodium. % RDI: 3% calcium, 11% iron, 1% vit A, 65% vit C, 10% folate.

Best-Ever Burgers

This basic beef patty formula is the foundation for many burgers to come. With a slice of cheese melted over the top and crowned with a curl of crisp bacon, it's a banquet burger. Add herbs or a dollop of pesto or finish with a barbecue sauce glaze and you have a whole new burger. Or switch the beef for lean ground pork, lamb, chicken or turkey – the formula works just as well.

1 **egg**
2 tbsp (30 mL) **water**
¼ cup (60 mL) **dry bread crumbs**
1 small **onion,** grated
1 tbsp (15 mL) **Dijon mustard**
1 clove **garlic,** minced
½ tsp (2 mL) each **salt** and **pepper**
1 lb (500 g) **lean ground beef**

In large bowl, beat egg with water; stir in bread crumbs, onion, mustard, garlic, salt and pepper. Add beef; mix just until combined. Shape into four ¾-inch (2 cm) thick patties. *(Make-ahead: Layer between waxed paper in airtight container and refrigerate for up to 24 hours or freeze for up to 1 month. Thaw in refrigerator.)*

Place on greased grill over medium heat; close lid and grill, turning once, until digital thermometer inserted sideways into centre registers 160°F (71°C), about 15 minutes.

Makes 4 servings. PER SERVING: about 280 cal, 25 g pro, 15 g total fat (6 g sat. fat), 7 g carb, 1 g fibre, 110 mg chol, 468 mg sodium. % RDI: 4% calcium, 19% iron, 2% vit A, 2% vit C, 10% folate.

IT'S BETTER WITH BUTTERS

A thin slice of one of these deliciously seasoned butters melting over a roasted fish fillet, burger, pork chop or flank steak pays big flavour dividends. Try a dab on a bowl full of vegetables – brussels sprouts, broccoli and corn are especially divine. Or spread on bread or melt over a baked potato.

• In bowl, soften ¼ cup (60 mL) butter at room temperature, then mash in these seasonings.

• <u>Mixed Peppercorn:</u> 2 tsp (10 mL) coarsely ground mixed peppercorns. Doll up with 1 tsp (5 mL) chopped fresh thyme or generous pinch dried thyme, if desired.

• <u>Horseradish Mustard:</u> 2 tbsp (30 mL) minced fresh parsley; 1 tbsp (15 mL) prepared horseradish; 2 tsp (10 mL) grainy Dijon mustard; and generous pinch pepper.

• <u>Mixed Herb:</u> 2 tbsp (30 mL) minced fresh chives or green part of green onion; 2 tsp (10 mL) each Dijon mustard and minced fresh tarragon; and generous pinch pepper.

• <u>Ginger Green Onion:</u> 2 tbsp (30 mL) minced green onion; 1 tsp (5 mL) grated fresh ginger or ½ tsp (2 mL) ground ginger; ½ tsp (2 mL) Worcestershire sauce; and generous pinch pepper.

• <u>Lemon Dill:</u> 1 tbsp (15 mL) minced fresh dill; 2 tsp (10 mL) grated lemon zest; 1 tsp (5 mL) lemon juice; and generous pinch pepper.

Grilled Liver with Mushrooms and Onions

Calves' liver is mild and tender, but a bit on the pricey side. If using less-expensive beef liver, soak in milk in the fridge for up to 4 hours before using. Drain, pat dry and cook.

3 cups (750 mL) sliced **mushrooms**
1 **onion,** sliced
3 tbsp (45 mL) **balsamic vinegar**
1 tbsp (15 mL) **butter,** melted
½ tsp (2 mL) crumbled **dried sage**
½ tsp (2 mL) each **salt** and **pepper**
1 tsp (5 mL) **Dijon mustard**
1 lb (500 g) thinly sliced calves' or beef **liver**
1 tbsp (15 mL) **vegetable oil**
2 tbsp (30 mL) minced **fresh parsley**

Cut 16-inch (40 cm) length of heavy-duty foil; arrange mushrooms and onion on one half. Drizzle with 1 tbsp (15 mL) of the vinegar and butter; sprinkle with sage and half each of the salt and pepper. Fold foil over vegetables; fold in sides and seal. Place on grill over medium heat; close lid and cook, turning once, until tender, about 10 minutes.

Meanwhile, in small bowl, whisk remaining vinegar with mustard; set aside. Pat liver dry; brush with oil and sprinkle with remaining salt and pepper. Add to greased grill; close lid and grill for 2 minutes. Turn and brush with half of the vinegar mixture; close lid and grill for 2 minutes. Turn and brush with remaining vinegar mixture; close lid and grill until glazed, browned on both sides and still slightly pink inside, about 1 minute. Serve with mushrooms and onions. Sprinkle with parsley.

Makes 4 servings. PER SERVING: about 252 cal, 24 g pro, 11 g total fat (4 g sat. fat), 14 g carb, 1 g fibre, 410 mg chol, 418 mg sodium. % RDI: 2% calcium, 62% iron, 897% vit A, 40% vit C, 89% folate.

Beef Koftas with Minted Yogurt

A change of shape, seasonings and condiments and you have a brand-new take on the humble burger.

1 cup (250 mL) lightly packed **fresh parsley leaves**
3 **green onions,** coarsely chopped
2 tsp (10 mL) **dried mint**
½ tsp (2 mL) each **ground cumin, sweet paprika** and **salt**
¼ tsp (1 mL) **pepper**
1 **egg**
1 lb (500 g) **lean ground beef**
½ cup (125 mL) **plain yogurt**
2 tbsp (30 mL) minced **fresh parsley**
4 **whole wheat pitas**

In food processor, purée parsley leaves, green onions, half of the mint, the cumin, paprika, salt and pepper. Transfer to large bowl; beat in egg. Mix in beef and 2 tbsp (30 mL) water.

Shape beef mixture by heaping 2 tbsp (30 mL) into small sausage shapes; thread each lengthwise onto metal or soaked wooden skewer.

Place skewers on greased grill over medium heat; close lid and grill, turning once, until no longer pink inside and digital thermometer inserted into several koftas registers 160°F (71°C), about 12 minutes. (Or broil, turning once, for 7 minutes.)

Meanwhile, combine yogurt with remaining mint and minced parsley. Grill or broil pitas, turning once, until hot and lightly crisped, about 4 minutes; cut each into quarters. Serve koftas with pita quarters and yogurt.

Makes 4 servings. PER SERVING: about 393 cal, 31 g pro, 14 g total fat (5 g sat. fat), 37 g carb, 5 g fibre, 109 mg chol, 712 mg sodium. % RDI: 10% calcium, 41% iron, 14% vit A, 42% vit C, 36% folate.

Grilled Sausage Spiedini

Spiedini are Italian brochettes threaded with chunks of baguette and other tasty things, such as sausage and onion. Serve with mustard and grilled peppers drizzled lightly with balsamic vinegar.

4 **Italian sausages** (about 1 lb/500 g)
2 tbsp (30 mL) **extra-virgin olive oil**
1 clove **garlic,** minced
Pinch each **salt** and **pepper**
1 **baguette** (8 inches/20 cm), cut in 1-inch (2.5 cm) cubes
Half **red onion,** cut in 1-inch (2.5 cm) cubes

Prick sausages with fork. Place on microwaveable plate; cover and microwave at high until no longer pink, about 5 minutes. (*Make-ahead: Refrigerate until cold; wrap and refrigerate for up to 24 hours.*) Cut into 1½-inch (4 cm) pieces.

Meanwhile, in bowl, whisk together oil, garlic, salt and pepper. Alternately thread sausage, bread cubes and onion onto metal or soaked wooden skewers; brush bread with oil mixture.

Place skewers on greased grill over medium heat; close lid and grill, turning 3 times, until crisped, browned and onion is tender, about 10 minutes.

Makes 4 servings. PER SERVING: about 354 cal, 19 g pro, 23 g total fat (7 g sat. fat), 17 g carb, 1 g fibre, 48 mg chol, 854 mg sodium. % RDI: 4% calcium, 14% iron, 5% vit C, 11% folate.

Ginger Pork Sandwiches

Start with one pork tenderloin and finish with a casual supper for four.

2 tbsp (30 mL) **sesame oil**
½ tsp (2 mL) **ground ginger**
½ tsp (2 mL) each **salt** and **pepper**
1 **pork tenderloin** (12 oz/375 g)
½ cup (125 mL) **light mayonnaise**
2 **green onions,** thinly sliced
1 tsp (5 mL) **unseasoned rice vinegar**
4 **kaiser rolls,** halved
8 **lettuce leaves**
8 thin slices **tomato**

In shallow dish, combine oil, ginger and half each of the salt and pepper; add pork and roll to coat all over. Place on greased grill over medium-high heat; close lid and grill, turning once, until juices run clear when pork is pierced and just a hint of pink remains inside, about 18 minutes. Transfer to cutting board and tent with foil; let stand for 5 minutes before slicing.

Meanwhile, in bowl, mix together mayonnaise, green onions, vinegar and remaining salt and pepper; spread on cut sides of rolls. Sandwich pork, lettuce and tomato in rolls.

Makes 4 servings. PER SERVING: about 457 cal, 27 g pro, 21 g total fat (4 g sat. fat), 38 g carb, 2 g fibre, 55 mg chol, 888 mg sodium. % RDI: 8% calcium, 26% iron, 6% vit A, 18% vit C, 38% folate.

Lemon Dill Salmon Skewers

A grilled lemon wedge adds a classy restaurant touch to salmon. Just brush thick wedges with oil and grill alongside the salmon. The hot juice literally bursts out of them!

4 **skinless centre-cut salmon fillets** (about 6 oz/175 g each)
3 tbsp (45 mL) chopped **fresh dill**
2 tbsp (30 mL) **extra-virgin olive oil**
½ tsp (2 mL) grated **lemon zest**
2 tbsp (30 mL) **lemon juice**
½ tsp (2 mL) **salt**
¼ tsp (1 mL) **pepper**
Dash **hot pepper sauce**
1 **lemon,** cut in 8 wedges

Cut salmon into 1½-inch (4 cm) cubes to make 24 pieces.

In large glass bowl, mix together dill, oil, lemon zest and juice, salt, pepper and hot pepper sauce. Add salmon cubes and toss to coat; let stand for 10 minutes.

Beginning and ending with lemon wedge, thread salmon loosely onto 4 metal or soaked wooden skewers, reserving marinade. Place on greased grill over medium heat; brush with remaining marinade. Close lid and grill, turning twice, until fish flakes easily when tested, about 10 minutes.

Makes 4 servings. PER SERVING: about 338 cal, 29 g pro, 23 g total fat (4 g sat. fat), 2 g carb, trace fibre, 84 mg chol, 368 mg sodium. % RDI: 2% calcium, 4% iron, 2% vit A, 23% vit C, 21% folate

Two-Bean Packet

8 oz (250 g) each **green** and **yellow beans,** trimmed
1 tbsp (15 mL) **butter** or extra-virgin olive oil
Pinch each **salt** and **pepper**

Arrange green and yellow beans on large piece of heavy-duty foil. Dot with butter; sprinkle with salt and pepper. Fold up sides and seal to form packet. Place on grill over medium heat; close lid and cook until tender-crisp, about 20 minutes.

Makes 4 servings. PER SERVING: about 106 cal, 5 g pro, 3 g total fat (2 g sat. fat), 15 g carb, 6 g fibre, 9 mg chol, 32 mg sodium. % RDI: 4% calcium, 10% iron, 6% vit A, 8% vit C, 24% folate.

TIP
Make life easier at the grocery store by using 1 lb (500 g) of all one colour bean – choose whatever looks freshest.

Grilled Pork Chops and Apple Rings

There is no better way to cook pork chops than on a grill or grill pan. The fat crisps and, as long as you don't grill it past the hint-of-pink-inside stage, the meat is totally toothsome.

4 **pork loin centre chops** (1¼ lb/625 g)
½ tsp (2 mL) **salt**
¼ tsp (1 mL) **ground cumin**
¼ tsp (1 mL) **ground ginger**
¼ tsp (1 mL) **cinnamon**
Pinch **cayenne pepper**
2 **Golden Delicious apples**
2 tsp (10 mL) **maple syrup** or liquid honey

Trim fat from pork chops; slash edges at ½-inch (1 cm) intervals to prevent curling. In small bowl, combine salt, cumin, ginger, cinnamon and cayenne pepper; rub on both sides of chops.

Place on greased grill or in grill pan over medium-high heat; close lid for barbecue and grill, turning once, until juices run clear when pork is pierced and just a hint of pink remains inside, 8 to 10 minutes.

Meanwhile, cut apples into ½-inch (1 cm) thick rings. Add to grill with pork chops; grill, turning once, until grill-marked and tender, about 4 minutes. Brush with maple syrup. Arrange apples and pork chops on platter.

Makes 4 servings. PER SERVING: about 198 cal, 21 g pro, 7 g total fat (3 g sat. fat), 13 g carb, 2 g fibre, 58 mg chol, 336 mg sodium. % RDI: 3% calcium, 8% iron, 7% vit C, 2% folate.

Corn and Zucchini Sauté

1 tbsp (15 mL) **vegetable oil**
3 **green onions,** sliced
1 **zucchini,** halved lengthwise and sliced
½ tsp (2 mL) **dried oregano**
¼ tsp (1 mL) each **salt** and **pepper**
2 cups (500 mL) **frozen corn kernels**

In large skillet, heat oil over medium heat; fry green onions until softened, about 3 minutes.

Add zucchini, oregano, salt and pepper. Fry, stirring occasionally, until zucchini is tender-crisp, about 3 minutes. Stir in corn; fry until hot, about 3 minutes.

Makes 4 servings. PER SERVING: about 104 cal, 3 g pro, 4 g total fat (trace sat. fat), 18 g carb, 2 g fibre, 0 mg chol, 150 mg sodium. % RDI: 2% calcium, 5% iron, 3% vit A, 10% vit C, 16% folate.

Barbecued Chicken Pizzas

You need already-grilled chicken for these personal pizzas, but it's a snap to prepare. Brush or spritz 3 boneless skinless chicken breasts lightly with oil and sprinkle with salt and pepper. Place on greased grill over medium-high heat; close lid and grill until no longer pink inside, about 12 minutes.

3 grilled **boneless skinless chicken breasts**
1 lb (500 g) **pizza dough**
⅓ cup (75 mL) **barbecue sauce**
2 cups (500 mL) shredded **Monterey Jack cheese**
1 **sweet green pepper,** cut in rings
½ tsp (2 mL) **hot pepper flakes**
½ tsp (2 mL) **dried oregano**

Cut chicken crosswise into slices; set aside.

On lightly floured surface, divide dough into quarters; shape each into disc. Roll out each into 8-inch (20 cm) oval. Place on greased grill over medium heat; close lid and grill, turning once, until crisp, about 7 minutes. Remove from grill.

Brush with half of the barbecue sauce. Sprinkle evenly with half of the cheese. Arrange chicken over top; drizzle with remaining barbecue sauce. Add green pepper; sprinkle with remaining cheese, hot pepper flakes and oregano.

Return to grill; close lid and grill until cheese is melted and bubbly and crust is golden, about 10 minutes.

Makes 4 servings. PER SERVING: about 649 cal, 46 g pro, 24 g total fat (13 g sat. fat), 60 g carb, 3 g fibre, 114 mg chol, 1,070 mg sodium. % RDI: 43% calcium, 27% iron, 19% vit A, 38% vit C, 25% folate.

TIP
You can vary the toppings to include a mix of sliced peppers and thinly sliced red onion, jalapeño pepper and Cheddar cheese.

VARIATION
Baked Chicken Pizzas
•Instead of grilling, bake pizzas on bottom rack of 500°F (260°C) oven for 12 minutes.

NEVER ORDER PIZZA AGAIN

Believe it or not, it takes less time to make a pizza from scratch than it does to wait for the delivery guy. Here's how.

•**Stock Up.** Freeze prepared pizza bases, pita breads or tortillas and stockpile jars of pizza or pasta sauce. Keep some stretchy cheese, such as mozzarella or provolone – already shredded if you like – on hand in the fridge. When you shop, fill your cart with favourite toppings: pepperoni; smoked or cured sausage; ham or smoked turkey; olives; onions; peppers (raw or roasted); mushrooms; pesto; anchovies; or sliced pineapple. Don't forget leftover or ready-made grilled or roasted vegetables.

•**Measure Out.** For each 12-inch (30 cm) pizza (enough for 2 adults), you need about ¾ cup (175 mL) pizza or pasta sauce, 2 cups (500 mL) shredded cheese and 2 cups (500 mL) toppings.

•**Build.** Place base on pizza pan or baking sheet; spread with sauce. Sprinkle with half of the cheese, all of the toppings, then the rest of the cheese.

•**Bake.** On bottom rack of 500°F (260°C) oven until base is crisp and cheese is bubbly, about 12 minutes.

Green Onion Pork Burgers

Serve these Chinese-inspired burgers topped with Napa Slaw (recipe, right) on sesame buns.

1 **egg**
1 cup (250 mL) finely chopped
   green onions
⅓ cup (75 mL) **dry bread crumbs**
1 **green hot pepper,** seeded and minced
   (optional)
1 clove **garlic,** minced
1 tbsp (15 mL) **soy sauce**
1 tbsp (15 mL) **fish sauce** or soy sauce
1 tbsp (15 mL) **Chinese rice wine** or dry
   sherry (or 1 tsp/5 mL balsamic vinegar)
2 tsp (10 mL) grated **fresh ginger**
2 tsp (10 mL) **sesame oil**
½ tsp (2 mL) **white pepper**
¼ tsp (1 mL) **hot pepper sauce**
1 lb (500 g) **lean ground pork**

In large bowl, whisk together egg, onions, bread crumbs, hot pepper (if using), garlic, soy sauce, fish sauce, wine, ginger, sesame oil, white pepper and hot pepper sauce; mix in pork. Shape into four ¾-inch (2 cm) thick patties.

Grill on greased grill over medium heat, turning once, until no longer pink inside or digital thermometer inserted sideways registers 160°F (71°C), about 15 minutes.

Makes 4 burgers. PER BURGER: about 309 cal, 25 g pro, 18 g total fat (6 g sat. fat), 10 g carb, 1 g fibre, 116 mg chol, 763 mg sodium. % RDI: 6% calcium, 16% iron, 6% vit A, 15% vit C, 13% folate.

Napa Slaw

2 tbsp (30 mL) **unseasoned rice vinegar**
2 tsp (10 mL) **granulated sugar**
1 tsp (5 mL) **sesame oil**
½ tsp (2 mL) **salt**
Pinch **hot pepper flakes**
3 cups (750 mL) shredded **napa cabbage**
1 small **carrot,** shredded
½ cup (125 mL) thinly sliced **sweet**
   red pepper

In large bowl, whisk together vinegar, sugar, sesame oil, salt and hot pepper flakes. Add cabbage, carrot and red pepper; toss to coat. Let stand for 15 minutes before serving.

Makes 1½ cups (375 mL), or 4 servings. PER SERVING: about 38 cal, 1 g pro, 1 g total fat (trace sat. fat), 7 g carb, 1 g fibre, 0 mg chol, 297 mg sodium. % RDI: 4% calcium, 2% iron, 53% vit A, 87% vit C, 23% folate.

Chicken Pita Skewers

Small chunks of chicken need less marinating time than whole breasts or thighs.

2 tbsp (30 mL) **lemon juice**

2 tbsp (30 mL) **extra-virgin olive oil**

2 cloves **garlic,** minced

¼ tsp (1 mL) **ground allspice**

¼ tsp (1 mL) each **salt** and **pepper**

2 large **boneless skinless chicken breasts**
  (1 lb/500 g total)

4 **Greek-style (pocketless) pitas**

1 cup (250 mL) shredded **romaine lettuce**

1 small **tomato,** diced

GARLIC MAYONNAISE:

½ cup (125 mL) **light mayonnaise**

1 clove **garlic,** minced

2 tbsp (30 mL) **lemon juice**

1 tbsp (15 mL) minced **fresh parsley**

Dash **hot pepper sauce**

In large bowl, combine lemon juice, oil, garlic, allspice, salt and pepper. Cut chicken into 1½-inch (4 cm) cubes; add to bowl and toss to coat. Cover and refrigerate for 1 hour. (*Make-ahead: Refrigerate for up to 4 hours.*)

GARLIC MAYONNAISE: Meanwhile, in bowl, whisk together mayonnaise, garlic, lemon juice, parsley and hot pepper sauce. (*Make-ahead: Cover and refrigerate for up to 24 hours.*)

Thread chicken onto metal or soaked wooden skewers. Place on greased grill over medium-high heat; brush with any remaining marinade. Close lid and grill, turning once, until no longer pink inside, about 12 minutes.

Toast pitas on grill, turning once, until light golden, 3 minutes. Spread Garlic Mayonnaise over half of each pita. Push chicken off skewers onto pitas. Top with lettuce and tomato; fold pita over. Wrap end in waxed paper to secure.

Makes 4 servings. PER SERVING: about 455 cal, 32 g pro, 18 g total fat (3 g sat. fat), 39 g carb, 2 g fibre, 76 mg chol, 749 mg sodium. % RDI: 7% calcium, 18% iron, 6% vit A, 22% vit C, 31% folate.

STANDBY MARINADES

Marinate chewier cuts of beef, lean pork, chicken thighs or legs, or tofu in these marinades. There's enough of each for about 1½ lb (750 g). Always marinate in the refrigerator and only for up to 24 hours – no longer.

RED WINE MARINADE

• **Combine ¼ cup (60 mL) red wine; 2 tbsp (30 mL) olive oil; 1 tbsp (15 mL) each herbes de Provence and wine vinegar; 2 cloves garlic, minced; 1 shallot or small onion, finely diced; and ¼ tsp (1 mL) each salt and pepper. Makes about ½ cup (125 mL).**

SUBSTITUTION

No red wine? Use white wine, or 3 tbsp (45 mL) broth and 1 tbsp (15 mL) wine vinegar.

TASTE OF THAILAND MARINADE

• **Combine ¼ cup (60 mL) minced fresh cilantro; 3 tbsp (45 mL) water; 2 tbsp (30 mL) each vegetable oil and lime juice; 1 tbsp (15 mL) fish sauce or soy sauce; 2 cloves garlic, minced; 1 green onion, minced; 1 tsp (5 mL) granulated sugar; and generous splash hot pepper sauce. Makes about ¾ cup (175 mL).**

Grilled Chicken Salad

This light but filling salad is perfect anytime.

4 small **boneless skinless chicken breasts** (1 lb/500 g total)

8 oz (250 g) **green beans,** trimmed

2 large **tomatoes,** cut in 8 wedges each

4 cups (1 L) torn **Boston lettuce** or Bibb lettuce

⅓ cup (75 mL) pitted **black olives**

DRESSING:

¼ cup (60 mL) **extra-virgin olive oil**

2 tbsp (30 mL) **white wine vinegar**

2 tsp (10 mL) **lemon juice**

1 tsp (5 mL) **granulated sugar**

½ tsp (2 mL) **herbes de Provence** or dried thyme

½ tsp (2 mL) **sweet paprika**

¼ tsp (1 mL) each **salt** and **pepper**

DRESSING: In jar, shake together oil, vinegar, lemon juice, sugar, herbes de Provence, paprika, salt and pepper. Pour 3 tbsp (45 mL) into bowl; add chicken and turn to coat. Let stand for 10 minutes. (*Make-ahead: Cover and refrigerate for up to 8 hours.*)

Place chicken on greased grill over medium-high heat; close lid and grill, turning once, until no longer pink inside, about 12 minutes. Slice thinly.

Meanwhile, in pan of boiling salted water, cover and blanch beans until tender-crisp, about 2 minutes. Drain; chill in cold water. Drain well.

In large bowl, toss together beans, tomatoes, lettuce, olives and remaining dressing; divide among plates. Arrange chicken alongside.

Makes 4 servings. PER SERVING: about 301 cal, 28 g pro, 17 g total fat (3 g sat. fat), 11 g carb, 3 g fibre, 67 mg chol, 425 mg sodium. % RDI: 6% calcium, 16% iron, 15% vit A, 37% vit C, 32% folate.

Grilled Turkey Breast

Oil, salt and pepper are the essentials, but add crumbled dried sage and Dijon mustard to the oil if you like.

1½ lb (750 g) **boneless turkey breast**

2 tsp (10 mL) **extra-virgin olive oil**

Pinch each **salt** and **pepper**

Brush turkey with oil; sprinkle with salt and pepper. Place on greased grill over medium heat; close lid and grill, turning twice, until juices run clear when turkey is pierced, about 40 minutes. Let stand for 10 minutes; slice. (*Make-ahead: Wrap and refrigerate for up to 24 hours.*)

Makes 6 servings. PER SERVING (WITHOUT SKIN): about 136 cal, 25 g pro, 4 g total fat (1 g sat. fat), 0 g carb, 0 g fibre, 54 mg chol, 50 mg sodium. % RDI: 1% calcium, 8% iron, 2% folate.

TIP

Because tomatoes are soft, they are rarely sold fully ripe. So buy tomatoes a few days ahead of making Grilled Chicken Salad and let them ripen at room temperature. You can speed up the process by enclosing them in a paper bag with an apple or a banana. Works every time, thanks to the ethylene gas these fruits emit.

Tofu Skewers with Jerk Barbecue Sauce and Grilled Coleslaw

Tofu is best when it takes on strong flavours, such as the ones in this Jamaican-style sauce.

1 pkg (454 g) firm or extra-firm **tofu**

2 cloves **garlic,** finely minced

2 tbsp (30 mL) **sodium-reduced soy sauce**

1 tbsp (15 mL) **vegetable oil**

1 each **sweet red, orange** and **yellow pepper**

6 **green onions** (white parts only)

JERK BARBECUE SAUCE:

1 cup (250 mL) **bottled strained tomatoes** (passata)

2 tbsp (30 mL) **fancy molasses**

1 to 2 tbsp (15 to 30 mL) **prepared jerk sauce**

2 tsp (10 mL) **malt vinegar**

¼ tsp (1 mL) **dried thyme**

GRILLED COLESLAW:

1 small **cabbage,** cut in sixths

Half **red onion,** cut in 3 pieces

1 large **carrot,** grated

2 tbsp (30 mL) **mayonnaise**

2 tbsp (30 mL) **malt vinegar** or cider vinegar

¼ tsp (1 mL) **celery seed**

¼ tsp (1 mL) each **salt** and **pepper**

JERK BARBECUE SAUCE: In pan, bring tomatoes, molasses, jerk sauce, vinegar and thyme to boil. Reduce heat and simmer until reduced to ½ cup (125 mL), 10 to 15 minutes. Set aside.

Meanwhile, cut tofu into 24 cubes. In bowl, toss together tofu, garlic, soy sauce and oil; let stand for 10 minutes.

Cut each red, orange and yellow pepper into 24 pieces; cut each onion in half. Thread vegetables and tofu alternately onto soaked wooden skewers; brush with barbecue sauce.

Place on greased grill over medium-high heat; close lid and cook, turning and brushing with barbecue sauce, until vegetables are tender and slightly browned.

GRILLED COLESLAW: Meanwhile, grill cabbage and onion over medium heat until outer layers start to soften, about 10 minutes. Thinly slice.

In bowl, toss together cabbage, onion, carrot, mayonnaise, vinegar, celery seed, salt and pepper. Serve with tofu skewers.

Makes 4 to 6 servings. PER EACH OF 6 SERVINGS: about 201 cal, 9 g pro, 10 g total fat (2 g sat. fat), 23 g carb, 4 g fibre, 2 mg chol, 639 mg sodium, 575 mg potassium. % RDI: 22% calcium, 24% iron, 31% vit A, 197% vit C, 28% folate.

Grilled Peanut Tofu Salad

This dish entertains your mouth! It's crunchy, crisp, fresh, soft and nicely coated with peanut sauce.

⅓ cup (75 mL) **natural peanut butter**
¼ cup (60 mL) **lime juice**
2 cloves **garlic,** minced
2 tbsp (30 mL) each **liquid honey** and **soy sauce**
½ tsp (2 mL) each **salt** and **pepper**
1 pkg (454 g) **firm tofu**
1 tbsp (15 mL) **vegetable oil**
8 cups (2 L) torn **leaf lettuce**
2 cups (500 mL) shredded **carrots**
1 cup (250 mL) **bean sprouts**
2 **green onions,** thinly sliced
¼ cup (60 mL) chopped **roasted peanuts**

In bowl, whisk together peanut butter, lime juice, garlic, 2 tbsp (30 mL) hot water, honey, soy sauce and half each of the salt and pepper.

Cut tofu horizontally into 4 slices; pat dry. Brush with oil; sprinkle with remaining salt and pepper. Place on greased grill over medium-high heat; close lid and grill, turning once, until grill-marked, about 10 minutes. Cut each into quarters.

Arrange lettuce on 4 plates. Top each with 4 pieces tofu, carrots, then bean sprouts. Drizzle with dressing; sprinkle with green onions and chopped peanuts.

Makes 4 servings. PER SERVING: about 386 cal, 21 g pro, 24 g total fat (3 g sat. fat), 32 g carb, 7 g fibre, 0 mg chol, 844 mg sodium. % RDI: 30% calcium, 36% iron, 177% vit A, 58% vit C, 63% folate.

GREAT GLAZES

Instead of store-bought barbecue sauce, try out this pair of glazes when grilling or roasting chops, pork tenderloins, salmon fillets, chicken pieces, burgers or steaks. Just remember to apply the glaze in the last few minutes of grilling or roasting so the sweetness in the sauce doesn't burn. Each glaze makes enough for about 1½ lb (750 g).

BALSAMIC HONEY GLAZE

• In saucepan, bring 1¼ cups (300 mL) balsamic vinegar and ½ cup (125 mL) liquid honey to boil over medium-high heat. Boil until reduced to ¾ cup (175 mL), about 15 minutes. Mix 1 tsp (5 mL) cornstarch with 1 tbsp (15 mL) cold water; stir into glaze and boil until thickened, about 1 minute. Let cool. Makes about ¾ cup (175 mL).

BOURBON MUSTARD GLAZE

• In saucepan, bring ⅔ cup (150 mL) orange juice; ¼ cup (60 mL) strained apricot jam; and dash hot pepper sauce to boil over medium-high heat. Boil until reduced to ⅔ cup (150 mL), about 5 minutes. In small bowl, stir together 3 tbsp (45 mL) bourbon or rye whisky; 1 tbsp (15 mL) each grainy mustard and water; and 2 tsp (10 mL) cornstarch. Stir into glaze and boil until thickened, about 2 minutes. Let cool. Makes about ¾ cup (175 mL).

CHAPTER 10

Make It Tonight... for Company

Goat Cheese–Stuffed Chicken Breasts

Your guests will never suspect that this fancy-looking chicken is a cinch to whip up.

6 oz (175 g) **goat cheese**
2 cloves **garlic,** minced
1 **green onion,** minced
1 tsp (5 mL) **dried thyme**
½ tsp (2 mL) **dried marjoram**
Pinch **cayenne pepper**
4 **boneless skinless chicken breasts**
2 tbsp (30 mL) **extra-virgin olive oil**
½ tsp (2 mL) each **ground cumin** and
    sweet paprika
¼ tsp (1 mL) each **salt** and **pepper**

In small bowl, combine goat cheese, garlic, green onion, thyme, marjoram and cayenne until smooth; set aside.

Trim any fat from chicken. With knife held horizontally and starting at thinner side, cut chicken in half almost but not all the way through; open like book. Spread 1 side of each with one-quarter of the cheese mixture. Fold uncovered side over; secure edge with small skewer or toothpicks.

In bowl, whisk together oil, cumin, paprika, salt and pepper; brush all over chicken.

Place on greased grill over medium-high heat; close lid and grill, turning once, until golden brown and chicken is no longer pink inside, about 16 minutes.

Makes 4 servings. PER SERVING: about 327 cal, 39 g pro, 18 g total fat (8 g sat. fat), 2 g carb, trace fibre, 98 mg chol, 370 mg sodium. % RDI: 7% calcium, 15% iron, 15% vit A, 2% vit C, 5% folate.

COMPANY ON A WEEKNIGHT? ARE YOU CRAZY?

Not at all – the trick is planning. First, keep it simple: choose a make-ahead, freeze-ahead, barbecue or slow cooker entrée. Then do the following to make it a nice, relaxing evening.

• <u>Serve a dish you're comfortable making.</u> It's fine to use your recipes over and over. Who knows? You could become famous for your roasted salmon or cranberry-glazed pork chops.

• <u>Prep early.</u> Shop ahead of time, and wash and trim vegetables and salad ingredients.

• <u>Serve a starter.</u> Soup or salad are both good. While guests are enjoying them, the main course and sides can simmer, grill or roast away.

• <u>Enlist helpers.</u> Get the rest of the household to set the table and deal with beverages, ice and glasses before dinner. One guest or family member can serve during dinner. Nobody to help? Set up the night before or take guests up on their offer to help. This is not an admission of incompetence – it's a sign of hospitality.

• <u>Preheat plates, bowls and platters.</u> Warm plates and bowls in microwave on high for about 3 minutes with a bowl containing 1 cup (250 mL) water. The boiling water warms everything nicely. Warm platters in an oven that's been heated and turned off.

• <u>Make dessert ahead.</u> Or serve fresh fruit with a rich sauce. See page 213 for inspiration.

• <u>Enjoy your company.</u> People want to visit and talk, not enjoy a flawless performance.

• <u>Wash up tomorrow.</u> Stack dishes neatly and save them for the night after. Hit the hay – you've earned it!

Smoked Trout Spread

Whole grain crackers and rye flatbreads are particularly well suited to the Nordic flavour of this dip.

10 oz (300 g) skinless boneless **smoked trout**
4 oz (125 g) **light cream cheese,** softened
3 tbsp (45 mL) **light mayonnaise**
1 tbsp (15 mL) **prepared horseradish**
2 tsp (10 mL) **lemon juice**
Pinch each **salt** and **cayenne pepper**
¼ cup (60 mL) minced **green onions**

In food processor, whirl together trout, cream cheese, mayonnaise, horseradish, lemon juice, salt and cayenne pepper until smooth. Add all but 2 tsp (10 mL) of the green onions; pulse just until blended. *(Make-ahead: Refrigerate in airtight container for up to 2 days.)*

Scrape into serving dish; garnish with remaining green onions.

Makes 2½ cups (625 mL). PER 2 TBSP (30 mL): about 48 cal, 5 g pro, 3 g total fat (1 g sat. fat), 1 g carb, 0 g fibre, 16 mg chol, 344 mg sodium. % RDI: 1% calcium, 1% iron, 2% vit A, 2% vit C, 1% folate.

Herbed Feta Dip

Serve this creamy dip with an assortment of vegetables. It's especially popular for family entertaining occasions, as kids never seem to tire of vegetables and dip.

¾ cup (175 mL) finely crumbled **feta cheese**
½ cup (125 mL) each **light sour cream** and **light mayonnaise**
2 tbsp (30 mL) minced **fresh parsley**
1 tbsp (15 mL) minced **fresh oregano** (or ½ tsp/2 mL dried)
1 small clove **garlic,** minced
Dash **hot pepper sauce**

In bowl, mash together feta cheese, sour cream, mayonnaise, parsley, oregano, garlic and hot pepper sauce. Cover and refrigerate for 1 hour. *(Make-ahead: Refrigerate for up to 24 hours.)*

Makes 1½ cups (375 mL). PER 1 TBSP (15 mL): about 31 cal, 1 g pro, 3 g total fat (1 g sat. fat), 1 g carb, 0 g fibre, 6 mg chol, 84 mg sodium. % RDI: 3% calcium, 1% iron, 1% vit A, 1% folate.

TIP
If your crudité selection includes carrots, slice them on a slight diagonal for easy scooping.

Mussels in Fennel Tomato Sauce

A pot of mussels, a crusty baguette and a bottle of wine: the recipe for a fun, relaxed evening.

2 lb (1 kg) **mussels**
1 can (14 oz/398 mL) **tomatoes**
1 tbsp (15 mL) **extra-virgin olive oil**
1 each **onion** and rib **celery,** diced
2 cloves **garlic,** minced
Half bulb **fennel,** diced
1 tsp (5 mL) each **dried basil** and **oregano**
1 **bay leaf**
½ tsp (2 mL) **salt**
¼ tsp (1 mL) **pepper**
¼ cup (60 mL) **white wine** or sodium-reduced chicken broth
1 tbsp (15 mL) **tomato paste**
¼ cup (60 mL) chopped **fresh parsley**

Scrub mussels, removing any beards. Discard any that do not close when tapped. Reserving juice, drain and dice tomatoes. Set aside.

In Dutch oven or large saucepan, heat oil over medium heat; fry onion, celery, garlic, fennel, basil, oregano, bay leaf, salt and pepper, stirring occasionally, until onion is softened, 5 minutes.

Add tomatoes, reserved juice, wine and tomato paste; bring to boil. Reduce heat; simmer until reduced by half, about 5 minutes.

Add mussels; cover and steam over medium-high heat, stirring once, until mussels open, about 5 minutes. Discard bay leaf and any mussels that do not open. Stir in parsley.

Makes 4 servings. PER SERVING: about 141 cal, 10 g pro, 5 g total fat (1 g sat. fat), 14 g carb, 3 g fibre, 18 mg chol, 587 mg sodium. % RDI: 7% calcium, 26% iron, 12% vit A, 50% vit C, 23% folate.

Maple Soy–Glazed Salmon

A quick broil at the end gives this salmon a golden, glazed finish. This recipe multiplies easily for a party.

4 **salmon fillets** (about 6 oz/175 g each)
¼ cup (60 mL) **maple syrup**
2 tsp (10 mL) **sodium-reduced soy sauce**
2 tsp (10 mL) **lime juice**
1 **jalapeño pepper,** seeded and minced
1 small clove **garlic,** minced
Pinch **pepper**

Place salmon in shallow dish. In bowl, combine maple syrup, soy sauce, lime juice, jalapeño pepper, garlic and pepper; pour half over salmon and turn to coat. Cover and refrigerate for 30 minutes, turning once.

Place salmon on parchment paper– or foil-lined rimmed baking sheet. Roast in 450°F (230°C) oven, brushing halfway through with remaining marinade, until fish flakes easily when tested, about 10 minutes. Broil until glazed, about 3 minutes.

Makes 4 servings. PER SERVING: about 330 cal, 30 g pro, 17 g total fat (3 g sat. fat), 14 g carb, trace fibre, 84 mg chol, 172 mg sodium. % RDI: 3% calcium, 6% iron, 2% vit A, 12% vit C, 21% folate.

Mushroom Pork Medallions for Two

You can replace the pork tenderloin with 12 oz (375 g) boneless skinless chicken breast, cut crosswise into ½-inch (1 cm) thick slices.

1 **pork tenderloin** (about 12 oz/375 g)
¼ tsp (1 mL) each **salt** and **pepper**
1 tbsp (15 mL) **vegetable oil**
1 **onion,** sliced
2 cups (500 mL) button or quartered **mushrooms**
Half small **sweet red pepper,** sliced
3 cloves **garlic,** minced
1 tsp (5 mL) crumbled **dried sage**
1¼ cups (300 mL) **sodium-reduced chicken broth**
1 tbsp (15 mL) **all-purpose flour**
2 **green onions,** sliced

Slice pork into 8 equal rounds; sprinkle with half each of the salt and pepper.

In large skillet, heat oil over medium-high heat; brown pork, turning once, about 2 minutes. Transfer to plate.

Drain any fat from pan. Add onion, mushrooms, red pepper, garlic, sage and remaining salt and pepper; sauté until onion and mushrooms are golden, about 5 minutes.

Add broth and bring to boil; boil for 2 minutes. Whisk flour with 2 tbsp (30 mL) water; whisk into sauce. Return pork to pan; simmer until sauce is thickened, juices run clear when pork is pierced and just a hint of pink remains inside, about 4 minutes. Sprinkle with green onions.

Makes 2 or 3 servings. PER EACH OF 3 SERVINGS: about 234 cal, 30 g pro, 8 g total fat (1 g sat. fat), 10 g carb, 2 g fibre, 67 mg chol, 504 mg sodium. % RDI: 3% calcium, 19% iron, 8% vit A, 67% vit C, 14% folate.

LEFTOVER SAFETY

• Always refrigerate or freeze any leftovers within 2 hours of serving.
• Carve large cuts of meat into slices and store in serving-size packets.
• Cover and refrigerate cooked rice within 1 hour of cooking; keep leftover rice for no longer than 24 hours.
• Transfer large quantities of thick food, such as stew or chili, to several shallow uncovered containers for quicker cooling in the fridge.
• Label and date wrapped leftovers in your fridge and eat within 3 days.
• Check the refrigerator once a week and discard old leftovers.

Stuffed Pork Tenderloin

One average tenderloin serves two or three. Double this quick recipe for more guests and do the same for the potato salad. In cold weather, grill the tenderloin on an indoor grill or grill pan. Cover with a domed lid or upside-down foil roasting pan to simulate the barbecue.

1 **pork tenderloin** (about 12 oz/375 g)
2 tbsp (30 mL) grated **Parmesan cheese**
2 tbsp (30 mL) minced **fresh parsley**
¼ tsp (1 mL) each **salt** and **pepper**
⅓ cup (75 mL) minced drained **oil-packed sun-dried tomatoes**

Cut pork lengthwise almost but not all the way through; open like book. Sprinkle with Parmesan cheese, parsley, salt and pepper. Sprinkle sun-dried tomatoes down centre. Fold pork over filling; secure with toothpicks.

Place pork on greased grill over medium-high heat; close lid and grill, turning occasionally, until juices run clear when pork is pierced and just a hint of pink remains inside, about 18 minutes. Transfer to cutting board; tent with foil and let stand for 5 minutes. Remove toothpicks and slice.

Makes 2 or 3 servings. PER EACH OF 3 SERVINGS: about 190 cal, 30 g pro, 6 g total fat (2 g sat. fat), 3 g carb, 1 g fibre, 65 mg chol, 339 mg sodium. % RDI: 6% calcium, 14% iron, 4% vit A, 27% vit C, 5% folate.

Warm Potato Salad

4 **potatoes** (2 lb/1 kg), peeled (if desired) and cubed
¼ cup (60 mL) **extra-virgin olive oil**
2 tbsp (30 mL) **wine vinegar**
1 tbsp (15 mL) **Dijon mustard**
½ tsp (2 mL) **salt**
¼ tsp (1 mL) **pepper**
½ cup (125 mL) each diced **celery** and **sweet green pepper**
2 tbsp (30 mL) chopped **fresh basil** or parsley

In saucepan of boiling salted water, cover and cook potatoes until tender, about 10 minutes. Drain and transfer to bowl; let cool for 10 minutes.

Meanwhile, in small bowl, whisk together oil, vinegar, mustard, salt and pepper; pour over potatoes. Add celery, green pepper and basil. Toss together.

Makes 4 servings. PER SERVING: about 274 cal, 3 g pro, 14 g total fat (2 g sat. fat), 36 g carb, 3 g fibre, 0 mg chol, 750 mg sodium. % RDI: 3% calcium, 6% iron, 2% vit A, 50% vit C, 11% folate.

Gremolata Rack of Lamb

Frenched refers to the way meat is prepared: the end of each rib bone is scraped clean to within 1 inch (2.5 cm) of the eye of the raw meat. It's a restaurant preparation worth doing for guests at home. Frozen imported racks of lamb are often frenched.

2 **racks of lamb**, frenched
  (about 1¼ lb/625 g each)
¼ tsp (1 mL) each **salt** and **pepper**
GREMOLATA:
½ cup (125 mL) minced **fresh parsley**
2 tbsp (30 mL) **extra-virgin olive oil**
4 tsp (20 mL) grated **lemon zest**
½ tsp (2 mL) **ground coriander**
2 cloves **garlic,** minced
¼ tsp (1 mL) each **salt** and **pepper**

GREMOLATA: In bowl, mix parsley, oil, lemon zest, coriander, garlic, salt and pepper.

Trim any outside fat from lamb; sprinkle with salt and pepper. Press gremolata onto rounded side. Place, gremolata side up, in roasting pan. (*Make-ahead: Cover and refrigerate for up to 12 hours.*)

Roast in 450°F (230°C) oven for 10 minutes. Reduce heat to 325°F (160°C); roast until meat thermometer registers 145°F (63°C) for medium-rare, about 15 minutes longer. (Or grill over medium heat for 20 minutes.)

Transfer to cutting board and tent with foil; let stand for 5 minutes before carving between bones.

Makes 4 servings. PER SERVING: about 253 cal, 24 g pro, 16 g total fat (5 g sat. fat), 2 g carb, 1 g fibre, 89 mg chol, 337 mg sodium. % RDI: 3% calcium, 17% iron, 4% vit A, 20% vit C, 5% folate.

THE WELL-STOCKED KITCHEN
ESSENTIAL SPICES AND HERBS

• <u>**Solo spices:**</u> salt, peppercorns to grind (worth the effort), cinnamon, paprika, cumin, ginger, dry mustard, and hot pepper flakes or cayenne
• <u>**Spice combos:**</u> chili powder, curry powder, Montreal Steak Spice, Cajun seasoning, five-spice powder and zaatar
• <u>**Solo herbs:**</u> thyme, basil, oregano, sage, rosemary, dillweed, mint and bay leaves
• <u>**Herb combos:**</u> dried Italian herb seasoning and herbes de Provence
• <u>**Handy additions:**</u> ground nutmeg, coriander seeds, allspice, cloves and fennel seeds

<u>**HOW TO STORE**</u>
Keep herbs and spices in a cool, dark spot – near the stove is a definite no-no. Try a drawer; label the tops of the jars and arrange alphabetically. Use them lavishly and renew every six months.

<u>**HOW TO BUY**</u>
For dried herbs, buy leaves, not powdered. In season, use fresh herbs; usually about three times the amount of dried called for.

Asian-Seasoned Steak with Cucumber Radish Pickle

Even if a dish is for entertaining, you can still think healthy. Red meat is one of the best sources of iron.

3 tbsp (45 mL) each **oyster sauce** and **sodium-reduced soy sauce**

4 tsp (20 mL) minced **fresh ginger**

4 tsp (20 mL) **granulated sugar**

4 tsp (20 mL) **sesame oil**

½ tsp (2 mL) **hot pepper sauce**

4 cloves **garlic,** minced

1 **top sirloin grilling steak,** 1 inch (2.5 cm) thick (about 2 lb/1 kg)

2 tsp (10 mL) toasted **sesame seeds**

CUCUMBER RADISH PICKLE:

3 cups (750 mL) sliced **English cucumber**

2 cups (500 mL) thinly sliced **radishes**

1 tsp (5 mL) **salt**

2 tbsp (30 mL) **unseasoned rice vinegar** or white wine vinegar

1 tbsp (15 mL) **granulated sugar**

1 tsp (5 mL) **sesame oil**

¼ tsp (1 mL) **hot pepper sauce**

In shallow bowl, whisk together oyster sauce, soy sauce, ginger, sugar, sesame oil, hot pepper sauce and garlic. Reserve ⅓ cup (75 mL) to heat and serve with steak; add steak to remaining marinade, turning to coat. Cover and refrigerate for 4 hours. (*Make-ahead: Refrigerate for up to 24 hours.*)

CUCUMBER RADISH PICKLE: In colander, toss together cucumber, radishes and salt; let stand for 15 minutes. Shake off liquid and pat dry; place in bowl. Add vinegar, sugar, sesame oil and hot pepper sauce; toss to coat.

Place steak on greased grill or in greased grill pan; close lid for barbecue and grill over medium-high heat, turning once, until medium-rare, about 16 minutes, or until desired doneness. Transfer to cutting board and tent with foil; let stand for 5 minutes before slicing and arranging on platter.

Heat reserved marinade; drizzle over steak. Sprinkle with sesame seeds. Serve with Cucumber Radish Pickle.

Makes 6 to 8 servings. PER EACH OF 8 SERVINGS: about 193 cal, 22 g pro, 8 g total fat (2 g sat. fat), 8 g carb, 1 g fibre, 51 mg chol, 547 mg sodium. % RDI: 3% calcium, 19% iron, 1% vit A, 15% vit C, 10% folate.

Pecan-Crusted Chicken Cutlets

This is not a new recipe, but it's one that never fails to please guests. Other nuts, especially walnuts, are good for the crust, too.

¼ cup (60 mL) **all-purpose flour**

½ tsp (2 mL) each **salt** and **pepper**

1 **egg**

¼ cup (60 mL) **milk**

1¼ cups (300 mL) finely chopped **pecans** or walnuts

4 small **boneless skinless chicken breasts** (about 4 oz/125 g each)

2 tbsp (30 mL) **vegetable oil**

1¼ cups (300 mL) **sodium-reduced chicken broth**

2 tbsp (30 mL) **Dijon mustard**

2 tsp (10 mL) chopped **fresh parsley**

2 tsp (10 mL) **butter**

2 tsp (10 mL) **liquid honey**

In shallow bowl, whisk together flour and half each of the salt and pepper. In separate bowl, whisk egg with milk. Pour pecans into third bowl.

Slice chicken in half horizontally to make 8 cutlets; sprinkle with remaining salt and pepper. Dip cut side of chicken into flour mixture; dip into egg mixture then pecans. Set aside.

In large skillet, heat 1 tbsp (15 mL) of the oil over medium-low heat; fry chicken, pecan side down, in batches and adding more oil if necessary, until pecans begin to darken and crisp, about 2 minutes. Turn and fry until chicken is no longer pink inside, 4 minutes. Transfer to platter. Cover and keep warm.

Drain any fat from pan. Add broth and bring to boil, scraping up brown bits from bottom of pan. Boil until reduced to about ½ cup (125 mL), about 5 minutes. Whisk in mustard, parsley, butter and honey. Serve with chicken.

Makes 4 servings. PER SERVING: about 479 cal, 32 g pro, 33 g total fat (5 g sat. fat), 15 g carb, 3 g fibre, 121 mg chol, 715 mg sodium. % RDI: 6% calcium, 14% iron, 6% vit A, 2% vit C, 12% folate.

Turkey Scaloppine with Leafy Salad

Scaloppine made from turkey or chicken are always tender. The salad is a fresh twist and a crunchy contrast to the turkey's crisp coating.

2½ cups (625 mL) **dry bread crumbs**
⅓ cup (75 mL) grated **Parmesan cheese**
2 tbsp (30 mL) minced **fresh parsley**
2 tsp (10 mL) **dried thyme**
⅓ cup (75 mL) **10% cream** or milk
4 **turkey scaloppine** or chicken scaloppine (about 1 lb/500 g)
3 tbsp (45 mL) **vegetable oil**
4 cups (1 L) torn **mixed salad greens**
1 tbsp (15 mL) **extra-virgin olive oil**
2 tsp (10 mL) **lemon juice**
½ tsp (2 mL) each **salt** and **pepper**
Lemon wedges

In shallow dish, combine bread crumbs, cheese, parsley and thyme. Pour cream into second shallow dish. Dip scaloppine into cream, letting excess drip back into dish. Press into bread-crumb mixture, turning to coat both sides. Place on rimmed baking sheet.

In large skillet, heat 2 tbsp (30 mL) of the vegetable oil over medium-high heat; fry scaloppine, turning once, in batches and adding remaining vegetable oil as necessary, until golden, about 4 minutes.

Meanwhile, in large bowl, toss salad greens, oil, lemon juice, salt and pepper. Serve salad on scaloppine. Garnish with lemon wedges.

Makes 4 servings. PER SERVING: about 587 cal, 39 g pro, 24 g total fat (6 g sat. fat), 53 g carb, 3 g fibre, 71 mg chol, 1,123 mg sodium. % RDI: 32% calcium, 46% iron, 16% vit A, 23% vit C, 34% folate.

TIP

If thin scaloppine are unavailable, make your own with thick turkey cutlets or slices of turkey breast. Place between sheets of plastic wrap and, with flat side of meat mallet, pound to scant ¼-inch (5 mm) thickness.

Ginger Lime Salmon Skewers

The marinade, with its nice balance of salty, sour, sweet and fresh flavours, complements the salmon beautifully and creates a shiny caramelized glaze.

4 **skinless centre-cut salmon fillets**
(about 6 oz/175 g each)

1 piece (1 inch/2.5 cm) **fresh ginger,** minced

1 **hot red pepper** or hot green pepper,
seeded and minced

3 tbsp (45 mL) chopped **fresh cilantro**

2 tbsp (30 mL) **sodium-reduced soy sauce**

1 tbsp (15 mL) **lime juice**

2 tsp (10 mL) **vegetable oil**

Pinch **granulated sugar**

4 **green onions,** cut in 1½-inch
(4 cm) pieces

1 **sweet red pepper,** cut in 1½-inch
(4 cm) pieces

4 **lime wedges**

Cut salmon into 1½-inch (4 cm) cubes to make 24 pieces.

In large glass bowl, mix together ginger, hot pepper, cilantro, soy sauce, lime juice, oil and sugar. Add salmon and toss to coat; let stand for 10 minutes. *(Make-ahead: Cover and refrigerate for up to 30 minutes.)*

Beginning and ending with green onions, thread salmon, red pepper and green onions loosely onto 4 metal or soaked wooden skewers, reserving marinade.

Place on greased grill over medium heat; brush with marinade. Close lid and grill, turning twice, until fish flakes easily when tested, about 10 minutes. Serve with lime wedges to squeeze over top.

Makes 4 servings. PER SERVING: about 316 cal, 31 g pro, 19 g total fat (4 g sat. fat), 5 g carb, 1 g fibre, 84 mg chol, 385 mg sodium. % RDI: 3% calcium, 8% iron, 17% vit A, 107% vit C, 27% folate.

Swiss Cheese Fondue

Fully ripened cheese and good-quality wine make the best fondue. Kirsch (cherry eau-de-vie) is the most traditional flavouring, but plum eau-de-vie (pflümli, pruneau or Slivovitz) and apple brandy, such as Calvados, are also recommended.

1 clove **garlic**
2 cups (500 mL) **dry white wine**
1 lb (500 g) **Emmenthal cheese,** shredded
   (4 cups/1 L)
1 lb (500 g) **Gruyère cheese,** shredded
   (4 cups/1 L)
2 tbsp (30 mL) **cornstarch**
¼ tsp (1 mL) **pepper**
Pinch **grated nutmeg**
2 tbsp (30 mL) **kirsch**
2 **baguettes,** cut in 1-inch (2.5 cm) cubes
1 each **apple** and **pear,** cored and cubed

Cut small slits in garlic clove; rub clove all over inside of fondue pot. Pour in all but 2 tbsp (30 mL) of the wine; bring to simmer over medium heat on stove top.

Add Emmenthal and Gruyère cheeses; stir with wooden spoon until melted. Dissolve cornstarch in remaining wine; stir into fondue pot along with pepper and nutmeg. Bring to simmer, stirring; simmer for 1 minute. Stir in kirsch.

Place over medium-low heat of fondue burner on table, stirring often and adjusting heat as necessary to maintain low simmer. Serve with bread, apple and pear cubes to skewer and dip into cheese mixture.

Makes 6 servings. PER SERVING: about 665 cal, 32 g pro, 28 g total fat (15 g sat. fat), 66 g carb, 4 g fibre, 83 mg chol, 868 mg sodium. % RDI: 77% calcium, 22% iron, 23% vit A, 5% vit C, 48% folate.

VARIATIONS
Garlic Fondue
• Instead of rubbing the pot with garlic, add 3 cloves garlic, thinly sliced, to white wine at beginning of cooking.

True Canadian Cheese Fondue
• Omit garlic. Substitute 1⅓ lb (670 g) Oka cheese, shredded (5½ cups/1.375 L), and 12 oz (375 g) extra-old Cheddar cheese, shredded (3 cups/750 mL) for Emmenthal and Gruyère cheeses. Along with pepper and nutmeg, stir in 1½ tsp (7 mL) Dijon mustard, 1 tsp (5 mL) Worcestershire sauce and pinch cayenne pepper. Substitute 1 tbsp (15 mL) whisky for kirsch.

Raclette

Classic meets modern in this selection of ingredients that you can prepare ahead. There's about 3 oz (90 g) cheese per person, but heartier appetites (and cheese lovers) may want to have 5 oz (150 g), which would increase the total to 2½ lb (1.25 kg).

1½ lb (750 g) **raclette cheese**

1½ lb (750 g) **cooked sausage** (such as knackwurst) or cured sausage (such as smoked turkey or kielbasa)

2 cups (500 mL) drained **pickles** (such as cornichons, gherkins and cocktail onions)

1 bunch **broccoli,** cut in florets

1 can (14 oz/398 mL) **whole baby corn**

24 small **new potatoes** (about 3 lb/1.5 kg)

Sweet paprika and **pepper**

Scrape away most of the tough rind from cheese. Thinly slice cheese into 3½-inch (9 cm) squares or cut to fit raclette pan. Arrange on serving plate.

Diagonally cut sausage into ½-inch (1 cm) thick slices; arrange on separate serving plate. Place pickles in bowls.

In large saucepan of boiling salted water, cover and cook broccoli until tender-crisp, 2 to 3 minutes. With slotted spoon, transfer to bowl of cold water to chill; drain and pat dry. Transfer to serving bowl.

Drain and rinse corn; pat dry. Place in serving bowl. (*Make-ahead: Cover all prepared ingredients and refrigerate for up to 24 hours.*)

In same saucepan of boiling salted water, cover and cook potatoes just until tender, 16 to 18 minutes; drain well. (*Make-ahead: Let cool; refrigerate for up to 24 hours. Reheat in microwave at high for 4 to 6 minutes.*) Transfer to cloth napkin–lined heatproof bowl; fold napkin over potatoes to keep warm.

To serve, choose one of the following.

• FOR THE PURIST: Quarter potatoes; place on plate. Place 1 slice cheese in raclette tray; broil under raclette broiler until melted and bubbly, about 2 minutes. Scrape over potatoes. Sprinkle with paprika and pepper to taste. Add pickles.

• FOR VARIETY: Arrange 1 piece each of the sausage, broccoli and baby corn in raclette tray; top with cheese and broil under raclette broiler.

• FOR ACTION: Chop potatoes; place in raclette tray. Top with cheese and broil under raclette broiler while grilling sausage on top portion of raclette grill.

Makes 8 servings. PER SERVING: about 800 cal, 40 g pro, 48 g total fat (24 g sat. fat), 57 g carb, 5 g fibre, 127 mg chol, 1,597 mg sodium. % RDI: 79% calcium, 21% iron, 31% vit A, 103% vit C, 33% folate.

TIP

Use top level of raclette grill to keep potatoes warm in a covered heatproof dish.

Coconut Curry Shrimp

A bag of frozen shrimp turns into an Asian feast with just a few simple pantry staples. Serve over rice or rice noodles.

1 can (400 mL) **coconut milk**
2 tbsp (30 mL) **fish sauce**
1 tbsp (15 mL) **mild curry powder**
2 tsp (10 mL) packed **brown sugar**
½ tsp (2 mL) each **salt** and **pepper**
2 lb (1 kg) thawed peeled deveined
   raw large shrimp
2 **sweet red peppers,** diced
4 **green onions,** chopped
½ cup (125 mL) **fresh cilantro leaves**
8 **lime wedges**

In large bowl, whisk together coconut milk, fish sauce, curry powder, brown sugar, salt and pepper. Add shrimp, red peppers, green onions and cilantro; toss to coat. Let stand for 5 minutes.

In wok or saucepan, stir-fry shrimp mixture over medium-high heat until shrimp are pink, about 6 minutes. Serve with lime wedges.

Makes 8 servings. PER SERVING: about 186 cal, 19 g pro, 10 g total fat (7 g sat. fat), 7 g carb, 1 g fibre, 129 mg chol, 626 mg sodium, 355 mg potassium. % RDI: 6% calcium, 28% iron, 16% vit A, 92% vit C, 11% folate.

CHAPTER 11

Make It Tonight... Breakfast for Dinner

Turkey Potato Patties

This recipe is quick if you have leftover mashed potatoes. If you don't, follow the tip. Serve with poached eggs, salsa and a salad.

1 **egg**
1½ cups (375 mL) diced **cooked turkey** or chicken
1 cup (250 mL) **mashed potatoes**
¼ cup (60 mL) **dry bread crumbs**
1 **green onion,** finely chopped
2 tbsp (30 mL) finely chopped **fresh parsley**
2 tsp (10 mL) **Dijon mustard**
¼ tsp (1 mL) each **dried thyme** and **sage**
¼ tsp (1 mL) each **salt** and **pepper**
1 tbsp (15 mL) **vegetable oil** (approx)

In bowl, beat egg; mix in turkey, potatoes, bread crumbs, green onion, parsley, mustard, thyme, sage, salt and pepper. Form into eight ½-inch (1 cm) thick patties. *(Make-ahead: Cover and refrigerate for up to 8 hours.)*

In large skillet, heat oil over medium heat; fry patties, turning once, reducing temperature if browning too quickly and adding more oil if necessary, until patties are crusty and golden, about 6 minutes.

Makes 4 servings. PER SERVING: about 184 cal, 14 g pro, 7 g total fat (1 g sat. fat), 16 g carb, 1 g fibre, 73 mg chol, 401 mg sodium. % RDI: 4% calcium, 11% iron, 3% vit A, 8% vit C, 8% folate.

TIP

To make mashed potatoes, peel and cube 2 potatoes. In saucepan of boiling salted water, cover and cook potatoes until tender, about 12 minutes. Drain and mash with potato masher.

EQUIPMENT

THE THREE MUST-HAVE KNIVES

1. **CHEF'S KNIFE**
2. **SERRATED BREAD KNIFE**
3. **PARING KNIFE**

FIND THE PERFECT CHEF'S KNIFE

This is the most important knife to have in your kitchen. Here's what you need to know to find the right one for you.
• Look for one with a forged blade rather than a lighter, less-dense stamped blade.
• A blade 8 inches (20 cm) long is ideal for home cooks. Get a longer one if you're tall and will use it professionally.
• The blade should extend from the tip of the knife right through the handle, where it's known as the tang.
• The handle can be metal, wood or moulded plastic – choose one that's comfortable to hold.
• A good chef's knife is a lifetime investment – buy quality and you'll only need to buy once.

HOW TO WASH AND STORE

Always hand-wash knives to avoid dulling the blades and damaging wooden handles. Store in a wooden block, in a drawer in a wooden knife insert or on a magnetic strip. Never store knives loose in a drawer, where edges can be dulled and an unsuspecting helper can get cut.

KEEP THEM SHARP

A butcher's steel is not a sharpener, but it will help maintain your knife's sharp edge. To use, hold the knife blade at a 20-degree angle and draw the knife along the length of the steel, angling with your wrist to ensure the entire length of the blade is honed. Six to eight strokes on each side should suffice. Have your knives sharpened regularly by a professional sharpener – cookware shops often offer this service.

Zucchini Pancakes

Top with sour cream or Feta Tomato Cream (recipe, right).

4 cups (1 L) coarsely grated **zucchini**
  (about 6, or 1 lb/500 g total)
1 tsp (5 mL) **salt**
2 **green onions,** minced
2 **eggs,** beaten
1 cup (250 mL) **buttermilk**
2 tbsp (30 mL) **vegetable oil**
⅔ cup (150 mL) **cornmeal**
½ cup (125 mL) **all-purpose flour**
1 tsp (5 mL) **granulated sugar**
¼ tsp (1 mL) each **baking soda** and **pepper**
2 tbsp (30 mL) **butter** (approx)

In colander, toss zucchini with salt; let stand for 20 minutes. Squeeze out as much liquid as possible; transfer zucchini to bowl. Stir in green onions, eggs, buttermilk and oil; set aside.

In large bowl, whisk together cornmeal, flour, sugar, baking soda and pepper. Pour zucchini mixture over top; stir just until blended.

In large skillet, heat half of the butter over medium heat. Spoon heaping 2 tbsp (30 mL) batter for each pancake into pan; flatten and spread with back of spoon. Fry, adding more butter if necessary, until bottoms are golden, about 2 minutes.

Turn and fry until edges are golden, about 2 minutes. Place on paper towel–lined baking sheet. (*Make-ahead: Let cool and stack between waxed paper; refrigerate in airtight container for up to 2 days. Reheat on baking sheet in 325°F/ 160°C oven, about 8 minutes.*)

Makes 4 servings. PER SERVING: about 335 cal, 9 g pro, 16 g total fat (5 g sat. fat), 38 g carb, 3 g fibre, 113 mg chol, 518 mg sodium. % RDI: 10% calcium, 13% iron, 13% vit A, 10% vit C, 28% folate.

Feta Tomato Cream

1 cup (250 mL) **grape tomatoes** or
  cherry tomatoes
½ cup (125 mL) crumbled **feta cheese**
  (about 2½ oz/75 g)
¼ cup (60 mL) **Balkan-style plain yogurt**
1 tbsp (15 mL) chopped **fresh mint**
1 tbsp (15 mL) **extra-virgin olive oil**
2 tsp (10 mL) **lemon juice**
Pinch each **salt** and **pepper**

Quarter tomatoes; place in small bowl. In food processor, blend feta cheese, yogurt, mint, oil, lemon juice, salt and pepper. Scrape over tomatoes; stir to blend. (*Make-ahead: Cover and refrigerate for up to 6 hours.*)

Makes 1¼ cups (300 mL). PER 1 TBSP (15 mL): about 20 cal, 1 g pro, 2 g total fat (1 g sat. fat), 1 g carb, 0 g fibre, 4 mg chol, 43 mg sodium. % RDI: 2% calcium, 1% iron, 1% vit A, 2% vit C, 1% folate.

Mushroom Fried Rice Omelette

Omelettes transition seamlessly from breakfast to dinner. This fried rice version is based on a diner-style dish commonly found in Japan.

3 tbsp (45 mL) **vegetable oil**
1 each **onion** and **carrot,** diced
1 cup (250 mL) chopped **cremini mushrooms**
1 cup (250 mL) **frozen peas,** thawed
½ tsp (2 mL) each **salt** and **pepper**
3 cups (750 mL) cooled **cooked rice**
3 tbsp (45 mL) **ketchup**
1 tbsp (15 mL) **sodium-reduced soy sauce**
3 **green onions,** chopped
8 **eggs**
4 tsp (20 mL) **butter**

In wok or large skillet, heat oil over medium-high heat; stir-fry onion and carrot until slightly tender, 2 to 3 minutes.

Add mushrooms; stir-fry for 1 minute. Add peas; stir-fry until hot. Add half each of the salt and pepper.

Stir in rice, ketchup and soy sauce; stir-fry until hot. Sprinkle with green onions. Set aside.

In bowl, whisk together eggs, remaining salt and pepper and 2 tbsp (30 mL) water just until blended but not frothy.

In 8-inch (20 cm) nonstick skillet, melt 1 tsp (5 mL) of the butter over medium heat. Add one-quarter of the egg mixture, making figure eight with spatula to combine. Cook until almost set, gently lifting edge to allow any uncooked eggs to flow underneath, 2 to 3 minutes or. Slide onto plate.

Spoon one-quarter of the rice mixture on bottom half of omelette; fold top half over. Repeat with remaining ingredients to make 4 omelettes.

Makes 4 servings. PER SERVING: about 533 cal, 19 g pro, 25 g total fat (6 g sat. fat), 58 g carb, 4 g fibre, 382 mg chol, 748 mg sodium. % RDI: 9% calcium, 18% iron, 58% vit A, 12% vit C, 40% folate.

Ham and Cheese Western Sandwiches

Tasty sandwiches are ideal for weeknights.

¼ cup (60 mL) **butter,** softened

Half each **onion** and **sweet green pepper,** diced

½ cup (125 mL) sliced **cremini mushrooms** or white mushrooms

½ tsp (2 mL) **dried oregano**

1 **green onion,** minced

¼ tsp (1 mL) each **salt** and **pepper**

8 **eggs**

½ cup (125 mL) diced **prosciutto**

½ cup (125 mL) shredded **provolone cheese**

8 slices **whole grain Italian bread**

1 cup (250 mL) **arugula** or baby spinach

In nonstick skillet, heat 1 tbsp (15 mL) of the butter over medium heat; cook onion, pepper, mushrooms and oregano until tender, 5 minutes. Stir in green onion, salt and pepper; cook for 2 minutes. Transfer to small bowl. In separate bowl, whisk eggs with ¼ cup (60 mL) water.

In same skillet, melt 1 tbsp (15 mL) of the remaining butter over medium heat. Add half each of the vegetable and egg mixtures, making figure 8 with spatula to combine. Sprinkle with half each of the prosciutto and provolone; cook, flipping halfway through, until set, 4 minutes. Cut into quarters. Repeat with remaining vegetable and egg mixtures.

Meanwhile, toast bread; spread with remaining butter. Sandwich egg mixture and arugula between toast.

Makes 4 servings. PER SERVING: about 575 cal, 27 g pro, 29 g total fat (14 g sat. fat), 52 g carb, 6 g fibre, 422 mg chol, 1,114 mg sodium. % RDI: 21% calcium, 31% iron, 32% vit A, 22% vit C, 33% folate.

Spinach, Ham and Cheese Strata

This strata is great for a group at brunch, lunch or supper. You can assemble it a day ahead, so it's suited to busy times.

1 loaf **sourdough bread**

1 pkg (10 oz/300 g) **frozen spinach,** thawed and squeezed dry

6 **green onions,** thinly sliced

1½ cups (375 mL) shredded **Swiss cheese**

1 cup (250 mL) **diced ham** or smoked turkey

8 **eggs**

2½ cups (625 mL) **milk**

1 tbsp (15 mL) **Dijon mustard**

¼ tsp (1 mL) each **salt** and **pepper**

Cut bread into 1-inch (2.5 cm) cubes to make about 12 cups (3 L). In large bowl, stir together bread, spinach, onions, cheese and ham. Spoon into greased 13- x 9-inch (3 L) baking dish.

In bowl, whisk together eggs, milk, mustard, salt and pepper; pour over bread mixture and let stand for 20 minutes, pressing occasionally. *(Make-ahead: Cover and refrigerate for up to 24 hours.)* Bake in 375°F (190°C) oven until puffed and golden, about 45 minutes.

Makes 8 servings. PER SERVING: about 383 cal, 25 g pro, 15 g total fat (7 g sat. fat), 37 g carb, 3 g fibre, 220 mg chol, 828 mg sodium. % RDI: 33% calcium, 20% iron, 35% vit A, 7% vit C, 47% folate.

Sausage and Potato Omelette

This thick omelette has it all – tomatoes, spinach, potatoes and sausage. While it's cooking, there's time to toss a salad and warm whole grain rolls.

2 **mild Italian sausages** (6 oz/175 g), thinly sliced

1 tbsp (15 mL) **extra-virgin olive oil**

1 small **onion,** chopped

1 cup (250 mL) **grape tomatoes** or cherry tomatoes

1 **potato,** peeled (if desired) and diced

6 **eggs**

¼ tsp (1 mL) each **salt** and **pepper**

¼ cup (60 mL) packed shredded **fresh spinach**

1 **green onion,** thinly sliced

½ cup (125 mL) shredded **mozzarella cheese** (optional)

In 9-inch (23 cm) cast-iron ovenproof skillet, brown sausages over medium-high heat. With slotted spoon, transfer to paper towel–lined plate. Drain fat from pan.

In same pan, heat oil over medium heat; fry onion, tomatoes and potato, stirring occasionally, until potato is tender, about 12 minutes. Return sausage to skillet.

Meanwhile, in bowl, whisk together eggs, salt and pepper; stir in spinach and green onion. Pour into skillet and stir to combine. Sprinkle with mozzarella (if using).

Cover and cook over medium-low heat until bottom and side are firm but top is still slightly runny, about 10 minutes.

Broil until golden and set, about 3 minutes. Cut into wedges.

Makes 4 servings. PER SERVING: about 288 cal, 17 g pro, 19 g total fat (6 g sat. fat), 12 g carb, 1 g fibre, 300 mg chol, 508 mg sodium. % RDI: 6% calcium, 13% iron, 16% vit A, 15% vit C, 24% folate.

EQUIPMENT

SPLATTER SCREEN

Skillets rarely have lids because moisture makes fried food soggy. When frying foods that tend to splatter, especially over high heat, a wire mesh antisplash lid placed over the skillet will help control fat spatters without making the food soggy. It also keeps the cook and the stove clean.

Folded Salsa Omelette

Here's a time-saver: replace homemade salsa with 1 to 2 cups (250 to 500 mL) store-bought salsa. We recommend the chunky variety.

8 **eggs**

Pinch each **salt** and **pepper**

4 tsp (20 mL) **butter** (approx)

½ cup (125 mL) shredded **Cheddar cheese**

SALSA:

1⅓ cups (325 mL) **cherry tomatoes,** quartered

⅓ cup (75 mL) chopped **sweet green pepper**

⅓ cup (75 mL) finely chopped **red onion**

4 tsp (20 mL) chopped **fresh cilantro** or parsley

1 tbsp (15 mL) **vegetable oil**

1 tbsp (15 mL) **white wine vinegar**

¼ tsp (1 mL) each **salt** and **pepper**

SALSA: In bowl, mix tomatoes, green pepper, onion, cilantro, oil, vinegar, salt and pepper; set aside.

In bowl, whisk together eggs, 2 tbsp (30 mL) water, salt and pepper just until blended but not frothy.

In 8-inch (20 cm) omelette pan or skillet, melt 1 tsp (5 mL) of the butter over medium heat. Pour one-quarter of the egg mixture into skillet; cook until almost set, gently lifting edge to allow any uncooked eggs to flow underneath, about 3 minutes.

Spoon ⅓ cup (75 mL) of the salsa onto half of the omelette; sprinkle 2 tbsp (30 mL) of the cheese over salsa. Fold uncovered half over top; cook for 2 minutes. Slide onto plate. Repeat with remaining ingredients, adding more butter as necessary. Serve with remaining salsa.

Makes 4 servings. PER SERVING: about 285 cal, 17 g pro, 22 g total fat (9 g sat. fat), 5 g carb, 1 g fibre, 399 mg chol, 397 mg sodium. % RDI: 14% calcium, 11% iron, 28% vit A, 33% vit C, 29% folate.

THE WELL-STOCKED KITCHEN
ESSENTIALS FOR COOL, DARK STORAGE

Remember, the space under the sink is too warm and moist for these foods. Keep them dry and cool for best results.
- Onions
- Garlic
- Potatoes: regular and sweet (store away from onions and garlic)
- Rutabaga
- Winter squash (in season)

Zucchini Red Pepper Omelettes

If the family arrives home at different times, leave the zucchini mixture, eggs and cheese ready in the fridge so the latecomers can have a fresh omelette.

8 **eggs**
¼ tsp (1 mL) each **salt** and **pepper**
4 tsp (20 mL) **butter** (approx)
FILLING:
1 tbsp (15 mL) **vegetable oil**
1 small **onion,** diced
1 small **zucchini** (about 4 oz/125 g), cubed
½ tsp (2 mL) **dried oregano**
½ cup (125 mL) sliced **roasted red peppers**
1 cup (250 mL) crumbled **feta cheese**

FILLING: In skillet, heat oil over medium heat; fry onion, zucchini and oregano, stirring occasionally, until tender, about 6 minutes. Stir in red peppers. Transfer to small bowl; set aside.

In bowl, whisk eggs, salt, pepper and 2 tbsp (30 mL) water just until blended but not frothy.

In 8-inch (20 cm) omelette pan or skillet, melt 1 tsp (5 mL) of the butter over medium heat. Add one-quarter of the zucchini mixture and one-quarter of the egg mixture. Make figure eight with spatula to combine. Sprinkle with one-quarter of the cheese. Cook until almost set, gently lifting edge with spatula to allow any uncooked eggs to flow underneath, about 3 minutes.

Fold in half; cook for 2 minutes. Slide onto plate. Repeat with remaining ingredients, adding more butter as necessary.

Makes 4 servings. PER SERVING: about 329 cal, 19 g pro, 26 g total fat (12 g sat. fat), 7 g carb, 1 g fibre, 417 mg chol, 767 mg sodium. % RDI: 23% calcium, 13% iron, 36% vit A, 70% vit C, 34% folate.

Simple Soda Bread

Home-baked bread, without the rising time? Absolutely. This recipe uses the leavening power of baking powder and buttermilk instead of yeast.

1 cup (250 mL) **all-purpose flour**
1 cup (250 mL) **whole wheat flour**
1 tbsp (15 mL) **granulated sugar**
2 tsp (10 mL) **baking powder**
½ tsp (2 mL) **baking soda**
¼ tsp (1 mL) **salt**
¼ cup (60 mL) **dried currants**
½ tsp (2 mL) **caraway seeds** (optional)
¾ cup (175 mL) **buttermilk**
3 tbsp (45 mL) **butter,** melted
1 **egg**

In large bowl, whisk together all-purpose flour, whole wheat flour, sugar, baking powder, baking soda and salt; stir in currants, and caraway seeds (if using).

Whisk together buttermilk, butter and egg; pour over flour mixture, tossing with fork to form sticky dough.

Scrape onto floured surface; gently knead 10 times. Transfer to parchment paper–lined baking sheet; press into 7-inch (18 cm) round. With sharp knife, score top into 8 wedges.

Bake in 350°F (180°C) oven until cake tester inserted in centre comes out clean, about 35 minutes.

Makes 1 loaf, or 8 slices. PER SLICE: about 188 cal, 6 g pro, 6 g total fat (4 g sat. fat), 30 g carb, 3 g fibre, 37 mg chol, 286 mg sodium, 171 mg potassium. % RDI: 8% calcium, 12% iron, 5% vit A, 1% vit C, 19% folate.

Gratin of Hard-Cooked Eggs

This creamy casserole – shared by *Canadian Living* reader Edie Warner of Winnipeg – fills the bill for breakfast or supper.

2 tbsp (30 mL) **butter**
3 tbsp (45 mL) **all-purpose flour**
1½ cups (375 mL) **milk**
Pinch each **salt** and **pepper**
Pinch **nutmeg**
1¼ cups (300 mL) shredded **Gruyère cheese,** or Cheddar or Swiss cheese
6 **hard-cooked eggs**
4 **green onions**
1¼ cups (300 mL) **frozen peas**
½ cup (125 mL) **fresh bread crumbs**

In saucepan, melt butter over medium heat; stir in flour and cook, stirring and without browning, for 2 minutes. Gradually whisk in milk; add salt, pepper and nutmeg. Bring to boil; reduce heat and simmer for 2 minutes. Remove from heat; stir in 1 cup (250 mL) of the cheese until melted.

Halve eggs lengthwise; chop onions into pea-size pieces. Arrange eggs, cut side up, in greased 6-cup (1.5 L) gratin or casserole dish; sprinkle with peas and onions. Pour sauce over top; sprinkle with bread crumbs and remaining cheese. (*Make-ahead: Cover and refrigerate for up to 6 hours.*)

Bake in 450°F (230°C) oven until bubbly and slightly browned, 25 to 30 minutes.

Makes 6 servings. PER SERVING: about 288 cal, 18 g pro, 18 g total fat (10 g sat. fat), 13 g carb, 2 g fibre, 229 mg chol, 237 mg sodium. % RDI: 34% calcium, 11% iron, 27% vit A, 7% vit C, 27% folate.

TIP

To hard-cook eggs, place in single layer in saucepan wide enough to fit number of eggs. Add enough cold water to come 1 inch (2.5 cm) over tops of eggs. Cover and bring to boil over high heat. Remove from heat; let stand for 20 minutes. Drain off water; chill eggs in cold water.

Make It Tonight...
Side Dishes and Salads

Lemon Brussels Sprouts

We toss tender-crisp vegetables, such as beans, asparagus and these sprouts, with lemon juice just before serving to keep their green colour vibrant.

8 cups (2 L) **brussels sprouts** (about 2 lb/1 kg), trimmed and halved
¼ cup (60 mL) **butter,** softened
2 tsp (10 mL) grated **lemon zest**
4 tsp (20 mL) **lemon juice**
Pinch each **salt** and **pepper**

In large saucepan of boiling salted water, cover and simmer brussels sprouts until tender-crisp, about 6 minutes. Drain and return to pan.

Add butter, lemon zest and juice, salt and pepper; heat, tossing, until butter is melted.

Makes 8 servings. PER SERVING: about 89 cal, 3 g pro, 6 g total fat (4 g sat. fat), 9 g carb, 4 g fibre, 15 mg chol, 287 mg sodium. % RDI: 3% calcium, 9% iron, 12% vit A, 102% vit C, 26% folate.

Asparagus with Creamy Lemon Sauce

Choose firm asparagus stalks with deep green or purplish closed tips. To keep asparagus fresh, store in refrigerator in plastic bag with woody ends wrapped in damp paper towel. Use within two days of purchase or, better still, within two days of picking!

3 tbsp (45 mL) **light mayonnaise**
2 tsp (10 mL) **lemon juice**
1 tsp (5 mL) minced **fresh chives** or green onion
Pinch **granulated sugar**
Pinch each **salt** and **pepper**
1 lb (500 g) **asparagus**

In small bowl, whisk together mayonnaise, 2 tsp (10 mL) water, lemon juice, chives, sugar, salt and pepper; set sauce aside.

Break woody ends off asparagus. Cover and steam on rack above 1 inch (2.5 cm) boiling water until tender-crisp, about 3 minutes for thin stalks or up to 7 minutes for thick stalks. Drain and arrange on plate; drizzle with sauce.

Makes 4 servings. PER SERVING: about 55 cal, 2 g pro, 4 g total fat (1 g sat. fat), 4 g carb, 2 g fibre, 4 mg chol, 87 mg sodium. % RDI: 2% calcium, 6% iron, 8% vit A, 12% vit C, 54% folate.

VARIATION
Asparagus with Creamy Mustard Sauce
•Replace lemon juice with 1 tsp (5 mL) Dijon mustard. Replace chives with parsley.

Roasted Cauliflower Salad

This is not your usual pasta, potato or grain salad but rather one that features the mellow flavour of roasted cauliflower. Anchovies, capers, olives and raisins add a touch of sun-drenched Sicily.

1 tsp (5 mL) **fennel seeds**
8 cups (2 L) **cauliflower florets**
  (1 large head)
¼ cup (60 mL) **extra-virgin olive oil**
¼ tsp (1 mL) each **salt** and **pepper**
2 tbsp (30 mL) **lemon juice**
1 tsp (5 mL) **anchovy paste**
½ cup (125 mL) **Kalamata olives,**
  pitted and quartered
¼ cup (60 mL) **golden raisins**
2 tbsp (30 mL) **capers,** drained and rinsed

Using mortar and pestle or bottom of pot, crush fennel seeds.

In large bowl, toss cauliflower with 2 tbsp (30 mL) of the oil, fennel seeds, salt and pepper; spread on large rimmed baking sheet. Roast in 450°F (230°C) oven until golden and tender-crisp, about 20 minutes. Let cool.

In serving bowl, whisk together remaining oil, lemon juice and anchovy paste. Cut cauliflower into ¼-inch (5 mm) thick slices or bite-size pieces; add to bowl. Add olives, raisins and capers. Toss to combine. (*Make-ahead: Cover and refrigerate for up to 24 hours.*)

Makes 8 servings. PER SERVING: about 128 cal, 2 g pro, 10 g total fat (1 g sat. fat), 9 g carb, 4 g fibre, 0 mg chol, 448 mg sodium. % RDI: 3% calcium, 5% iron, 75% vit C, 20% folate.

HOW TO WASH AND STORE GREENS, HERBS AND VEGETABLES

SALAD GREENS, CELERY AND HERBS Wash before storing – you're more likely to go to the bother of making a salad for supper if the greens are ready. Separate leaves or stalks and swish in cool water. Repeat, especially for sandy herbs and greens, such as cilantro and spinach. Spin dry, lay out in single layer on dry towels and roll loosely. Enclose in plastic bag and store in crisper.

BROCCOLI, BOK CHOY, BEANS, SPINACH, SWISS CHARD AND BRUSSELS SPROUTS Wrap in tea towels, enclose in a plastic bag and store in the crisper. Before cooking, dunk in a sinkful of cool water; swish leafy or sandy vegetables to remove dirt. Avoid soaking vegetables.

CARROTS, BEETS OR ANY VEGETABLES WITH TOPS Remove tops – use beet greens as a vegetable, like spinach. Wrap in tea towel, enclose in a plastic bag and store in the crisper. Before cooking carrots, peel and trim. For beets, scrub with vegetable brush to remove dirt. Cook with root and base of stems; scrape off peel, root and top bit when beets are fork-tender.

LEEKS Trim off dark green parts and root end. Slit from root end to close to pale green part. Swish, white ends up, in cool water, separating layers to ensure that none of the sand in which they grew remains between the layers.

Steamed Vegetables

Because water-soluble vitamins can't escape into the boiling liquid, steamed vegetables retain more nutrients and minerals than boiled ones. Steaming is suitable for small quantities because the steam can quickly cook each piece. Place steamer at least 1 inch (2.5 cm) above boiling water.

Asparagus
PREP: Snap off woody ends; peel thick stems if desired
TIME: 3 minutes (thin stalks) to 7 minutes (thick stalks)

Beets
PREP: Cut off tops; keep whole and unpeeled until after cooking
TIME: 40 minutes

Bok Choy
PREP: Trim and chop coarsely, or halve if small
TIME: 5 minutes

Broccoli
PREP: Cut into florets; peel and slice stalks
TIME: 7 minutes

Brussels Sprouts
PREP: Trim off wilted or coarse outer leaves; cut thin end off stem and score shallow X in bottom
TIME: 10 minutes

Cabbage
PREP: Remove coarse outer leaves, then quarter and remove core
TIME: 10 to 12 minutes

Carrots or Parsnips
PREP: Peel and cut into coins, sticks or chunks
TIME: 15 minutes

Cauliflower
PREP: Cut into florets
TIME: 10 minutes

Green Beans
PREP: Cut off stem end
TIME: 10 minutes

New Potatoes
PREP: Scrub well; cut if large
TIME: 30 minutes

EQUIPMENT
STEAMERS 101

VEGETABLE STEAMER
A collapsible basket made of perforated, interleaved panels that stands out of the water on three little legs and expands to fit inside saucepans between 5 inches (12 cm) and 9 inches (23 cm) in diameter. A central stem can be used to lift out the steamer or removed to accommodate a whole cauliflower or artichokes.

POT STEAMERS
If you are purchasing a new set of pots, a set with a steamer is a worthwhile investment. Or look for one with a perforated bottom and concentric ridges to fit over pots of various sizes.

CHINESE STEAMING POTS
An alternative to a wok and bamboo steamer combo is a lightweight aluminum or stainless-steel set consisting of a water pot base and two or three stackable steaming trays with a domed lid. Unlike a flat lid, the domed style directs condensed water droplets down the side and prevents them from dripping into the food.

Corn on the Cob

Choose your favourite way to cook husked cobs of corn. Any of the following yield tender, sweet corn ready for topping and crunching.
• Boil or steam for 8 to 10 minutes.
• Grill over medium-high heat for 10 to 15 minutes.
• Microwave at high for about 10 minutes.

CREATIVE CORN TOPPINGS

You can brush cooked corn on the cob with butter or olive oil and season with salt and pepper. Or get creative and dress them up with one of these butter, mayonnaise or olive oil toppings. Each topping makes about ⅓ cup (75 mL), enough for 6 cobs of corn.

PESTO Butter
Mix together ¼ cup (60 mL) butter, softened; 2 tbsp (30 mL) grated Parmesan cheese; 1 clove garlic, minced; and 1 tbsp (15 mL) minced fresh basil.

PROVENÇAL Butter
Mix together ¼ cup (60 mL) butter, softened; 1 tbsp (15 mL) Dijon mustard; and ¾ tsp (4 mL) herbes de Provence.

INDIAN-SPICED Olive Oil with Butter
Mix together 2 tbsp (30 mL) extra-virgin olive oil; 2 tbsp (30 mL) butter, softened; 1 tbsp (15 mL) minced fresh cilantro; 1 tsp (5 mL) curry paste; and ½ tsp (2 mL) lemon juice.

MEDITERRANEAN Olive Oil
Mix together 3 tbsp (45 mL) extra-virgin olive oil; 4 tsp (20 mL) minced sun-dried tomatoes; ½ tsp (2 mL) dried thyme; and pinch each salt and pepper.

SMOKY ORANGE Mayonnaise
Mix together ¼ cup (60 mL) light mayonnaise; 2 tsp (10 mL) barbecue sauce; and 1 tsp (5 mL) each chopped chipotle pepper and grated orange zest.

LEMON PEPPER Mayonnaise
Mix together ¼ cup (60 mL) light mayonnaise; 1 tsp (5 mL) each grated lemon zest and lemon juice; and ½ tsp (2 mL) pepper.

Roasted Parsnips

These parsnips come out of the oven nicely crisp, with just a hint of natural sweetness.

1½ lb (750 g) **parsnips**
2 tbsp (30 mL) **extra-virgin olive oil**
¼ tsp (1 mL) **salt**
Pinch **pepper**

Peel and cut parsnips into about 1½-inch (4 cm) thick sticks. Transfer to large bowl; toss with oil, salt and pepper.

Roast on greased baking sheet in 450°F (230°C) oven until tender and golden at edges, about 20 minutes.

Makes 4 servings. PER SERVING: about 165 cal, 2 g pro, 7 g total fat (1 g sat. fat), 25 g carb, 5 g fibre, 0 mg chol, 158 mg sodium. % RDI: 5% calcium, 6% iron, 32% vit C, 40% folate.

BONUS RECIPE

Garlic Mashed Parsnip Potatoes

• In large saucepan of boiling salted water, cook 3 parsnips, peeled and chopped; 2 potatoes, peeled and chopped; and 3 cloves garlic until tender, about 15 minutes. Drain and return to pan. Using potato masher, mash in 2 tbsp (30 mL) butter; ½ tsp (2 mL) Dijon mustard; and ¼ tsp (1 mL) salt until smooth. Makes 4 servings.

TECHNIQUE
CHOPPING

Sounds simple, doesn't it? But mastering this technique guarantees less prep time and more cooking and eating time. You need a sharp chef's knife and a large chopping board to contain the mess. Space makes a big difference.

TO CHOP AN ONION, SHALLOT, GARLIC CLOVE OR OTHER ROUND VEGETABLE:
• Peel, keeping root end intact. On cutting board, cut in half lengthwise (root to stem); place cut sides down. With rounded knuckles and keeping fingertips curled under, hold root end of one half firmly on board. With knife held horizontally, make 2 or 3 cuts through stem end, almost but not all the way through to root, depending on thickness desired.
• With knife held vertically and keeping vegetable steady, cut lengthwise from stem end almost but not all the way through to root end, into same-size thick slices.
• With tip of knife constantly on board, slice across vegetable with rocking motion, moving curled fingers away from blade and toward root end while chopping, finishing with and discarding root.

TIP: Generally, dicing refers to cutting a food into ⅛- to ¼-inch (3 to 5 mm) cubes, and cubing refers to cutting it into ½-inch (1 cm) cubes. Chopping denotes a slightly coarser, more irregular cut.

Tri-Colour Pepper Sauté

Red and yellow peppers take three to six weeks longer than green to develop sweetness and change colour. No wonder they taste so good! Maximize their use in recipes when they're in season.

4 **sweet peppers** (red, yellow and green)
2 tbsp (30 mL) **extra-virgin olive oil**
2 cloves **garlic,** minced
1 **shallot** (or half small onion),
   finely chopped
¼ tsp (1 mL) each **salt** and **pepper**
1 tbsp (15 mL) **white balsamic** or
   wine vinegar

Seed, core and cut sweet peppers into ½-inch (1 cm) wide strips. In large skillet, heat oil over medium heat; fry garlic and shallot until softened, about 2 minutes.

Add sweet peppers, salt and pepper; fry, stirring often, until tender-crisp, about 7 minutes.

Add vinegar; cook, stirring, just until evaporated, about 1 minute.

Makes 4 servings. PER SERVING: about 100 cal, 1 g pro, 7 g total fat (1 g sat. fat), 10 g carb, 2 g fibre, 0 mg chol, 146 mg sodium. % RDI: 1% calcium, 5% iron, 18% vit A, 253% vit C, 9% folate.

TECHNIQUE
JULIENNE

It may seem fancy, but it's just a French cooking term for cutting food into matchstick-shaped pieces or strips. These strips can vary in size and length from matchstick- to pinky-size. This technique is particularly suited to long vegetables, such as carrots and parsnips, but can be used for celery, squash, sweet potatoes, potatoes and apples. The secret is to create a flat base so the object to be sliced is steady on the cutting board.

TO JULIENNE A CARROT, PARSNIP OR OTHER LONG VEGETABLE:
• Peel vegetable.
• Cut crosswise into 2-inch (5 cm) lengths. Trim thin strip off 1 side to create flat side. Place on flat side and cut lengthwise into about ⅛-inch (3 mm) thick slices.
• Stack slices; cut lengthwise into about ⅛-inch (3 mm) thick matchstick-size strips.

Lightened-Up "Creamed" Spinach

The rich, decadent taste and creamy texture of the original isn't lost in this healthier version of the classic spinach side dish.

¼ cup (60 mL) light or regular **herbed
  cream cheese**
2 tbsp (30 mL) **milk**
2 tsp (10 mL) **lemon juice**
Pinch each **salt** and **pepper**
Pinch **nutmeg**
1 bag (10 oz/284 g) **spinach,**
  cooked and drained

In skillet or saucepan, whisk together cream cheese, milk, lemon juice, salt, pepper and nutmeg over medium-low heat until melted and smooth.

Finely chop spinach; add to cheese sauce and cook, stirring, until blended and hot, about 2 minutes.

Makes 2 or 3 servings. PER EACH OF 3 SERVINGS: about 70 cal, 5 g pro, 4 g total fat (2 g sat. fat), 5 g carb, 2 g fibre, 13 mg chol, 204 mg sodium. % RDI: 14% calcium, 23% iron, 77% vit A, 17% vit C, 60% folate.

HOW TO COOK SPINACH

Trim ends of stems, and coarse veins if desired, from 1 bag fresh spinach (bag sizes vary slightly). Rinse spinach; shake off excess water. In large saucepan or Dutch oven, cover and steam spinach over medium-high heat, with just the water clinging to leaves and stirring once, until wilted, about 5 minutes. In sieve, press out liquid. *(Make-ahead: Let cool; cover and refrigerate for up to 24 hours.)* One 10-oz (284 g) bag makes about 1½ cups (375 mL), enough for 2 or 3 servings.

Beets with Feta

The fresh mint and tangy, creamy cheese match well with the earthy taste of beets. Make sure you save your greens to sauté later (see recipe, below).

2 bunches **beets** (about 2 lb/1 kg), 6 to 8
1 tbsp (15 mL) **extra-virgin olive oil**
2 tsp (10 mL) **white wine vinegar**
Pinch each **salt** and **pepper**
Pinch **granulated sugar**
¼ cup (60 mL) crumbled **feta cheese**
1 tbsp (15 mL) shredded **fresh mint**

Leaving root end intact, trim green tops from beets, leaving about 1-inch (2.5 cm) stem; set greens aside for another use.

In saucepan of boiling salted water, cover and cook beets until fork-tender, about 25 minutes. Let cool. Slip off skins and cut into wedges.

Meanwhile, in bowl, whisk together oil, vinegar, salt, pepper and sugar.

Arrange beets on platter; drizzle with dressing. Sprinkle with cheese and mint.

Makes 4 servings. PER SERVING: about 88 cal, 3 g pro, 6 g total fat (2 g sat. fat), 8 g carb, 2 g fibre, 9 mg chol, 338 mg sodium. % RDI: 6% calcium, 6% iron, 2% vit A, 5% vit C, 29% folate.

BONUS RECIPE
Sautéed Beet Greens
• Soak 2 bunches beet greens in a few changes of water to remove any grit; rinse and shake off water. In large nonstick skillet, heat 2 tbsp (30 mL) extra-virgin olive oil over medium-high heat; cover and cook beet greens; 1 clove garlic, minced; and ½ tsp (2 mL) each salt and pepper, stirring occasionally, until wilted, about 4 minutes. Makes 4 to 6 servings.

Stir-Fried Vegetables

This Chinese-style dish is also lovely with broccoli or other types of greens.

1 tbsp (15 mL) **sesame seeds**

Half small **napa cabbage**

3 cups (750 mL) **bok choy,** Shanghai cabbage or spinach

3 small **carrots**

4 tsp (20 mL) **vegetable oil**

2 **green onions** (white part only), coarsely chopped

1 clove **garlic,** sliced

1 piece (1 inch/2.5 cm) **fresh ginger,** sliced

1 cup (250 mL) **snow peas,** trimmed

1 tbsp (15 mL) **Chinese rice wine** or dry sherry (optional)

1 tsp (5 mL) **light-coloured soy sauce** or sodium-reduced soy sauce

Pinch **granulated sugar**

2 tsp (10 mL) **sesame oil**

In skillet, toast sesame seeds over medium-low heat until light golden, 2 minutes. Set aside.

Cut cabbage into 1½-inch (4 cm) wide strips to make about 3 cups (750 mL). Coarsely chop bok choy. Cut carrots in half lengthwise; thinly slice crosswise on diagonal. Set aside.

In wok or large skillet, heat oil over medium-high heat; stir-fry onions, garlic and ginger for 1 minute. Stir in carrots and snow peas; stir-fry for 30 seconds. Add 2 tbsp (30 mL) water; cover and steam until vegetables are tender, 2 minutes. Add cabbage, bok choy, wine (if using), soy sauce and sugar; stir-fry until greens are wilted, about 3 minutes. Drizzle with sesame oil, tossing to coat. Sprinkle with sesame seeds.

Makes 4 servings. PER SERVING: about 119 cal, 3 g pro, 9 g total fat (1 g sat. fat), 10 g carb, 4 g fibre, 0 mg chol, 93 mg sodium. % RDI: 13% calcium, 12% iron, 88% vit A, 72% vit C, 53% folate.

Vinaigrette Cabbage Salad

This useful little keeper will last for up to seven days in the refrigerator. It's a fantastic side dish for everything from stews to grilled meat.

2 tbsp (30 mL) **vegetable oil**

2 tbsp (30 mL) **cider vinegar** or white wine vinegar

2 tsp (10 mL) **Dijon mustard**

2 tsp (10 mL) **granulated sugar**

½ tsp (2 mL) **celery seeds**

½ tsp (2 mL) each **salt** and **pepper**

1 clove **garlic,** minced

6 cups (1.5 L) shredded **green cabbage**

1 **carrot,** shredded

2 **green onions,** chopped

In large bowl, whisk together oil, vinegar, mustard, sugar, celery seeds, salt, pepper and garlic. Add cabbage, carrot and green onions; toss to coat. Let stand for 15 minutes before serving. (*Make-ahead: Cover and refrigerate for up to 1 week.*)

Makes 6 servings. PER SERVING: about 74 cal, 1 g pro, 5 g total fat (trace sat. fat), 8 g carb, 2 g fibre, 0 mg chol, 232 mg sodium. % RDI: 4% calcium, 6% iron, 39% vit A, 42% vit C, 16% folate.

Lemon Garlic Broccolini

Broccolini is the trademarked name for a hybrid of broccoli and gai lan (Chinese kale). Its long thin stalks topped with florets or buds have a mild broccoli flavour. Tender and sweet, Broccolini is best lightly seasoned and quickly cooked (steamed, sautéed or stir-fried).

2 bunches **Broccolini** (about 12 oz/ 375 g total)
2 tbsp (30 mL) **extra-virgin olive oil**
2 cloves **garlic,** sliced
¼ tsp (1 mL) **salt**
1 tsp (5 mL) grated **lemon zest**
1 tbsp (15 mL) **lemon juice**

Trim tough ends from Broccolini. In large skillet, heat oil over medium-high heat; sauté garlic and salt until fragrant, about 1 minute.

Add Broccolini, ¼ cup (60 mL) water and lemon zest; cover and steam until tender and no water remains, about 6 minutes. Stir in lemon juice.

Makes 4 servings. PER SERVING: about 98 cal, 3 g pro, 7 g total fat (1 g sat. fat), 7 g carb, 1 g fibre, 0 mg chol, 169 mg sodium. % RDI: 6% calcium, 6% iron, 14% vit A, 95% vit C.

VARIATIONS

Spicy Garlic Broccolini
•Add ¼ tsp (1 mL) hot pepper flakes along with garlic. Omit lemon zest and juice.

Lemon Garlic Broccoli
•Use 1 bunch broccoli instead of Broccolini. Cut into florets; peel and slice stems. Cook for 2 minutes longer.

Never Buy Dressing Again

Say goodbye to the salad dressing aisle with these simple make or shake versions. Or do as they do in Italy: drizzle greens with a 3:1 ratio of extra-virgin olive oil to wine vinegar, then sprinkle with sea salt and grind a bit of fresh black pepper over top. *Bellissimo!*

Two-Minute Oil and Vinegar Dressing

On a busy day after work and school, making a salad may seem like the last thing you want to do. But if the lettuce is washed and waiting and there's a superior homemade dressing in the fridge, chances are you will make that salad. Here is a classic dressing to have on hand. One-third cup (75 mL) is enough to dress 6 to 8 cups (1.5 to 2 L) salad greens, which serves four.

2 cloves **garlic,** quartered
½ tsp (2 mL) **salt**
½ cup (125 mL) **canola oil** or
    extra-virgin olive oil
¼ cup (60 mL) **wine vinegar**
2 tsp (10 mL) **Dijon mustard**
Pinch each **granulated sugar** and **pepper**

On cutting board and using fork, crush garlic with salt. In jar, shake together garlic, oil, vinegar, mustard, sugar and pepper until blended. (*Make-ahead: Refrigerate for up to 1 week.*)

Makes about ¾ cup (175 mL). PER 1 TBSP (15 mL): about 83 cal, trace pro, 9 g total fat (1 g sat. fat), trace carb, 0 g fibre, 0 mg chol, 107 mg sodium.

Creamy Lemon Dill Dressing

This is wonderfully thick and tangy, but if you prefer a thinner dressing, stir in 2 tbsp (30 mL) milk. Either way, it's perfect for tossing with salad greens, whether all at once to dress 12 cups (3 L) or in smaller salads to suit your family. It's also delicious as a dip.

⅓ cup (75 mL) each **light sour cream** and
    light mayonnaise
2 tbsp (30 mL) chopped **fresh dill**
    (or 1 tsp/5 mL dried dillweed)
4 tsp (20 mL) **lemon juice**
2 tsp (10 mL) **Dijon mustard**
¼ tsp (1 mL) each **salt** and **pepper**

In small bowl, whisk together sour cream, mayonnaise, dill, lemon juice, mustard, salt and pepper. (*Make-ahead: Refrigerate in airtight container for up to 5 days.*)

Makes ¾ cup (175 mL). PER 1 TBSP (15 mL): about 29 cal, 1 g pro, 2 g total fat (2 g sat. fat), 1 g carb, 0 g fibre, 3 mg chol, 114 mg sodium. % RDI: 1% calcium, 1% iron, 2% vit C.

VARIATION
Creamy Blue Cheese Dressing
•Omit dill. Replace lemon juice with 1 tbsp (15 mL) wine vinegar. Stir in ¼ cup (60 mL) crumbled blue cheese and 1 tbsp (15 mL) chopped fresh chives.

Shaker Dressings

Shake up these dressings in screw-top jars. They're excellent tossed with warm cooked vegetables, such as potatoes, green beans, asparagus or carrots, or with cool salad greens or fresh tomatoes. They're also delicious drizzled over grilled fish, poultry or chops.

Mustard Honey Vinaigrette

In jar, shake together ¾ cup (175 mL) vegetable oil; ⅓ cup (75 mL) wine vinegar; 2 tbsp (30 mL) Dijon mustard; 2 tbsp (30 mL) liquid honey; and ¼ tsp (1 mL) each salt and pepper. (*Make-ahead: Refrigerate for up to 2 weeks. Shake well before using.*)

Makes 1⅓ cups (325 mL). PER 1 TBSP (15 mL): about 76 cal, 0 g pro, 8 g total fat (1 g sat. fat), 2 g carb, 0 g fibre, 0 mg chol, 46 mg sodium. % RDI: 1% iron.

Oregano Vinaigrette

In jar, shake together ⅓ cup (75 mL) each extra-virgin olive oil and vegetable oil; 3 tbsp (45 mL) red wine vinegar; 2 tbsp (30 mL) water; 2 tsp (10 mL) Dijon mustard; 1 clove garlic, minced; 1 tsp (5 mL) dried oregano; and ½ tsp (2 mL) each salt and pepper. (*Make-ahead: Refrigerate for up to 3 days. Shake well before using.*)

Makes about 1 cup (250 mL). PER 1 TBSP (15 mL): about 81 cal, 0 g pro, 9 g total fat (1 g sat. fat), trace carb, 0 g fibre, 0 mg chol, 80 mg sodium. % RDI: 1% iron.

Cranberry Shallot Dressing

In jar, shake together ½ cup (125 mL) frozen cranberry concentrate, thawed; ¼ cup (60 mL) each vegetable oil, water and wine vinegar; 2 tsp (10 mL) grainy or Dijon mustard; 2 small shallots, minced; and ½ tsp (2 mL) each salt and pepper. (*Make-ahead: Refrigerate for up to 3 days. Shake well before using.*)

Makes about 1 cup (250 mL). PER 1 TBSP (15 mL): about 49 cal, trace pro, 3 g total fat (trace sat. fat), 5 g carb, trace fibre, 0 mg chol, 80 mg sodium. % RDI: 1% iron, 12% vit C.

Lemon Thyme Dressing

In jar, shake together ¾ cup (175 mL) vegetable oil; 1 tbsp (15 mL) grated lemon zest; ¼ cup (60 mL) lemon juice; 1 tsp (5 mL) dried thyme; and ¼ tsp (1 mL) each salt and pepper. (*Make-ahead: Refrigerate for up to 2 weeks. Shake well before using.*)

Makes 1 cup (250 mL). PER 1 TBSP (15 mL): about 92 cal, 0 g pro, 10 g total fat (1 g sat. fat), trace carb, 0 g fibre, 0 mg chol, 36 mg sodium. % RDI: 1% iron, 3% vit C.

Mango Melon Salad

Refreshing and light, this salad is the perfect showcase for summer produce. Cut the melon and mango into ½-inch (1 cm) cubes.

3 tbsp (45 mL) **lime juice**
3 tbsp (45 mL) **liquid honey**
2 cups (500 mL) cubed peeled **mango**
2 cups (500 mL) cubed peeled **cantaloupe**
2 cups (500 mL) cubed seedless
   watermelon
¼ cup (60 mL) **pine nuts** (optional),
   lightly toasted
1 tbsp (15 mL) chopped **fresh mint**

In microwaveable bowl, microwave lime juice with honey on high for 30 seconds; whisk until honey is dissolved. Let cool.

Add mango, cantaloupe, watermelon, pine nuts (if using) and mint; toss to combine.

Makes 4 to 6 servings. PER EACH OF 6 SERVINGS: about 103 cal, 1 g pro, trace total fat (trace sat. fat), 27 g carb, 2 g fibre, 0 mg chol, 12 mg sodium. % RDI: 2% calcium, 4% iron, 43% vit A, 65% vit C, 10% folate.

Blueberry Nectarine Salad

Basil isn't just for spaghetti sauce. It's a surprisingly delicious partner to fresh fruit.

¼ cup (60 mL) **granulated sugar**
1 tsp (5 mL) grated **lemon zest**
6 **nectarines** or peaches (or combination),
   cut into ¾-inch (2 cm) cubes
¾ cup (175 mL) **fresh blueberries**
1 tbsp (15 mL) **lemon juice**
½ tsp (2 mL) minced **fresh ginger**
3 large **basil leaves,** chopped

In microwaveable bowl, microwave sugar, lemon zest and 1 cup (250 mL) water at high for 30 seconds; whisk until sugar is dissolved. Let cool.

Add nectarines, blueberries, lemon juice, ginger and basil; toss to combine.

Makes 4 to 6 servings. PER EACH OF 6 SERVINGS: about 103 cal, 2 g pro, 1 g total fat (0 g sat. fat), 26 g carb, 2 g fibre, 0 mg chol, 1 mg sodium. % RDI: 1% calcium, 3% iron, 5% vit A, 17% vit C, 4% folate.

Creamy Cucumber Salad

This Scandinavian-inspired salad is easy to prepare and full of lively accents. Salting and draining the cucumber is essential to prevent a watery salad.

3 cups (750 mL) thinly sliced peeled
   English cucumber
1 tsp (5 mL) **salt**
½ cup (125 mL) thinly sliced **red onion**
¼ cup (60 mL) light or regular **sour cream**
1 tbsp (15 mL) chopped **fresh dill** (or 1 tsp/
   5 mL dried dillweed)
1 tbsp (15 mL) **white wine vinegar**
1 tsp (5 mL) **granulated sugar**

In colander, sprinkle cucumber with salt; let drain for 30 minutes. Pat dry.

Meanwhile, soak onion in cold water for 15 minutes; drain and pat dry.

In bowl, whisk together sour cream, dill, vinegar and sugar. Add cucumber and onion; toss to coat.

Makes 4 servings. PER SERVING: about 38 cal, 2 g pro, 1 g total fat (1 g sat. fat), 6 g carb, 1 g fibre, 2 mg chol, 302 mg sodium. % RDI: 4% calcium, 1% iron, 1% vit A, 7% vit C, 7% folate.

Green Bean and Sweet Onion Salad

Here's a bright, crisp salad tossed with a sassy jalapeño dressing.

4 cups (1 L) **green beans**
   (about 8 oz/250 g), trimmed
½ cup (125 mL) thinly sliced **sweet onion,**
   such as Vidalia or Spanish
2 tbsp (30 mL) **toasted slivered almonds**
JALAPEÑO DRESSING:
1 **jalapeño pepper** (or 1 tsp/5 mL minced
   pickled jalapeño)
¼ cup (60 mL) **extra-virgin olive oil**
2 tbsp (30 mL) **wine vinegar**
½ tsp (2 mL) each **salt** and **pepper**

In large pot of boiling salted water, cover and cook green beans until tender-crisp, about 3 minutes. Drain and chill in cold water. Drain and pat dry.

JALAPEÑO DRESSING: Wearing rubber gloves, seed and mince jalapeño. In large bowl, whisk together jalapeño, oil, vinegar, salt and pepper.

Add green beans and onion; toss to coat. (*Make-ahead: Cover and refrigerate for up to 8 hours.*) Sprinkle with almonds.

Makes 4 servings. PER SERVING: about 187 cal, 3 g pro, 16 g total fat (2 g sat. fat), 10 g carb, 3 g fibre, 0 mg chol, 516 mg sodium. % RDI: 5% calcium, 11% iron, 9% vit A, 27% vit C, 17% folate.

CHAPTER 13

Make It Tonight... Sweets and Treats

Raspberry Rhubarb Sundaes

Sundaes are decadent, right? Not always. This one certainly tastes sinful, but it's loaded with healthy fruit and nuts and lightened up with frozen yogurt instead of rich ice cream.

¼ cup (60 mL) **slivered almonds**
8 scoops **vanilla frozen yogurt** (4 cups/1 L)
RASPBERRY RHUBARB SAUCE:
3 cups (750 mL) chopped **fresh rhubarb**
1 cup (250 mL) **frozen raspberries**
½ cup (125 mL) **granulated sugar**

RASPBERRY RHUBARB SAUCE: In large microwaveable bowl, toss together chopped rhubarb, raspberries and granulated sugar; cover and microwave at high until rhubarb is tender but chunky, about 10 minutes. (Or combine in saucepan and bring to boil; simmer over medium heat for 15 minutes.) Let cool.

Meanwhile, in small skillet, toast almonds over medium heat until lightly browned, about 5 minutes. Set aside.

Place 1 scoop frozen yogurt in each of 4 dishes or glasses; top with half of the rhubarb sauce. Repeat layers. Sprinkle with almonds.

Makes 4 servings. PER SERVING: about 481 cal, 11 g pro, 15 g total fat (7 g sat. fat), 80 g carb, 4 g fibre, 19 mg chol, 122 mg sodium. % RDI: 34% calcium, 6% iron, 6% vit A, 20% vit C, 10% folate.

VARIATION
Strawberry Peach Sundaes
•Omit Raspberry Rhubarb Sauce and almonds. In saucepan, combine 2 cups (500 mL) sliced peeled peaches or nectarines, ¼ cup (60 mL) granulated sugar and pinch cinnamon; bring to boil over medium heat. Reduce heat and simmer, stirring gently once or twice, until peaches are tender, about 10 minutes. Add 1 cup (250 mL) sliced strawberries; let cool. In 4 glasses or bowls, alternately layer sauce and frozen yogurt. Garnish with 4 whole strawberries or replace strawberries with blackberries, blueberries or raspberries.

Sundae Sauces

Both homemade sauces are easy to make and so much more delectable than store-bought. The caramel is gooey; the chocolate, wickedly rich.

CARAMEL SAUCE:
1½ cups (375 mL) **granulated sugar**
⅔ cup (150 mL) **whipping cream**
¼ cup (60 mL) **butter**

In heavy saucepan over medium heat, stir sugar with ⅓ cup (75 mL) water until sugar is dissolved; brush down side of pan with pastry brush dipped in cold water. Bring to boil; boil vigorously, without stirring but brushing down side of pan, until dark amber, about 6 minutes.

Standing back and averting face, add cream; whisk until smooth. Whisk in butter until smooth. Let cool. *(Make-ahead: Refrigerate in airtight container for up to 1 week; rewarm to liquefy.)*

Makes 1½ cups (375 mL). PER 2 TBSP (30 mL): about 173 cal, trace pro, 8 g total fat (5 g sat. fat), 25 g carb, 0 g fibre, 29 mg chol, 44 mg sodium. % RDI: 1% calcium, 8% vit A.

CHOCOLATE SAUCE:
1 cup (250 mL) **whipping cream**
2 tbsp (30 mL) **corn syrup**
6 oz (175 g) **bittersweet chocolate,** chopped

In small saucepan, bring cream and corn syrup to boil; remove from heat. Add chocolate; whisk until smooth. Let stand until thickened, about 15 minutes. *(Make-ahead: Refrigerate in airtight container for up to 1 week; rewarm to liquefy.)*

Makes 1⅔ cups (400 mL). PER 2 TBSP (30 mL): about 139 cal, 1 g pro, 11 g total fat (7 g sat. fat), 10 g carb, 1 g fibre, 23 mg chol, 10 mg sodium. % RDI: 2% calcium, 4% iron, 6% vit A.

Pineapple with Kirsch Syrup

This is a delicious twist on fresh fruit for dessert. It is especially recommended after a meal of Swiss Cheese Fondue (recipe, page 176).

½ cup (125 mL) **granulated sugar**
⅓ cup (75 mL) **kirsch** or orange juice
1 **golden pineapple,** peeled and cored

In small saucepan, bring sugar, kirsch and 2 tbsp (30 mL) water to boil over medium-high heat, swirling to dissolve sugar. Let cool. *(Make-ahead: Refrigerate in airtight container for up to 2 days.)*

Cut pineapple into bite-size pieces; place in large glass bowl. *(Make-ahead: Cover and refrigerate for up to 4 hours.)* Add half of the syrup; toss. Divide among dessert dishes; pass remaining syrup.

Makes 8 servings. PER SERVING: about 115 cal, trace pro, trace total fat (0 g sat. fat), 25 g carb, 1 g fibre, 0 mg chol, 1 mg sodium. % RDI: 1% calcium, 1% iron, 55% vit C, 5% folate.

Sabayon

Sabayon (or *zabaglione* in Italian) is a luscious, foamy custard that is made by whisking together egg yolks, sugar and wine over gently simmering water. It's lovely poured over fresh fruit (especially berries), cake or ice cream – and is simply delicious all by itself.

4 **egg yolks**
½ cup (125 mL) **fruity white wine** (such as Riesling) or dry Marsala
¼ cup (60 mL) **granulated sugar**

In large heatproof bowl over saucepan of gently simmering water, whisk together egg yolks, wine and sugar until thick enough to mound softly on spoon, 5 to 7 minutes. Serve immediately.

Makes 2 cups (500 mL), or 6 servings. PER SERVING: about 83 cal, 2 g pro, 4 g total fat (1 g sat. fat), 9 g carb, 0 g fibre, 136 mg chol, 6 mg sodium. % RDI: 2% calcium, 4% iron, 6% vit A, 8% folate.

Creamy Orange Honey Dip with Fruit

This light dessert is elegant enough for company and simple to whip up for the cook. Garnish with strips of orange zest, if desired. And don't forget to set out sturdy skewers for spearing the fruit.

1 cup (250 mL) **light sour cream**
2 tbsp (30 mL) thawed **orange juice concentrate**
1 tbsp (15 mL) **liquid honey**
Strip **orange zest** (optional)
Assorted **fresh fruit** (such as cubed watermelon, cantaloupe, honeydew melon, strawberries and grapes)

In small bowl, combine sour cream, orange juice concentrate and honey. *(Make-ahead: Cover and refrigerate for up to 24 hours.)*

Place in centre of large serving plate; garnish with orange zest (if using). Arrange fruit around dip.

Makes 1¼ cups (300 mL). PER 1 TBSP (15 mL) WITHOUT FRUIT: about 20 cal, 1 g pro, 1 g total fat (trace sat. fat), 3 g carb, 0 g fibre, 2 mg chol, 11 mg sodium. % RDI: 2% calcium, 1% vit A, 5% vit C, 1% folate.

Creamy Rice Pudding

The hint of spice adds just the right amount of flavour to this ever-popular simple dessert. You can add 2 tbsp (30 mL) golden raisins or cranberries, or garnish with a sprinkle of toasted sliced almonds. If you want to serve it cold, place plastic wrap directly on surface of warm pudding and refrigerate; stir in ¼ cup (60 mL) milk before serving.

2 tbsp (30 mL) **butter**
½ cup (125 mL) **short-grain rice**
¼ tsp (1 mL) **ground cardamom** or cinnamon
¼ tsp (1 mL) **cinnamon**
2½ cups (625 mL) **milk**
2 tbsp (30 mL) **granulated sugar**
1 tsp (5 mL) grated **orange zest**

In small saucepan, melt butter over medium heat. Add rice, cardamom and cinnamon; stir to coat.

Stir in milk and sugar; bring to boil. Reduce heat, cover and simmer, stirring often, until most of the liquid is absorbed and rice is tender, about 25 minutes.

Stir in orange zest. Serve warm.

Makes 4 servings. PER SERVING: about 241 cal, 7 g pro, 9 g total fat (5 g sat. fat), 34 g carb, trace fibre, 30 mg chol, 135 mg sodium. % RDI: 17% calcium, 2% iron, 13% vit A, 2% vit C, 4% folate.

VARIATION
Coconut Rice Pudding
•Replace milk with 1 can (400 mL) coconut milk and ¾ cup (175 mL) milk.

DESSERT DRESS-UPS

You don't have to be a pastry chef or buy from a high-end bakery to serve stylish desserts.

•Sauces dress up scoops of good-quality ice cream, frozen yogurt and sorbet. Chocolate Sauce or Caramel Sauce (recipes, page 213) are handy to keep in the fridge. For a quick raspberry sauce (the kind restaurants call coulis), purée a package of frozen raspberries in syrup and press through a sieve to remove the seeds. Add a splash of raspberry liqueur or kirsch if you like. Serve over peaches and ice cream for a classic peach Melba. It's also lovely over fresh strawberries.

•For a vanilla crème anglaise, or pouring custard, let high-quality vanilla ice cream melt. Stir in a little vanilla or rum if you like.

•Buy little squirt bottles. Any of the sauces above are attractive on a square or a plate of ice cream and fruit. Drizzle over or around the dessert – you don't need much to make a great impression.

•Bananas to the rescue: Melt a couple spoonfuls of butter in a skillet; add about the same amount of brown sugar and let melt together. Add chunks of firm but ripe bananas (1 small banana per person) and turn to coat with sauce. Stir in some rum if you like and spoon out of the pan before the bananas soften. Serve immediately over scoops of vanilla or chocolate ice cream.

•Dust on some icing sugar. It's amazing how a fine shower of this sweet stuff over a homemade brownie or crumble elevates the ordinary to chic. Use a small fine sieve – carefully fill with a spoonful of icing sugar, place over the dessert and tap lightly so the icing sugar snows down evenly and delicately.

Buttermilk Panna Cotta with Strawberry Coulis

Buttermilk adds a slight tartness to this creamy, custard-like Italian dessert. The bright red coulis made from frozen berries couldn't be easier to make.

1 tbsp (15 mL) **unflavoured gelatin**
1 cup (250 mL) **whipping cream**
⅓ cup (75 mL) **granulated sugar**
2 tsp (10 mL) **vanilla**
1 cup (250 mL) **buttermilk**
STRAWBERRY COULIS:
1 pkg (425 g) **frozen strawberries**
    in syrup, thawed

In small saucepan, sprinkle gelatin over 2 tbsp (30 mL) of the cream; let stand for 5 minutes. Stir over medium-low heat until dissolved.

In separate saucepan, heat together remaining cream, sugar and vanilla over medium heat until steaming; remove from heat. Stir in gelatin mixture and buttermilk. Pour into six 6-oz (175 mL) ramekins. Cover and refrigerate until set, about 4 hours. (*Make-ahead: Refrigerate for up to 2 days.*)

STRAWBERRY COULIS: In food processor, whirl strawberries until smooth; press through fine strainer into bowl. Run knife around edge of each ramekin; turn out onto dessert plate. Drizzle coulis attractively onto plate.

Makes 6 servings. PER SERVING: about 236 cal, 4 g pro, 14 g total fat (9 g sat. fat), 24 g carb, 0 g fibre, 52 mg chol, 61 mg sodium. % RDI: 7% calcium, 2% iron, 13% vit A, 53% vit C, 6% folate.

MEASURING UP

Follow either the metric or the imperial measures throughout a recipe, not a combination. And use the right cup for the job: there are different ones for dry ingredients and for wet.

•Dry ingredient measures come in sets of different sizes: ¼ cup (60 mL), ⅓ cup (75 mL), ½ cup (125 mL) and 1 cup (250 mL).
•Liquid ingredient glass measuring cups have a spout and are marked on the outside.
•Measuring spoons are used for both dry and liquid ingredients and come in four sizes: ¼ tsp (1 mL), ½ tsp (2 mL), 1 tsp (5 mL) and 1 tbsp (15 mL).

DRY INGREDIENTS
•Lightly spoon dry ingredients into dry measure.
•Do not pack down or tap measure on counter (except for brown sugar, which should be packed enough to keep cup shape when dumped out).
•Fill measure until heaping. Then, working over canister, push straight edge of knife across top of measure.

LIQUID INGREDIENTS
•Place liquid measuring cup on counter. Pour in liquid to desired level, then bend down to check measurement at eye level.
•If liquid doesn't come exactly to desired mark on outside, pour off a little or add a little as needed.

Crispy Ice-Cream Sandwiches

Everyone's favourite treat of crispy rice squares gets even better with ice cream, chocolate and sprinkles.

2 cups (500 mL) **vanilla ice cream**
8 oz (250 g) **semisweet chocolate,** chopped
¼ cup (60 mL) **coloured sprinkles**
RICE CRISP SQUARES:
5 cups (1.25 L) **marshmallows** (about 40)
¼ cup (60 mL) **butter**
1 tsp (5 mL) **vanilla**
5 cups (1.25 L) **rice crisp cereal**

Line bottom of 13- x 9-inch (3.5 L) cake pan with parchment paper; grease sides. Set aside.

RICE CRISP SQUARES: In large saucepan, melt marshmallows with butter over medium-low heat, stirring constantly, until smooth, about 5 minutes. Remove from heat; stir in vanilla.

Add half of the cereal; stir until combined. Add remaining cereal; stir to coat completely. Scrape into greased bowl; let cool enough to handle, about 5 minutes. With greased hands, press into prepared pan; let cool completely.

Run knife around edges of pan; remove from pan and peel off paper. Cut crosswise in half. Spread 1 half evenly with ice cream; top with remaining half. Wrap in plastic wrap; freeze in airtight container until firm, about 4 hours. Cut into 6 squares; cut each in half diagonally.

Meanwhile, in heatproof bowl over saucepan of hot (not boiling) water, melt chocolate; let cool. Dip 1 corner of triangle halfway into chocolate; smooth with knife. Place coloured sprinkles on waxed paper; press chocolate edge into sprinkles. Wrap individually in plastic wrap; freeze in airtight container until firm, at least 4 hours. (*Make-ahead: Freeze for up to 2 days.*)

Makes 12 servings. PER SERVING: about 297 cal, 3 g pro, 11 g total fat (7 g sat. fat), 47 g carb, 1 g fibre, 22 mg chol, 197 mg sodium. % RDI: 3% calcium, 16% iron, 6% vit A, 6% folate.

Chocolate Peanut Butter Pudding Cake

You can bake this luscious little number in the oven or the slow cooker. Talk about convenient!

¾ cup (175 mL) **all-purpose flour**
⅓ cup (75 mL) **granulated sugar**
1 tsp (5 mL) **baking powder**
⅓ cup (75 mL) **milk**
1 **egg,** beaten
3 tbsp (45 mL) **natural peanut butter**
¾ cup (175 mL) packed **brown sugar**
¼ cup (60 mL) **cocoa powder**
1 cup (250 mL) **boiling water**

In large bowl, whisk together flour, granulated sugar and baking powder. Whisk together milk, egg and peanut butter; stir into flour mixture. Scrape into greased 8-inch (2 L) square baking dish.

In heatproof bowl, whisk brown sugar with cocoa powder; whisk in boiling water until smooth. Pour over cake; do not stir. Bake in 350°F (180°C) oven until cake is firm to touch, about 30 minutes. Let cool for 10 minutes.

Make 4 to 6 servings. PER EACH OF 6 SERVINGS: about 281 cal, 6 g pro, 6 g total fat (1 g sat. fat), 54 g carb, 2 g fibre, 32 mg chol, 81 mg sodium. % RDI: 7% calcium, 16% iron, 2% vit A, 17% folate.

VARIATION

Slow Cooker Chocolate Peanut Butter Pudding Cake:
• Scrape batter into greased slow cooker. Pour cocoa mixture over top; do not stir. Cover and cook on high until cake is firm to touch, about 2 hours.

SIFTING

• All-purpose flour does not require sifting.
• Sift cake-and-pastry flour before measuring.
• Sift cocoa powder and icing sugar after measuring to eliminate lumps.

Chocolate Fondue for Two

This melty chocolate dip is a treat on almost any kind of fruit. Try the types we've called for or experiment with other favourites, such as melon chunks, grapes or sliced pear.

1 cup (250 mL) bite-size peeled **fresh pineapple** chunks

1 **navel orange,** peeled and cut in segments

2 **kiwifruit,** peeled and sliced

1 **Red Delicious apple,** cored and sliced

6 **cookies** (optional)

CHOCOLATE FONDUE:

⅓ cup (75 mL) **whipping cream**

3 oz (90 g) **bittersweet chocolate,** chopped

2 oz (60 g) **milk chocolate,** chopped

1 tbsp (15 mL) **amaretto,** brandy or rum

GARNISH (OPTIONAL):

Cape gooseberries or sliced bananas

CHOCOLATE FONDUE: In saucepan, heat cream until boiling. Pour over bittersweet and milk chocolates in fondue pot; whisk until melted. Whisk in amaretto. Keep warm.

Meanwhile, arrange pineapple, orange, kiwi, apple, and cookies (if using) on platter.

GARNISH: Garnish with gooseberries (if using). Serve with fondue.

Makes 2 servings. PER SERVING: about 692 cal, 8 g pro, 40 g total fat (24 g sat. fat), 82 g carb, 12 g fibre, 57 mg chol, 45 mg sodium. % RDI: 15% calcium, 21% iron, 17% vit A, 167% vit C, 19% folate.

TIP
For best flavour and texture, use quality chocolate, such as Lindt.

Blueberry Streusel Muffins

For this Canadian favourite, fresh wild blueberries are best. Out of season you can stir frozen wild berries straight from the freezer into the batter.

2 cups (500 mL) **all-purpose flour**
1 cup (250 mL) packed **brown sugar**
¾ tsp (4 mL) **baking soda**
½ tsp (2 mL) **salt**
1 **egg**
1 cup (250 mL) **buttermilk**
¼ cup (60 mL) **butter,** melted
1 tsp (5 mL) **vanilla**
½ tsp (2 mL) grated **lemon zest**
1 cup (250 mL) fresh or frozen
  wild blueberries
STREUSEL:
⅓ cup (75 mL) packed **brown sugar**
¼ cup (60 mL) **slivered almonds**
¼ cup (60 mL) **all-purpose flour**
¼ tsp (1 mL) grated **nutmeg**
2 tbsp (30 mL) **butter,** melted

Line muffin cups with paper liners or grease; set aside.

STREUSEL: In bowl, stir together brown sugar, almonds, flour and nutmeg. Drizzle with butter; toss with fork. Set aside.

In large bowl, whisk together flour, sugar, baking soda and salt. In separate bowl, whisk egg, buttermilk, butter, vanilla and lemon zest. Pour over dry ingredients; stir twice. Sprinkle with blueberries; stir just until dry ingredients are moistened.

Spoon into prepared muffin cups; sprinkle with streusel. Bake in 375°F (190°C) oven until tops are firm to the touch, about 25 minutes. *(Make-ahead: Let cool in pan for 2 minutes. Transfer to rack and let cool completely. Store in airtight container for up to 1 day. Or wrap individually in plastic wrap; freeze in airtight container for up to 2 weeks.)*

Makes 12 muffins. PER MUFFIN: about 264 cal, 4 g pro, 8 g total fat (4 g sat. fat), 45 g carb, 1 g fibre, 265 mg sodium. % RDI: 5% calcium, 12% iron, 6% vit A, 15% folate.

Mocha Snacking Cake

This tender, moist cake is terrific on its own, dusted with icing sugar, or dressed up with ice cream or whipped cream and berries. If you don't have strong brewed coffee, make it with 2 tbsp (30 mL) instant coffee.

⅔ cup (150 mL) **butter,** softened
1½ cups (375 mL) **granulated sugar**
2 **eggs**
1 tsp (5 mL) **vanilla**
1⅔ cups (400 mL) **all-purpose flour**
¾ cup (175 mL) **cocoa powder**
1 tsp (5 mL) each **baking soda** and
　 baking powder
¼ tsp (1 mL) **salt**
1⅓ cups (325 mL) **strong brewed coffee,**
　 cooled

Grease sides of 8-inch (2 L) square cake pan; line bottom with parchment or waxed paper. Set aside.

In large bowl, beat butter with sugar until fluffy; beat in eggs, 1 at a time, just until incorporated. Stir in vanilla.

In separate bowl, sift together flour, cocoa, baking soda, baking powder and salt; add to butter mixture alternately with coffee, making 2 additions of dry ingredients and 1 of coffee. Beat until almost smooth. Scrape into prepared pan; spread evenly.

Bake in 350°F (180°C) oven until cake tester inserted in centre comes out clean, 45 to 50 minutes. Let cool in pan on rack. (*Make-ahead: Wrap in plastic wrap and store for up to 3 days. Or overwrap with heavy-duty foil and freeze for up to 2 weeks.*)

Makes 12 servings. PER SERVING: about 275 cal, 4 g pro, 12 g total fat (7 g sat. fat), 41 g carb, 2 g fibre, 63 mg chol, 283 mg sodium. % RDI: 2% calcium, 13% iron, 11% vit A, 19% folate.

THE WELL-STOCKED KITCHEN
ESSENTIAL BAKING SUPPLIES

- **Sugar:** Granulated, brown and icing
- **Liquid sweeteners:** Honey and corn syrup
- **Flour:** All-purpose, whole grain and cake-and-pastry
- **Leaveners:** Baking powder and baking soda
- **Cornstarch**
- **Vanilla:** Vanilla extract (preferably pure)
- **Spices:** Cinnamon and nutmeg
- **Chocolate:** Cocoa powder, chocolate chips, bittersweet and unsweetened chocolate
- **Dried fruit:** Raisins, and dried cranberries and blueberries
- **Nuts:** Slivered almonds, and pecan and walnut halves
- **Rolled oats:** Large-flake

Baked Apples with Figs and Almonds

Just a spoonful of almond liqueur boosts the almond flavour of this rustic, homey dessert.

4 **baking apples**
¼ cup (60 mL) **whole almonds** (with skin)
½ cup (125 mL) chopped dried **Mission figs** or pitted prunes
2 tbsp (30 mL) packed **brown sugar**
1 tbsp (15 mL) **almond liqueur** (such as amaretto) or maple syrup
4 tsp (20 mL) **butter**
½ cup (125 mL) **apple juice**

Using melon baller or spoon, core apples, leaving ¼-inch (1 cm) base. Pierce each apple 4 times with fork or knife. Set aside.

On baking sheet, toast almonds until golden and fragrant, about 10 minutes. Let cool and finely chop.

In bowl, stir together figs, almonds, sugar and liqueur. Spoon into apple centres. Top each with 1 tsp (5 mL) butter.

Place apples in 8-inch (2 L) square baking dish; pour in apple juice. Bake in 375°F (190°C) oven until tender, about 45 minutes.

Makes 4 servings. PER SERVING: about 249 cal, 3 g pro, 9 g total fat (3 g sat. fat), 44 g carb, 6 g fibre, 10 mg chol, 35 mg sodium, 398 mg potassium. % RDI: 6% calcium, 9% iron, 5% vit A, 10% vit C, 3% folate.

Ginger Pear Muffins

Muffins are the ultimate in easy baking. These moist mini gingerbread cakes are packed with spices and chunks of ripe pear.

2½ cups (625 mL) **all-purpose flour**

1 tsp (5 mL) **baking soda**

1 tsp (5 mL) **ground ginger**

½ tsp (2 mL) **salt**

½ tsp (2 mL) **cinnamon**

¾ cup (175 mL) packed **brown sugar**

⅓ cup (75 mL) **vegetable oil**

1 **egg**

1 cup (250 mL) **buttermilk**

2 cups (500 mL) chopped peeled **pears**

TOPPING:

⅓ cup (75 mL) packed **brown sugar**

2 tsp (10 mL) **butter,** melted

¼ tsp (1 mL) **ground ginger**

Line muffin cups with paper liners or grease; set aside.

In bowl, whisk together flour, baking soda, ginger, salt and cinnamon. In separate bowl, whisk brown sugar with oil; whisk in egg and buttermilk. Pour over dry ingredients; sprinkle with pears and stir just until dry ingredients are moistened. Spoon into prepared muffin cups.

TOPPING: In bowl, combine brown sugar, butter and ginger; sprinkle over batter. Bake in 350°F (180°C) oven until tops are firm to the touch, about 25 minutes.

Makes 12 muffins. PER SERVING: about 254 cal, 4 g pro, 8 g total fat (1 g sat. fat), 43 g carb, 1 g fibre, 18 mg chol, 234 mg sodium. % RDI: 5% calcium, 12% iron, 1% vit A, 2% vit C, 16% folate.

Peach Betty

Betties or Brown Betties are puddings of fruit tossed with sugar and spices and layered with buttered crumbs, which soak up all the fruit juices. They're as simple as fruit crisps but with a slight twist.

2 cups (500 mL) coarse **fresh bread crumbs**

¼ cup (60 mL) **salted butter,** melted

8 cups (2 L) thickly sliced peeled **peaches** (about 3 lb/1.5 kg)

⅔ cup (150 mL) packed **brown sugar**

½ tsp (2 mL) grated **lemon zest**

Pinch each **nutmeg** and **cinnamon**

3 tbsp (45 mL) **water**

2 tsp (10 mL) **lemon juice**

In bowl, toss bread crumbs with butter; spread one-quarter in 8-inch (2 L) square baking dish.

In large bowl, toss peaches, brown sugar, lemon zest, nutmeg and cinnamon; spread half over crumbs in dish. Top with another quarter of the bread crumb mixture; spread remaining peach mixture over top. Drizzle with water and lemon juice. Sprinkle with remaining crumb mixture.

Bake in 375°F (190°C) oven until golden and fruit is tender, about 45 minutes.

Makes 8 servings. PER SERVING: about 215 cal, 3 g pro, 7 g total fat (4 g sat. fat), 40 g carb, 4 g fibre, 15 mg chol, 105 mg sodium, 403 mg potassium. % RDI: 4% calcium, 8% iron, 11% vit A, 20% vit C, 8% folate.

HOW TO PEEL PEACHES

With slotted spoon, lower a few peaches at a time into pot of boiling water; blanch until skin starts to peel away, about 30 seconds. Submerge immediately in bowl of ice water until cool enough to handle; peel off skins.

Plum Hazelnut Crumble

Enjoy this fruity, nutty dessert warm or cool, with frozen yogurt or ice cream.

6 cups (1.5 L) **sliced plums** (or part nectarines), about 2¼ lb (1.125 kg) whole fruit

⅓ cup (75 mL) packed **brown sugar**

2 tbsp (30 mL) **all-purpose flour**

¼ tsp (1 mL) **cinnamon**

1 tbsp (15 mL) **icing sugar**

HAZELNUT CRUMBLE:

¾ cup (175 mL) **hazelnuts**

¾ cup (175 mL) **all-purpose flour**

½ cup (125 mL) packed **brown sugar**

½ cup (125 mL) cold **butter**

Grease 8-inch (2 L) square baking dish; set aside.

HAZELNUT CRUMBLE: On rimmed baking sheet, toast hazelnuts in 350°F (180°C) oven until fragrant, about 10 minutes. Briskly rub nuts in tea towel to remove as much of the skins as possible.

In food processor, finely chop nuts. Pulse in flour, sugar and butter until in fine crumbs with a few larger pieces. (Or with knife, chop nuts. In bowl, mix nuts, flour and sugar; cut in butter with pastry blender or 2 knives.) Set aside.

In large bowl, toss plums, brown sugar, flour and pinch of the cinnamon. Spread in prepared dish. Sprinkle with Hazelnut Crumble. Bake in centre of 350°F (180°C) oven until topping is crisp and filling is tender and bubbly, about 40 minutes. Serve warm or let cool on rack.

In small bowl, whisk icing sugar with remaining cinnamon; sprinkle over crumble.

Makes 6 to 8 servings. PER EACH OF 8 SERVINGS: about 394 cal, 4 g pro, 21 g total fat (8 g sat. fat), 52 g carb, 4 g fibre, 36 mg chol, 126 mg sodium. % RDI: 5% calcium, 12% iron, 14% vit A, 15% vit C, 13% folate.

Quick Apple Rhubarb Turnover

We recommend butter puff pastry sold boxed in rolls in the freezer section of your supermarket.

2 large **apples,** peeled, cored
   and thinly sliced
1 cup (250 mL) chopped **rhubarb**
¼ cup (60 mL) **granulated sugar**
2 tbsp (30 mL) **all-purpose flour**
1 tsp (5 mL) **lemon juice**
¼ tsp (1 mL) **cinnamon**
Half pkg (450 g pkg) **butter puff pastry**
1 **egg yolk**
2 tsp (10 mL) **granulated sugar**

Line rimmed baking sheet with parchment paper or grease; set aside.

In large bowl, toss together apples, rhubarb, sugar, flour, lemon juice and cinnamon.

Unroll pastry onto prepared pan. Spoon apple mixture lengthwise along half of the pastry, leaving ½-inch (1 cm) border uncovered. Whisk egg yolk with 1 tsp (5 mL) water; lightly brush some over border. Using parchment paper to lift, fold uncovered pastry over filling; with fork, press edges to seal. Brush top with egg yolk mixture. Cut 4 evenly spaced 2-inch (5 cm) slashes on top; sprinkle with sugar.

Bake in 375°F (190°C) oven until golden and filling is tender, about 40 minutes.

Makes 6 servings. PER SERVING: about 439 cal, 6 g pro, 23 g total fat (4 g sat. fat), 54 g carb, 3 g fibre, 51 mg chol, 144 mg sodium. % RDI: 4% calcium, 14% iron, 5% vit A, 7% vit C, 18% folate.

INDEX

CREDITS

Photography
Michael Alberstat: pages 74 and 227.
Yvonne Duivenvoorden: pages 14, 18, 24, 37, 38, 40, 56, 62, 68, 81, 88, 103, 108, 138, 145, 165, 175, 196, 205, 209 and 221.
Geoff George: page 107.
Edward Pond: pages 17, 43, 93, 115, 118, 123 and 224.
Jodi Pudge: pages 11, 12, 32, 126, 160, 202, 219 and 228.
David Scott: pages 21, 51, 94, 183, 184 and 201.
Andreas Trauttmansdorff: page 189.
Felix Wedgwood: page 157.

Food styling
Donna Bartolini: pages 68, 74 and 227.
Carol Dudar: page 21.
Ian Muggridge: page 228.
Christine Picheca: page 157.
Lucie Richard: pages 11, 12, 14, 17, 18, 51, 56, 62, 81, 88, 93, 94, 103, 108, 145, 165, 175, 183, 201, 205, 209 and 224.
Claire Stancer: pages 37, 38 and 196.
Claire Stubbs: pages 24, 40, 43, 115, 118, 123, 138, 160, 184, 189 and 202.
Rosemarie Superville: page 221.
Nicole Young: pages 32, 107, 126 and 219.

Prop styling
Laura Branson: pages 14, 40, 56, 62 and 228.
Catherine Doherty: pages 11, 12, 17, 38, 43, 93, 107, 157, 160, 189, 221 and 224.
Marc-Philippe Gagné: pages 18, 24 and 81.
Catherine MacFadyen: page 74.
Oksana Slavutych: pages 21, 32, 37, 51, 68, 88, 94, 103, 108, 115, 118, 123, 126, 138, 165, 175, 183, 184, 196, 201, 202, 205, 209 and 227.
Genevieve Wiseman: page 145.

Recipes
All recipes were developed by
The Canadian Living Test Kitchen.

TRANSCONTINENTAL BOOKS

1100 René-Lévesque Boulevard West
24th Floor
Montreal, Que. H3B 4X9
Tel: 514-340-3587
Toll-free: 1-866-800-2500
canadianliving.com

Bibliothèque et Archives nationales
du Québec and Library and Archives
Canada cataloguing in publication

Main entry under title :
Make it tonight
2nd ed.
Includes index.
ISBN 978-0-9813938-6-5
1. Cooking. 2. Quick and easy cooking. I. Canadian
Living Test Kitchen.

TX714.B353 2011   641.5   C2011-940696-9
Project editor: Christina Anson Mine
Copy editor: James Doyle
Indexer: Gillian Watts
Art direction and design: Chris Bond

Printed in Canada
© Transcontinental Books, 2011
Legal deposit – 2nd quarter 2011
National Library of Quebec
National Library of Canada
ISBN 978-0-9813938-6-5

We acknowledge the financial support of
our publishing activity by the Government
of Canada through the Canada Book Fund.

For information on special rates for
corporate libraries and wholesale purchases,
please call 1-866-800-2500.

About Our Nutrition Information

To meet nutrient needs each day, moderately active women 25 to 49 need about 1,900 calories, 51 g protein, 261 g carbohydrate, 25 to 35 g fibre and not more than 63 g total fat (21 g saturated fat).

Men and teenagers usually need more. Canadian sodium intake of approximately 3,500 to 4,500 mg daily should be reduced, whereas the intake from food sources of potassium should be increased to 4,700 mg per day.

Percentage of recommended daily intake (% RDI) is based on the highest recommended intakes (excluding those for pregnant and lactating women) for calcium, iron, vitamins A and C, and folate.

Figures are rounded off. They are based on the first ingredient listed when there is a choice and do not include optional ingredients or those with no specified amounts.

Abbreviations:
cal = calories
pro = protein
carb = carbohydrate
sat. fat = saturated fat
chol = cholesterol

tested till perfect — Our Tested-Till-Perfect guarantee means we've tested every recipe, using the same grocery store ingredients and household appliances as you do, until we're sure you'll get perfect results at home.